ARTHUR LOWE

ARTHUR LOWE

GRAHAM LORD

ORION

Copyright © Graham Lord 2002

The right of Graham Lord to be identified as the author
of this work has been asserted by him in accordance
with the Copyright, Designs and Patents Act 1988.

First published in Great Britain in 2002 by
Orion
An imprint of Orion Books Ltd
Orion House, 5 Upper St Martin's Lane,
London WC2H 9EA

Third impression November 2002

A CIP catalogue record for this book
is available from the British Library

ISBN 0 75284 184 X

Pictures supplied by kind permission of
Tony and Lesley Keen, Tony Oliver, Norman
Littlechild, Martin Benson and A. L. Hewitt.

Every effort has been made to trace the copyright holders,
but if any have been inadvertently overlooked, the publishers
will be pleased to make the necessary arrangements at the
first opportunity.

Typeset by Selwood Systems, Midsomer Norton

Printed in Great Britain by
Butler & Tanner Ltd, Frome and London

For
Clive Dunn,
Ian Lavender,
Bill Pertwee,
Frank Williams
and
Pam Cundell

Contents

Acknowledgements

I am especially grateful to Arthur Lowe's son, Stephen, and stepson, David Gatehouse, for their help and permission to quote from Stephen's book about his father, *Arthur Lowe: A Life*, and from their parents' diaries and letters; to Lesley and Tony Keen for allowing me complete access to Arthur and Joan Lowe's diaries, letters, records and photographs, and for helping to assess and copy them; to the *Dad's Army* experts Richard Webber and David Homewood for generously sharing all their own incredibly encyclopedic research; and to Tony Oliver for showing me his Lowe memorabilia and photographs.

For hours of wonderfully entertaining interviews I must thank the surviving stars of *Dad's Army* – Clive Dunn, Ian Lavender, Bill Pertwee, Frank Williams and Pamela Cundell – as well as David Croft, Jimmy Perry, John le Mesurier's widow, Joan, and James Beck's widow, Kay. I am equally grateful to the many other actors, playwrights and producers who told me about Arthur's early days in repertory theatre, on the West End stage, in films, and on television: Daniel Albineri, Avril Angers, John Barron, Colin Bean, Derek Benfield, Christopher and Peggy Bond, Edward Bond, Richard Briers, Ian Carmichael, Betty Driver, Paul Gane, Derek Granger, John Hodges, John Inman, Richard Leech, Alec McCowen, Sarah Miles, Michael Morris, John Newman, Nancy Powell, Paul Scofield, Dick Sharples, Harold Snoad, John Warner and Tony Warren.

For invaluable glimpses of the Lowes' private lives I am indebted to their close friend Phyllis Bateman; Joan's first husband, Richard Gatehouse, and his wife, Barbara Bliss; Joan's sister, Margaret Stapleton; Ted Shine, the son of their close friends Bill and Diana Shine; their theatrical agent, Peter Campbell; and their accountant, Lawrence Newman.

For memories of the Lowes' visits to Arthur's birthplace, Hayfield in Derbyshire, I owe a great deal to Ann and Trevor Middleton, Bill and Helen Higginbottom, and Alice MacDonald, as well as to Lynn and Mike Atkinson, George Benham, George Cooper, Charles Hadfield, Jim Harrison, Les Huddlestone, Ethel and Fred Hulme, Jon James, Mary Miller, Ken Rangeley, Richard Rowbottom, Richard Sinclair, Eric Smith and Victor Turner. Paul Beattie and Judith Phillips of the Derbyshire Record Office and Katy Goodrum of the Cheshire Record Office were extremely helpful, and for assistance with research into Arthur Lowe's early years in Manchester I am grateful to Sylvia Dugdale of Levenshulme Library, the librarians of Manchester Central Library and the Manchester Local Archive Library, Gary Kershaw of Chapel Road Primary School, Pat Jones of Alma Park Central School PTA, Gilly Girling and David Graham of Brown Brothers, Diane Wallwork of Williams Fairey Engineering Ltd, and Terry Hamilton of the *Manchester Evening News*.

I could not have written of Lowe's barmy army career in such detail without the vivid evidence of Norman Littlechild and Martin Benson as well as that of Harry Hartill, Norman Hewitt, Colin Mills and Ernie Skidmore. I should also thank Paul Aubin, Val Doonican, Albert Finney, Ray Galton, Sheila Hancock, Sir Edward Heath, Doris Lessing, Dennis Quilley, Reggie Salberg, Alan Simpson and Warren Taylor for their kind replies to my questions.

I could not have begun to work on this book without access to the remarkable resources of the British Library and National Record Archive at St Pancras, London, which continually astonishes me with the richness of its material and the helpfulness of its staff. For initial guidance I am very grateful for the generous help of Rebecca Sandiford of Watchmaker Productions, Jack Wheeler of the *Dad's Army* Appreciation Society, Mrs E. O. Marland, Mark Lewisohn, Sylvia Gatehouse and the Ministry of Defence. For help in researching newspaper archives I am particularly grateful to Lynda Iley and Steve Baker of *The Times* library, Gavin Fuller of the *Daily Telegraph* library, the *Daily Mail*'s chief librarian Steve Torrington, and Gemma Field of the Royal National Theatre. And for letting me see so many of Arthur Lowe's forgotten old films I am indebted to Kathleen Dickson and Alexander Marlow-Man of the British Film Institute.

Several television and radio documentaries were extremely useful, most notably Bill Pertwee's *The Arthur Lowe Story* (BBC Radio 2, 1993), Terry Wogan's *A Life on the Box: Arthur Lowe* (BBC1, 1998), and *The Unforgettables: Arthur Lowe* (Watchmaker Productions, 2000). I am grateful to the following copyright owners or their estates for permission to quote from their scripts and songs: W. W. Jacobs for *The Monkey's Paw*; Guy Bolton for *Larger Than Life*; James Elroy Flecker for *Hassan*; George Abbott, Richard Bissell, Richard Adler and Jerry Ross for *The Pajama Game*; Irving Berlin, Howard Lindsay and Russel Crouse for *Call Me Madam*; John O'Hara, Richard Rodgers and Lorenz Hart for *Pal Joey*; Harry Warren and Mack Gordon for 'At Last'; Frank Wells and Robert Gow for *Ann Veronica*; Jimmy Perry for 'Who Do You Think You Are Kidding, Mr Hitler?'; David Croft and Jimmy Perry for *Dad's Army*; Walter Ridley and Miles Rudge for 'My Little Boy, My Little Girl'; Roy Clarke for *Potter*; Ray Galton and Alan Simpson for *Car Along the Pass*; John Masefield for 'Sea-Fever'; and E. Maschwitz for 'A Nightingale Sang in Berkeley Square'.

And finally I owe much to the authors of the following books, plays, and documents:

Rodney Ackland, *A Dead Secret* (Samuel French, 1958); *Alma Park Central School, Levenshulme, Log Book* (Manchester Education Committee, 1926–1937); Lt-Col J. D. Bastick, MBE, *Trumpet Call: The Story of the Duke of Lancaster's Own Yeomanry* (Duke of Lancaster's Own Yeomanry, 1973); Colin Bean, *Who Do You Think You Are Kidding!* (Minerva Press, 1998); Gerald Boardman (ed.), *The Oxford Companion to American Theatre* (Oxford University Press, 1992); Guy Bolton, *Larger Than Life* (Samuel French, 1950); John Braine, *J. B. Priestley* (Weidenfeld and Nicolson, 1978); John Brereton, *Chain Mail: The History of the Duke of Lancaster's Own Yeomanry* (Picton, 1992); Elaine Burrows (ed.), *The British Cinema Source Book* (British Film Institute, 1995); Michael Feeney Callan, *Richard Harris: A Sporting Life* (Sidgwick and Jackson, 1990); Judith Cook, *Priestley* (Bloomsbury, 1997); Clive Dunn, *Permission to Laugh* (Michael O'Mara, 1996) and *Permission to Speak* (Century, 1986); Kate Dunn, *Exit Through the Fireplace: The Great Days of Rep* (John Murray, 1998); Richard Dyer, Christine Gerachty, Marion Jordan, Terry Lovell, Richard Patterson, John Stewart, *Coronation Street* (BFI Publishing, 1981); Walter Ellis, *Bedtime Story: A Light Comedy in Three Acts* (Fortune Press, 1942); Stephen Fay, *Power Play: The Life and Times of Peter Hall* (Hodder & Stoughton, 1995); Richard Fawkes, *Fighting for a Laugh: Entertaining the British and American Armed Forces 1939–1946* (Macdonald and Jane's, 1978); Michael Freedland, *Peter O'Toole* (W. H. Allen, 1983); John Galsworthy, *The Silver Box* (Duckworth, 1910); *Peter Hall's Diaries*, ed. by John Goodwin (Hamish Hamilton, 1983); Peter Hall, *Making an Exhibition of Myself* (Sinclair-Stevenson, 1993); Hayfield Civic Trust, *Hedfeld to Hayfield* (n.d.); Hayfield Parish Council, *Hayfield, Derbyshire: Official Guide to the Parish* (1951); Peter Helm and Gay Sussex, *Looking Back at Rusholme and Fallowfield* (Willow, 1985); *Hereford: City of the Marches* (Hereford City Council Leisure Services, 1997); Arnold P. Hinchliffe, *John Osborne* (Twayne, Boston, 1984); Clive Hopwood (ed.), *Memories: Reminiscences of Rusholme* (Rusholme Project, 1992); Sir Michael Hordern with Patricia England, *A World Elsewhere* (Michael O'Mara, 1993); Edward Houghton, *History of Hayfield* (unpublished ms, Derbyshire Library Service); John Graven Hughes, *The Greasepaint War: Show Business 1939–1945* (New English Library, 1976); W. W. Jacobs, *The Monkey's Paw*, dramatised by Louis N. Parker (Samuel French, 1910); Graeme Kay, *Coronation Street: Celebrating 30 Years* (Boxtree, 1990); *Kelly's Directory of Derbyshire* (1912, 1916, 1922, 1936, 1941); Susan Lake, *The Story of Brown Brothers 1889–1989* (Brown Brothers, 1989); Colin Larkin (ed.), *The Guinness Who's Who of Stage Musicals* (Guinness, 1994); Joan le Mesurier, *Lady Don't Fall Backwards* (Sidgwick and Jackson, 1988) and *Dear John* (Sidgwick and Jackson, 2001); John le Mesurier, *A Jobbing Actor* (Elm Tree Books, 1984); *Levenshulme Local Defence Committee Minute Book* (1940); Henry Livings, *Kelly's Eye* (Methuen, 1964) and *The Rough Side of the Boards* (Methuen, 1994); Pamela W. Logan, *Jack Hylton Presents* (British Film Institute Publishing, 1995); Stephen Lowe, *Arthur Lowe: a Life* (Nick Hern, 1996); Chris Makepeace, *A Century of Manchester* (Sutton, 1999) and *Manchester As It Was* (Hendon Publishing, 1976); Graham McCann, *Dad's Army* (Fourth Estate, 2001) and *Morecambe and Wise* (Fourth Estate, 1998); Sarah Miles, *Serve Me Right* (Macmillan, 1994); David Mondey and Michael J.

H. Taylor, *The Guinness Book of Aircraft* (Guinness, 1988); Allan Monkhouse, *The Grand Cham's Diamond* (Gowans and Gray, 1924); Eric Morecambe and Ernie Wise with Michael Freedland, *There's No Answer to That!* (Arthur Barker, 1981); Gary Morecambe and Martin Sterling, *Morecambe and Wise: Behind the Sunshine* (Robson, 1994); Graham Nown (ed.), *Coronation Street: 25 Years, 1960–1985* (Ward Lock, 1985); Eugene O'Neill, *Bound East For Cardiff* (Frank Shay, 1916); John Osborne, *Almost a Gentleman* (Faber, 1991); Barbara Paskin, *Dudley Moore* (Sidgwick and Jackson, 1997); Jimmy Perry, David Croft and Richard Webber, *Dad's Army: The Complete Scripts of Series 1–4* (Orion, 2001); Bill Pertwee, *A Funny Way to Make a Living!* (Sunburst Books, 1996) and *Dad's Army: The Making of a Television Legend* (PRC Publishing, 1997); Roy Plomley with Derek Drescher, *Desert Island Lists* (Hutchinson, 1984); Bill Podmore with Peter Reece, *Coronation Street: The Inside Story* (Macdonald, 1990); Lawrence Quirk, *The Films of Warren Beatty* (Citadel Press, 1990); H. W. Radcliffe, *Reminiscences* (unpublished ms, 1978); Terence Rattigan, *Flare Path* (Hamish Hamilton, 1942); Jeffrey Richards, *Films and British National Identity: From Dickens to Dad's Army* (Manchester University Press, 1997); William Roache with Stan Nicholls, *Ken and Me* (Simon and Schuster, 1993); Joe Roberts, *With Spanners Descending* (Bluecoat Press, 1996); Roger Rolls, *Variety at Hulme Hippodrome, Manchester, 1920–1940* (Print Designs, Wilmslow, Cheshire, 2000); George Rowell and Anthony Jackson, *The Repertory Movement: A History of Regional Theatre in Britain* (Cambridge University Press, 1984); Derek Salberg, *A Mixed Bag* (Cortney Publications, 1983); Pauline Scudamore, *Spike Milligan* (Granada, 1985); Gus Smith, *Richard Harris* (Robert Hale, 1990); Harry Stanley, *Can You Hear Me, Mother?: Sandy Powell's Lifetime of Music Hall* (Jupiter Books, 1975); Elizabeth Sussex, *Lindsay Anderson* (Studio Vista, 1969); Gay Sussex, Peter Helm, Andrew Brown, *Looking Back at Levenshulme and Burnage* (Willow, 1987); Robert Tanitch, *Guinness* (Harrap, 1989); Eric Taylor, *Showbiz Goes to War* (Robert Hale, 1992); John W. R. Taylor, *Fairey Aviation* (Chalford 1997); Rod Taylor, *The Guinness Book of Sitcoms* (Guinness, 1994); Harry Thompson, *Peter Cook* (Hodder and Stoughton, 1997); Ben Travers, *A-Sitting on a Gate* (W. H. Allen, 1978); John Walker (ed.), *Halliwell's Film and Video Guide* (HarperCollins, 1997); Max Wall with Peter Ford, *The Fool on the Hill*

(Quartet, 1975); Nicholas Wapshott, *Peter O'Toole* (New English Library, 1983); J. P. Wearing, *The London Stage 1950–1959* (Scarecrow Press, 1993); Richard Webber, *Dad's Army: A Celebration* (Virgin, 1999); Richard Webber with Jimmy Perry and David Croft, *The Complete A–Z of Dad's Army* (Orion, 2000); Don B. Wilmeth and Christopher Bigsby (eds.), *The Cambridge History of American Theatre* (Cambridge University Press, 2000); Terry Wyke and Nigel Rudyard, *Manchester Theatres* (Bibliography of N. W. England, 1994).

CHAPTER I

A Derbyshire Village

(1915–1916)

When Arthur Lowe was born in a tiny working-class terrace cottage in a tranquil Derbyshire village in September 1915 his arrival was greeted by a thunderous 1,387-gun salute 300 miles away on the Western Front as the deadlocked British and French armies of the First World War bombarded 30 miles of German trenches with heavy guns and chlorine gas three days before launching a suicidal attack that was to win a few yards of ground at a cost of 383,000 lives.

It was a tragic but appropriate start to the life of an infant who was himself to become one of the most famous soldiers in British history, albeit a fictional one: Captain George Mainwaring, the much-loved star of *Dad's Army*, the television series about the Home Guard during the next world war. He was born on 22 September in his maternal grandfather's two-up, two-down cottage in the High Peak hamlet of Hayfield, which had its own Home Guard already, one that was just as shambolic as *Dad's Army* was to be on television. After a year of war the boys in the trenches were still able to joke about it because none of the lads from Hayfield had yet been killed or severely wounded. A couple of weeks after Arthur was born, a brave young soldier from Hayfield wrote home from Belgium a determinedly jolly letter as he and several other boys from the village were about to be relieved after spending 16 hellish days in the trenches.

We have had a pretty warm time recently and have been presented with a daily allowance of German shells. Yesterday we were bombarded for three hours, but only lost a few sandbags and a bit of sleep. Our officer detailed his daily trench report as follows: 'Enemy's shelling caused nine casualties – eight mice and one frog wounded.' This again proves the Hun's frightfulness in killing non-combatants.

But a few weeks later, in January 1916, the first two Hayfield lads to be killed in battle died in France: 21-year-old Private Willie Francis and 22-year-old Private Percy Hibbert. Thirty-seven more Hayfield men were to die before the war ended nearly three years later.

Far from the carnage, Arthur was born in the rustic peace of his grandfather Joe Ford's cottage in Spring View Terrace, which still stands but is now either 61 or 63 Kinder Road: no one today is sure. To the locals Arthur would be known for the rest of his life as Little Arthur or Young Arthur to distinguish him from his father, Big Arthur or Old Arthur, a huge, 27-year-old man with a deep, booming voice. Big Arthur was a clerk at the local railway station who could sink pint after pint of beer with little effect and who walked with his massive feet at the clock-face position of ten to two. Neither Big nor Little Arthur was given a second Christian name: they were simple country people; so simple that Big Arthur's father, Tom, an illiterate railway platelayer, had signed his name with a cross when he had registered Big Arthur's birth in November 1888.

Little Arthur's mother, Nan, had been born and raised in Hayfield. Her family was posher than Big Arthur's, for when her father, a journeyman tailor, had registered her birth in June 1885 he had given her two names, Mary Annie, and had signed his name properly; later, he gave up tailoring and became a fireman. Nan's mother or grandmother had worked as a servant in a big house, and the family sideboard glittered with cut glass and silver – presents perhaps from grateful employers. But Nan had not been too posh to set her cap at Big Arthur as soon as he had come to Hayfield from his home village of Godley, five miles away in Cheshire, to work at the railway station as a booking clerk for the Grand Central Railway in 1906, when he was 18. They looked an odd couple as they walked together through the village, he a young giant, she so tiny and birdlike that the landlady of the Railway Inn told her: 'You look like a stork in knickers.' Nan was a girl of apparently delicate health, one of those frail creaking gates who always have something wrong with them yet somehow live much longer than anyone else, in Nan's case until she was 96. They married in Hayfield parish church in the summer of 1910, when Big Arthur was 21 and Nan 25, though she fibbed on the marriage certificate that she was only 24. It was 'a very pretty wedding', reported the local newspaper, the *High Peak Reporter*, and after the ceremony 'about 60 guests sat down to an excellent repast at the bride's home, where dancing and singing were largely indulged in'. Big Arthur had definitely married above himself. By the time Little Arthur was born his parents had returned to live in Godley, at 220 Mottram Road, near Big Arthur's parents, Tom and Mary, but Nan returned to Hayfield to give birth in her parents' home to the baby who would be her only child.

In 1915 Hayfield was a bleak scattering of small, grey stone buildings with a population of nearly 3,500 people just 15 miles east of the bustling city of Manchester, but in spirit 1,000 miles away, nestling in a beautiful little valley beneath the looming 2,088-foot peak of Kinder Scout, straddling a trout stream and the country lane between Glossop and Chapel-en-le-Frith, and surrounded by woods and hillsides dotted with sheep and divided by sturdy dry-stone walls. So beautiful is the area that in summer thousands of people would pass through the village – as they did that August Bank Holiday a month before Little Arthur was born – to walk the Sett Valley Trail and to climb up high on to the rugged Pennine Way and to hike across the Peak District. The feudal lord of the manor was the Duke of Devonshire, who lived at nearby Chatsworth House, and the names of Hayfield's streets are still redolent of a bygone age: Fairy Bank Road, Cock Robin Row, Swallow House Lane, Fishers Bridge, Steeple End Fold, Rhubarb Square. At the Anglican Church of St Matthew's, where Nan and Big Arthur were married and John Wesley preached in 1755, the gravestones in the churchyard are carved with the stern biblical names of a stout northern breed of canny, tight-lipped, tight-fisted, God-fearing Englishmen: Caleb Shaw, Josiah Bowden, Ebenezer Adamson, Moses Chatterton, Abraham Massey, Lemuel Wild, Israel Barrington, Aaron Collier. It was the kind of English village where the local poet, Edward Fife, could write a verse that begins:

'And here I am wi' both mi sleeves up
Sweepin' all these bally leaves up.'

In 1915 there were three Methodist chapels as well as the established church, though none of the Lowes was ever much interested in religion. There were two hotels (the George, dating from 1533, and the Royal), three inns (the Toll Bar, the Bull's Head, and the Pack Horse, the last dating from 1577), three ale-house drinking dens, two primary schools, a doctor, Liberal and Conservative Clubs, a cricket club, a branch of the Manchester and County Bank, and a stationer and post office, where the sub-postmaster was also called Arthur Lowe – Arthur *Howard* Lowe, who saw to it that letters were delivered by horse and trap twice a day and even on Sundays. The village was still firmly rooted in the nineteenth century, with its resident blacksmith, wheelwright, cooper, tripe dresser, carpenter, coal merchant and three bootmakers, and it also enjoyed the services of six confectioners, five butchers, five drapers, four grocers, two fruiterers, a baker, greengrocer, druggist, chemist, ironmonger, and hairdresser. There was also a co-op and a gas company. For the farmers there was a shepherds' market twice a year and cattle fairs in May and October. Because of the abundance of river water, there were two large calico-printing works, two paper mills, a paper-printing works, and a cotton mill, providing plenty of jobs. Hayfield also had a reputation for being a wonderfully healthy place to live, thanks to its pure mountain air and sparkling mountain water, and both Nan and Big Arthur were to enjoy long lives. It was a good place for Little Arthur Lowe to be born.

The first weekend of his life was the start of Old Wakes Week, an ancient holiday when the whole village stopped work and feasted for six or seven days, relishing on Wakes Sunday itself the traditional dinner of beef, mashed turnips, potatoes and pickles, followed by rice pudding with currants; maybe that too was a portent, for Little Arthur was to grow up with a deep love of his grub. Because of the war, however, there was little to celebrate, and it was the quietest Wakes Week for years. Christmas Day was also much quieter than usual, even thought the village band played hymns and carols in the streets, and it ended with a miserable, wet evening. Nature seemed unsettled. On New Year's Eve an earthquake shook the village so violently that people sitting at home in their chairs were shunted across the floor, and a few weeks later the village was blanketed by a great snowstorm.

When Little Arthur was nine months old, the *High Peak Reporter* informed its readers that 'the Hayfield Platoon of Home Guards were inspected on Wednesday evening on the cricket field by Colonel Wilkinson and Adjutant Lees, of Buxton. The men were kept on the move for nearly two hours, and gave the large audience of spectators quite a surprise.' Afterwards the Colonel exhorted the platoon to 'play the game and do your best'. He reminded the men that 'their duty was to act in case of invasion or disturbance' and that 'every man must be able to use a rifle and be ready to use it if required' – a pointless instruction since the Home Guard still had no rifles at all, let alone any ammunition, after nearly two years of war.

In August the war came to Hayfield itself when a Zeppelin flew overhead while the village was full of summer day-trippers. As the autumn days shortened into winter, strict lighting restrictions were introduced, so that all the street lamps were extinguished and the village became extremely dark at night. To add to all the gloom and unhappiness of that year, it was a bitterly cold winter of icy roads, deep snowdrifts and biting winds, and the village's only medical man, Dr Frank Pritchard, decided to go and live elsewhere, leaving the villagers at the mercy of the district nurse, Nurse Loose. None of this dismayed the local Home Guard, which was renamed the Hayfield Platoon of Volunteers and marched about importantly, rifleless, to the raucous accompaniment of a drum and bugle band under the beady eye of its leader, Captain Walter Bowden, who was land steward to one of the two main landowners in the area.

Big Arthur was doing well with the railway and in 1916 he became a clerk in Manchester at the busy mainline London Road station (now Piccadilly Station), and he and Nan rented a humble little house three miles south-east of the city centre, at 112 Hemmons Road in the suburb of Levenshulme. But in 1916, too, the government passed a bill conscripting all men between the ages of 18 and 41, even if they were married. The first day of the four-month Battle of the Somme had just cost 60,000 British casualties and the generals were running out of bodies. Big Arthur was called to do his duty. He was 28. His country needed him, and he was sent to France to join the rest of the cannon fodder.

Manchester
(1916–1939)

Manchester in 1916 was Britain's second city and fourth largest port, despite the fact that the cotton and textile industry that had fuelled its growth was in terminal decline. It was a bustling, raucous centre of heavy industry and commerce; a frenetic metropolis teeming with two and a half million people and hundreds of horses, cars and trams, its factory chimneys belching smoke into the damp, foggy, atmosphere; the home of a great newspaper (the *Manchester Guardian*), orchestra (the Hallé), school (Manchester Grammar) and university. The southern suburb of Levenshulme was still a quiet village surrounded by farms and open fields, where the rustic silence was broken only now and then by a train rattling past on its way to London or a tram clattering down the cobbled main street, Stockport Road. To the south there were more than 50 open fields, a golf course, two brooks, and a 54-acre public park, Cringle Fields.

The house that the Lowes rented was on the edge of open country and just a few yards from Crowcroft Park, Yew Tree Farm, two football grounds, a cricket pitch, and some bowling greens. It was a mean little house in a terraced row of tiny, two-up, two-down, redbrick municipal units that, by the time I saw them in 2000, looked unloved and badly rundown, with filthy windows and peeling paint. The area had become an Asian ghetto, the street was punctuated with potholes and decorated with litter and graffiti, and many of the houses had broken or boarded-up windows. In fact, by 2000 all of central Levenshulme was a tatty place of ugly, dwarfish buildings, shabby little shops and litter.

It was probably less of a slum in 1916 but it was still a poor, cramped, working-class area. It must have come as a shock to Nan and Big Arthur after the rural charms of Hayfield and Godley, though old photographs show that in the early 1900s Stockport Road was at least wide and clean, with not a trace of litter anywhere, and its buildings comparatively salubrious. Horses, carts and carriages still clopped and rattled along the streets, which were lit by tall gas lamps, and everyone wore a hat, children as well as adults, the men in caps or straw boaters. Milk from one of the local farms was delivered by horse-drawn cart, and a couple of regular street vendors pushed barrows around the village selling vinegar from a big barrel and a wide variety of fish: cod, plaice, skate, shrimps, jellied eels. Another street vendor would push a cart around the village, ringing a bell and shouting 'Pies! Muffins! Pikelets!' (Pikelets are thin crumpets.)

Here young Arthur Lowe was to live for more than a third of his life, until he was 24. His earliest years were probably very similar to those of other working-class children who lived in the area, like Queenie Needham, who told Clive Hopwood for his book *Memories: Reminiscences of Rusholme*:

> There was no radio or television, so we had to amuse ourselves drawing, knitting, playing draughts, or trying to sew. But mostly children used to play in the street – cars were almost non-existent then. We played with skipping ropes … the boys would sometimes pinch it and put it over the lamp arm of the gas street lamp and swing around and back … Then there was Rally-O, Puss in the Corner, Whip and Top, Hopscotch, and wall games. The boys played cricket at the gable ends, drawing wickets on opposite walls, and goalposts for football in winter.

It was a hard life, especially for the women, who were expected to cook lunch (since everyone came home at midday) as well as supper on a small gas fire or an old fire range that had to be black-leaded and emery-papered every week, and to clean the stone flags in the kitchen. Bathing was done in a tin bath that hung on a nail in the backyard when not in use, and the bathwater was heated by lighting a fire under the boiler in the kitchen, which also provided the hot water for boiling the laundry every Monday. Drying the laundry involved squeezing it through an old wringer in the backyard, hanging it out in the street to dry, and pressing it with a flat iron that had been heated in front of the fire. The houses themselves had gas lighting, just one cold tap and an outdoor lavatory. Life for working-class families then was frighteningly precarious. Mrs Needham remembered that a number of families, some with as many as 10 children, were so poor that they relied on their neighbours to give them a little food now and then.

> We were quite a close-knit community and neighbours were always ready to help one another [but] there were two families in the avenue where the husband had died and the families were sent to the parish, where they were given black bread and other ghastly food … In those days there was no help for these people; no child allowance, and in some cases the child had to go into a home.

Another contemporary, Derek McEleavey, told Mr Hopwood that menus rarely varied. On Monday harassed mothers would serve up bubble and squeak – fried potato and cabbage leftovers from the Sunday meal – and on Friday it was always fish. A good, cheap weekday standby was tripe – black tripe, honeycombed, thick seam or jellied tripe, sometimes cold with tomatoes and 'vinegar in every hole' – but Sunday was the day for 'a slap-up do', the one day that most people ate meat. By contrast with modern times, it was chicken that was rare and expensive then and beef that was cheap. 'After Christmas you'd save the carcass of the bird and for about a week you'd make soup out of it every day, boiling up the bones.' As for the biggest treat of all, 'if anyone had a tin of salmon they were rich. The only time you saw tinned salmon was at funerals.'

Since Big Arthur had a secure job at London Road station with the London and North Eastern Railway (the LNER) – otherwise known as the Late Never Early Railway – and since they had only themselves and Little Arthur to worry about, the Lowes would at first have been better off than most of their neighbours, but when Big Arthur was sent to fight in France life for Nan was much more difficult. Luckily her parents were only 15 miles away in Hayfield, and she and Little Arthur spent an increasing amount of time with them there, quite possibly living with them most of the time until Big Arthur returned from the war in 1918. Nan's apparently delicate health gave her the excuse to rely more and more on her mother, old Mrs Ford, whose names were also Mary Ann, to help with raising the child, and it is widely believed in Hayfield that it was Arthur's granny rather than his mother who really brought him up. This may have been fortunate for Arthur, since he told his own son, Stephen, that as a boy he had been bullied by his mother.

Against all the odds Big Arthur survived two terrible years in the trenches, those nightmare years of the Third Battle of Ypres, Passchendaele, the huge German offensives of 1918, and the final Battle of the Somme. He did suffer a mustard-gas attack that was to leave him with chronic bronchitis, but it did not stop him smoking cheroots for the rest of his life. 'Big Arthur never spoke of the First World War,' his grandson, Stephen, wrote in his vivid memoir *Arthur Lowe: A Life*, 'but he had some gruesome brass trophies converted to cigarette lighters and so on … Every time he lit up I thought I could smell German blood. He was a tall man and must have been powerful in his day, an infantryman with a bayonet and muddied boots. The British Tommy.'

Armistice Day, 11 November 1918, was celebrated with frenzied joy in Hayfield and even three-year-old Little Arthur must have felt the excitement. Everyone stopped work – the women even abandoned the laundry despite the fact that it was a washday Monday – and the streets were decorated with hundreds of flags and streamers. Captain Bowden told the Home Guard, the Platoon of Volunteers, that military drill would no longer be compulsory, and at 3 p.m. a brass band marched *oompah-oompah-oompah* through the streets, followed by a procession of Boy Scouts, children waving flags and banners, and a milk float carrying a group of soldiers who had already been discharged. The church bells rang all afternoon and evening, and that night there was a firework display – the last thing the soldiers needed after years of terrifying explosions on the Western Front. The street lamps were lit again for the first time in three years and at 7.30 p.m. a large congregation attended a service of thanksgiving in St Matthew's Church to remember the 39 men from the village who had died. Finally, the celebrations ended with a dance in the church schoolroom.

When Big Arthur returned from the war he moved Nan and Little Arthur back into the house in Levenshulme and resumed his job at London Road station. Little Arthur still spent a great deal of time with his grandparents in Hayfield, where his greatest pleasure as a boy was when his grandfather took him on Saturday afternoons to watch the cricket matches on the circular field in the middle of the village. 'Here was born my love for cricket,' he said many years later. 'For me, the real thing has always been played on the village green.'

When he was four he joined the infants' section of the Chapel Street Elementary Municipal School just a few streets away from Hemmons Road in the centre of Levenshulme, a solid, red-brick, one-storey building with high ceilings and two crowded playgrounds surrounded by sharp iron railings. The infants' section was in a temporary structure known as The Tin School. Little Arthur was not a pretty boy. A photograph of him in 1923 at the age of seven, dressed in grey flannel shorts, a tie, jacket and cap and standing haughtily on the back of a lorry during a High Bourne Chapel ladies' group Sunday outing, shows an unnerving miniature replica of the future Captain Mainwaring, right up to the big nose. Still, he was clever enough to be put into the A-stream classes at the Chapel Street school. His days there would have been little different from those experienced in the 1920s by Norman Worrell, who went to a similar school nearby. 'You sat at an old iron desk with an ink well on the top,' Mr Worrell told Clive Hopwood.

The seats tipped up. You took your own pen, and you had a sliding pencil box. You were provided with the ink, and if you were the monitor, you'd go around filling the ink wells. At playtime the boys used to rag each other. The girls were on the other side of the playground, separated by a railing …. As you got older you had a man teacher [and] they'd think nothing of getting hold of your ear and pulling you out to the front. One teacher there had been expelled from another school – his trick was to rap your knuckles with a wooden ruler until they bled. And you wouldn't be allowed to be left-handed; they'd tie your hand behind your back. If you were late for school you weren't allowed in the class, you had to stand outside. There used to be a punishment book, and if you went in it more than once you had to go to the headmaster. I remember a lad being caught smoking in the toilets, and the whole school had to assemble. The lad had to drop his pants and bend over a table. They said, 'Let this be a lesson to all of you.' He didn't smoke again!

Arthur's classmate Harold Grimshaw told Stephen Lowe that Arthur did well at school and that the most important teacher for his future was a Miss Crossley, an austere woman with short hair and a big nose, who taught him French and drama, and first ignited his interest in the theatre. Grimshaw also recalled that they became Boy Scouts and interested in girls – in Arthur's case a girl called Mildred Nuttall – and that they liked watching the girls playing basketball in their short skirts. In Hayfield Arthur befriended a much younger boy, Vic Turner, whose parents ran a draper's shop and lived a few doors away from Arthur's Ford grandparents in Kinder Road. 'Arthur lived with Mrs Ford,' Mr Turner told me in 2000. 'He was there all the time.' Young Vic was only seven and Arthur 11, a big gap at that age, but Arthur had no other friends in Hayfield. 'We saw each other every day and played together with my train set in my house,' said Mr Turner. Arthur had also discovered the pleasure of reading and said later that his favourite books as a boy had been those by R. M. Ballantyne, George Henty, H. Rider Haggard, P. C. Wren and Dornford Yates. No book, however, could match for sheer excitement the shocking murder in Little Hayfield in 1927 of the wife of Arthur Collinson, the landlord of the New Inn – now the Lantern Pike Inn – by an intruder who broke in to rob the pub. A local man, Jerry Hayward, was hanged for the murder, which must surely have made a vivid impression on 11-year-old Arthur and sharpened his budding sense of drama, especially if he knew both the victim and the murderer, as he may well have done.

Arthur left Chapel Street when he was nearly 12, in July 1927, after winning a scholarship to a grammar school. Many years later he told his *Dad's Army* colleague Bill Pertwee that he had been a grammar school boy, but neither of the two grammar schools in Manchester at the time has any record of him. According to Harold Grimshaw, he and Arthur went on to Alma Park Central School in Levenshulme, just a few blocks away from Chapel Street, but Alma Park mysteriously has no record of Arthur either. Equally mysteriously, the Chapel Street School records do not say where he went, though they list the later schools of most other pupils. The best guess is that Arthur was unable to take up his scholarship because his parents could not afford to send him to a grammar school, and that he did go to Alma Park but fibbed to Pertwee because he felt that at least he had won and deserved a grammar school place.

Alma Park Central was in the smart area of Errwood Road, a leafy residential avenue of elegant, two-storey houses with gardens, and close to the wide open spaces of Burnage House, High Farm and Cringle Fields Park. A low, red-brick building surrounded by a large asphalt playground, it had about 300 pupils, both boys and girls, and had been founded just two and a half years earlier. It may not have been a grammar school but it offered an impressive curriculum which included French, physics, chemistry and geography as well as the three Rs, art, handicrafts, cookery, needlework and organised games. The classes were large – five had 40 pupils and three had 30 – but it was easier to teach big classes in those days because teenagers were much more disciplined than they are today. The headmaster, Walter Moorfield, had a BSc degree as well as a BA, and four of the 15 other teachers (five men and 10 women) had degrees, while the other 11 all had teacher's certificates. As in any smart public school, the pupils were divided into four houses for sporting and scholarship rivalry: Alba, Libera, Magna and Alta. The school logbook for 1927 and 1928 is surprisingly dull, reporting nothing at all about individual pupils or incidents but recording only humdrum episodes such as 'Plumber repaired Boys' Lavatory taps' and 'Washing of School Towels by Laundry commenced.' No mention is made of cricket matches, school plays, hobbies, magazines, or any other extra-curricular activities, though in later years there are passing references to swimming, cricket and netball. Grimshaw told Stephen Lowe that he and Arthur used to enjoy informal boxing in a friend's basement and that Arthur 'was a handy boxer ... light on his feet and aggressive, hard to beat'.

The most entertaining logbook entries are those relating to the numerous absences of the headmaster, who was away 'ill' or with 'sprained shoulder and rheumatism' so often that one starts to suspect him of playing truant or enjoying an illicit affair during school hours. On 9 December 1929 comes the first record that may be connected definitely with Arthur: the pupils performed two one-act plays, one of them, *The Grand Cham's Diamond*, a play in which Grimshaw told Stephen Lowe he and Arthur had appeared and in which Arthur played a colonel, drew a gun and shot him. There is, in fact, no colonel among the five characters in *The Grand Cham's Diamond*, a silly, melodramatic play about a London family that suddenly finds an Eastern potentate's stolen jewel crashing in through their suburban window, but one character does indeed shoot another: the thief is shot by a Scotland Yard detective, so Arthur probably played the detective and Grimshaw the thief. The play was hardly a memorable debut and is packed with wonderfully absurd lines. When the suburban father, for instance, tells his wife that she has no right to keep the diamond because it belongs to the Grand Cham, she replies: ' 'e's a tyrant, 'e stole it off some nigger. Now it's come to me. It's mine.

It's mine as much as anyone's.' Still, this ludicrous play gave Arthur the first role we know of in his 53-year career in the theatre.

He was already taking an interest in the cinema and theatre. By 1927 there were 295 'picture palaces' in Greater Manchester and by the early 1930s Levenshulme had three cinemas, but it was probably in the neighbouring suburb of Rusholme that Arthur's thespian ambitions were first seriously ignited. Rusholme had two cinemas as well as a repertory theatre which put on a different play every week or fortnight with the help in 1930 of the future Dame Wendy Hiller, who was then its assistant stage manager. But the major attraction in Rusholme for Arthur was the local variety hall, Leslie's Pavilion, on the corner of Dickenson Road and Wilmslow Road, where a local shop assistant called Beryl Reid was to start her acting career.

Big Arthur had a good baritone voice and he, Nan and Little Arthur would often enjoy musical evenings around the piano with friends when Big Arthur would sing a current music-hall song like Tosti's 'Parted'. The Lowes loved music hall and took Little Arthur along with them. Right from an early age he revelled in the magic of the old-time variety shows which sadly were about to be killed off by the cinema, and he loved going to see the concert-party performances at Leslie's in those last years before it was forced to close in 1939. The Pavilion had been founded in 1904 by Harry Leslie, who had once been a clerk in a Manchester cotton office but had decided at the age of 28 that he was fed up with working in an office. 'Dad would have been drawn to a man like Harry Leslie like a can of spinach to a magnet,' said Stephen Lowe. 'He admired entrepreneurs, impresarios, theatre managers, risk-takers, men who stood or fell by their own decisions. He loved people who were just a little larger than life.' And 'Arthur loved the old comedians, like Harry Tate and Robb Wilton, and knew a lot about the variety theatre and music hall,' Bill Pertwee told me in 2000. 'Harry Tate and Robb Wilton were just like Arthur was later when he played Captain Mainwaring, that sort of character who said ridiculous things and pretended he was in control of everything but wasn't.'

In March 1930 the dreary Alma Park logbook suddenly springs to life, thanks to the dramatic exploits of two French teachers. On 11 March the regular French mistress, Mam'selle Winifred Hand BA, went absent with a medical certificate attesting that she had 'Nervous Depression'. She returned after nine days, but on the afternoon of 9 April was once again taken ill with nervous depression and had to be taken home. She was still absent 10 days later, so the Head engaged a replacement: Miss Gladys M. Smith, MA, a gloriously wacky character who might have been created by P. G. Wodehouse. After just three days of teaching 'Miss Smith left at 3.40 p.m. to travel to Hoylake (Tide 6.15) to take a yacht to Liverpool,' reported the logbook. The following morning she was late for school, returning at 9.45 a.m., 'delayed from Liverpool'. Five days later 'Miss Smith fainted 9.5 a.m. and resumed lessons later.' Six days after that, she and the Headmaster had a row and she flounced off to the Education Department offices to complain about him, which resulted in the arrival at Alma Park of two school inspectors to investigate the complaint.

The Whitsun holiday provided a brief, 10-day truce, but when the school reassembled it did so without a French mistress at all, for Mam'selle Hand was still suffering from nervous depression and 'unable to resume duties', and Mam'selle Smith was 'absent from duties' and had not bothered to explain why until she sent a telegram two days later reporting that she was suffering from 'biliousness'. A few days later Miss Smith was again absent without leave, and again a few days after that because of 'blood poison', though this time she did not bother to let the school know. Eventually the harassed Headmaster was able to get rid of Miss Smith – who nevertheless somehow persuaded the Education Department to pay her salary in full right through the ensuing holidays – only for two detectives to arrive and arrest three pupils for theft from a motor car. Young Arthur must have watched this farce with delight and filed its comic details away in his memory for future use. He had begun to develop a talent for mimicry and could hardly have resisted the temptation to lampoon the two neurotic French mistresses.

In December 1930 two more plays were performed by the pupils, and 15-year-old Arthur was probably in one of them since he said in later life that he had appeared in more than one play at school.

Arthur left Alma Park surprisingly early for a scholarship boy, just before his sixteenth birthday, maybe because he felt that his father could no longer afford to keep him at school, but he knew precisely what he wanted to do with his life and that it would need no great academic qualifications: he wanted to join the merchant navy. For years he had often watched with longing the huge vessels loaded with heavy machinery, locomotives, steam engines, machine tools and textiles casting off at the docks and slipping out through the Manchester Ship Canal and the Mersey estuary towards the Irish Sea, the open oceans and the big, wide world. He developed deeply romantic notions about ships and the sea, and hankered for a life on the ocean waves, but his dream was shattered when he failed the vital Board of Trade eye test just after he had left school. 'That was a terrible blow,' he confessed years later. 'If I had passed the eyesight test, I would be in the Merchant Navy and would never have become an actor at all.'

Suddenly he needed to find a job, and in 1931 the world was a cold and frightening place, for Manchester, like everywhere else, was in the grip of the Great Depression.

In July 1931 one man in six was out of work in Manchester compared with the national average of one in four, and heavy Manchester industries such as engineering were badly hit. There were queues outside every employment exchange. Early in October 10,000 protesters marched from All Saints to Quay Street, and four days later another march ended in a brawl between National Unemployment Workers Movement protesters and the police, and led to 26 arrests. Arthur's first job after leaving school was as a barrow boy for the big Manchester branch of the motor-accessory company Brown Brothers, and he pushed a handcart through the streets of Manchester for 10 shillings a week, which would be worth about £16 a week today. At least Big Arthur was doing well at work and had been promoted, so that he, Nan and Little Arthur were able to leave the poky little house in Hemmons Road in 1931 and move to a much nicer house and area a mile and a half away to the south-west at 3 Barcicroft Road. It was a much more spacious, semi-detached house, with a small garden at the front and back, three bedrooms, and a bow window in the living room – and it was brand new, one of the hundreds of municipal dwellings that had been built by Manchester Corporation on open green farmland beyond Burnage during a frenzy of suburban construction in the 1920s. A year later the Lowes moved again, this time just around the corner to 3 Barnfield Road, a similar but plainer, less attractive three-bedroom semi.

Little Arthur soon found himself a proper job as a clerk in the bicycle department of Brown Brothers, which was a huge national company with a dozen branches and warehouses all over Britain that specialised in motor cars and spares but also sold almost everything imaginable, from airguns and footballs to lawnmowers, prams, paint, radios, rollerskates, raincoats, tools and billiard tables. The company was also involved in the aircraft industry: it was a Brown Brothers mechanic who had assisted Wilbur Wright when he made his first 12-second flight in 1903, Brown Brothers that launched the first airmail service from Hendon aerodrome, and Brown Brothers that supplied the engine for Amy Johnson's solo flight to Australia in 1930. In fact the company claims that every aircraft built in Britain before 1945 had some parts that it had made.

The Manchester branch was in a big, old, three-storey, one-time jam factory with a haunted tower at 261–273 Deansgate, which still stands, close to where the television series *Coronation Street* is filmed – the series that was to make Arthur a TV star 30 years later. 'It was a wonderful firm,' I was told in 2001 by Mrs Ethel Hulme, who joined Brown Brothers in Manchester as a 15-year-old order-office clerk in 1934. 'I think Arthur enjoyed it there. It was a very pleasant, happy, easygoing place to work.' Each day Arthur would catch an early morning tram from Burnage into the city with Mrs Hulme's future husband, Fred, who was his age and also worked at Browns. They would work from 8.30 a.m. to 6 p.m. (8.30 till noon on Saturdays), with an hour off for lunch, which they would eat at one of the two cafés on the other side of Deansgate or at one of the chip shops down Liverpool Road. Among the 100 or so employees were 10 men in the cycle spares and accessories department on the first floor, where Arthur's job was to stand all day behind the counter keeping track of the stock using trays of stock cards, and ordering more supplies when particular items ran low or when a customer wanted something that was not in stock. His responsibilities covered hundreds of individual items stocked in the cycle department, from handlebars and saddles to pedals, wheels, spokes, sprockets, tyres, brakes, toolbags, chains, padlocks, gas lamps, hubs, mudguards, child carriers and even Brown Brothers' own-brand bike, the Vindec.

For working 51 hours a week he was paid £2 10s (the equivalent of about £80 a week today). 'Mind you,' said Mrs Hulme,

if you were earning £3 a week in those days you were well paid, and if you were earning £5 you were in the millionaire bracket! If you wanted a rise you had to go in and ask for it, and if you were lucky you got 2/6d a week more, but if the manager was in a bad mood he'd tell you to pick your window – which one you wanted to be thrown out of! Arthur's boss was Reg Green, a nice chappie. They were all nice in the cycle department, but a bit mad at times. When the window cleaner came to do the inside windows they nailed his bucket to the floor! But Arthur wasn't like the rest of the chaps there and kept himself to himself. He didn't mess about with the rest of the lads, because they were up to all sorts of tricks there which he never joined in. He was more reserved in those days and didn't have any friends there among the chappies that I ever heard about. They did think he was a bit standoffish and I think at first they used to take the mickey out of him a bit. He was well spoken and I wouldn't say he had any Manchester or Derbyshire accent. And he was definitely a bit pompous even then. Captain Mainwaring was not acting: that was Arthur; he was exactly like that when we knew him, even when he was 21. Even in those days he was already Captain Mainwaring.

Yet Arthur had a surprisingly flamboyant side to his nature. 'He used to wear a snakeskin tie, which was a very fast thing to do in those days,' said Mrs Hulme.

It was cream with dark brown markings on it. And he used to stand at the desk with his stock cards crooning like Al Bowlly. He was really good at it and had quite a decent voice, a Bing Crosby sort of voice, and the lads always referred to him as Al. He used to sing love songs like 'I'm in the Mood for Love' at the counter while he was working, but he never talked about acting or the theatre and we were astonished when he appeared later in *Coronation Street*.

Arthur relished the music of the big bands of the Thirties – Lou Stone, Roy Fox, Sydney Kyte, Jack Jackson – and another Manchester friend, Phyllis Bateman, remembered that in his teens he ran his own little dance band and played in dance halls. 'He played the saxophone,' she told me. 'I can see him here, sitting in a chair, acting silly, pretending to play one.'

When Arthur was 19 he started going out with Lillian Peake, an invoice typist at Browns. 'She was very nice, perhaps a year younger than Arthur, dark-haired, a good churchgoer,' said Mrs Hulme, 'and at one time she was the Rose Queen. I would imagine they did their courting in the back row of the cinema.' There were plenty of places in Manchester in the 1930s for a young couple to enjoy themselves, not only the dark back row of the cinema but also the 100-year-old Bellevue amusement park and zoo, which had an open-air dance floor and regular firework shows. If Arthur ever took Lillian home to Levenshulme they could have gone swimming in one of the two new swimming baths that had opened in Barlow Road in 1931, and they would have gone to Arthur's beloved music halls: Leslie's Pavilion and the Hulme Hippodrome in Preston Street, where numerous famous variety artistes had appeared, among them Bud Flanagan and Chesney Allen, George Formby, Tommy Handley, Fred Karno, Sandy Powell, Tommy Trinder, Max Wall, even Edward VII's mistress Lillie Langtry. There was another Hippodrome (in Warwick Street) as well as the richly ornate, 1,005-seat Manchester Palace of Varieties – with its huge entrance hall, green-and-white marble floor, polished mahogany doors and vast auditorium with lifesize Greek and Roman statues and golden chairs and carpets – where Charlie Chaplin, Gracie Fields, Will Hay, Harry Lauder, Dan Leno, Marie Lloyd, George Robey, Little Tich and Donald Wolfit had trod the boards. Stephen Lowe says in his book that Arthur actually worked at the Palace of Varieties, first as a scene shifter and then as assistant stage manager, and may even have played some small parts there, but he admitted to me that the story is apocryphal. In the 1970s Arthur himself said that until he started acting in the army in 1943 his only previous theatrical experience had been at school. Arthur's romance with Lillian lasted for two or three years but 'then it suddenly broke up – I don't know why – and poor Lillian was broken-hearted,' said Mrs Hulme. 'It was very tragic.' Lillian eventually married and lived to be over 80, dying in 2000.

Now that Arthur was 22 his father urged him to find a job with better prospects and suggested that he should train as a draughtsman with Fairey Aviation, which had a huge aircraft factory employing several thousand people at Crossley Road in Heaton Chapel, less than a mile from the Lowes' home in Barnfield Road. Arthur left Browns in 1936 to work at the Fairey factory as a progress chaser, which he explained years later was 'a sort of time-and-motion man chivvying the fellows along and seeing that they produced a certain amount of work each day'. There was in fact more to it than that: starting at eight o'clock each morning, he also had to ensure that the various bits and pieces necessary for building each plane were where they ought to be when they were needed on his section of the production line in the vast hangars.

Fairey was already renowned for several of its aircraft: the Fairey IIIF spotter-reconnaissance biplane, the Fox light bomber, the Hendon canti-lever monoplane heavy bomber, and the record-breaking Long Range Monoplane. During the Second World War it was to build numerous other aircraft: Albacores, Barracudas, Beaufighters, Fireflies, Fulmars, and Halifax bombers. When Arthur joined the company in 1938 a second world war looked inevitable and Fairey was frantically mass-producing two types of aircraft at Heaton Chapel for the Fleet Arm Arm: the Battle light bomber and the Swordfish torpedo-bomber reconnaissance plane, the gawky but magnificent fabric-covered 'Stringbag' that was to be one of the heroes of the war, sinking more enemy ships than any other plane and effectively destroying the German battleship *Bismarck* in 1941.

Arthur was not to know all this and found his new job dreadfully boring. To spice up his life he joined the Territorial Army of part-time soldiers in February 1939. He wanted to learn to ride a horse, so he signed up as a cavalry trooper in the Duke of Lancaster's Own Yeomanry, 'The Dukes', and began to enjoy playing soldiers on evenings and at weekends and attending the TA horseback summer camp at Lowther Park. By joining up he ensured that he would be among the very first men to be called up when war was finally declared on 3 September 1939. It meant that he also missed one of the finest moments at the Fairey Aviation factory in Heaton Chapel. In 1940, after the first German blitz of Manchester, King George VI visited the Fairey production line and stopped to talk to one of the workers. 'And what do *you* make?' he asked.

'Time and a half, Your Majesty,' the worker replied.

CHAPTER 3

Kidding Mr Hitler

(1939–1945)

At 7.30 p.m. on Friday, 1 September 1939 the 30 officers and 635 men of the Duke of Lancaster's Own Yeomanry were mobilised for war. Among them was 24-year-old Trooper 322499 Arthur Lowe, who joined the rest of A/C Squadron at their barracks in Whalley Road, Manchester. As a progress chaser at Fairey's Aviation, a vital wartime job, he could easily have claimed exemption from call-up, but he did not even consider it. Two days later the Prime Minister, Neville Chamberlain, made his fateful Sunday broadcast to tell the nation that once again Britain was at war with Germany. 'We were all sat round radio sets in the barracks,' I was told in 2001 by one of Arthur's army comrades, Norman ('Nobby') Hewitt. 'When Chamberlain declared war on Germany they all cheered, but not me, and I don't think Arthur did either. I felt like crying. I knew my life was going to change for ever. One lad fainted and had to be revived by the medical orderly. What a life!'

The Dukes had a noble history and had won regimental honours at 14 great battles during the First World War, but by 1939 an old-fashioned cavalry regiment was absurdly out of date. Officers were still expected to give orders by waving their swords about. So you want them to advance? Very well: swing the sword arm forward and point the sword to the front. Such ancient traditions might well have been adequate for dealing with the 'fuzzy-wuzzies' in the Sudan in 1885 but they were not going to be quite up to the job of stopping the Nazi tanks in 1940. Right from the start Arthur's war was to be as farcical as anything that the scriptwriters would dream up 30 years later for *Dad's Army*. His 21-year-old friend Bill Bateman's first wartime mission was to guard a coil of rope, a scene that could have been played to perfection by Ian Lavender as Private Pike. 'It was chaotic,' Bateman's widow, Phyllis, told me in 2001.

> They weren't organised at all. They had no proper uniforms and when one of the officers came round to pay them, he was a very grand gentleman and he used to say 'I'm so sorry it's so little', as if he was paying them out of his own pocket!

They had no horses nor even any knives and forks, and spent the first week drilling on foot, going on route marches, and attending map-reading classes and weapons training as well as cleaning and polishing their quarters. Day after day they had to clean their uniforms, swords and equipment to a gleaming finish: 57 pieces of brass on each uniform, buckles on the saddles, the saddles themselves, the boots.

The Army Remount Service bought hundreds of horses from pony clubs and private owners, who were loath to part with them. Some were thoroughbreds, some carthorses, and one that had previously pulled a milk float and was now expected to tow a gun carriage could be made to stop only if somebody shouted 'Milko!' One mare arrived with a poignant note attached to its head collar that read: 'Lizzie has been a family pet. Please look after her and bring her back safe. Thank you!' The owner of Arthur's horse, a small beast called Daisy, was so distressed to lose the animal that Arthur wrote to her regularly to reassure her that Daisy was not going to be forced to charge the German cannon. 'Some would take a five-barred gate in their stride,' wrote John Brereton in his history of the Duke of Lancaster's Own Yeomanry, *Chain Mail*, 'others could not be persuaded to negotiate a two-foot ditch. One of the latter was named "Blouse" by its rider. On being asked the reason for this odd choice, the trooper replied, "Well, sir, he ain't no bloody jumper." '

The Dukes' A/C Squadron was stationed at a disused, rundown, rat-infested cotton mill in the Lancashire village of Hawkshaw, between Bury and Bolton, where the men had to sleep on palliasses on the cold concrete floor and to get up at 5 a.m. each day to muck out the horses, a job that became decidedly unpleasant during that icy winter. Many of the soldiers went down with flu and some had to be sent to hospital, but Arthur never let the harsh conditions get him down. Bill Bateman told his wife that 'at night, when the lights had gone out, a little voice would come out of the corner where Arthur was sleeping and he'd suddenly say in a terrible Lancashire accent "This is Preston staaation mekin' traaain announcements", and then he'd reel off all the railway stations to Blackpool.' On other nights a sinister German voice would suddenly emerge from Arthur's dark corner: 'My name is Col-on-el von Kramm. Vel-come to my vaur.' Over the months Arthur developed the character of this imaginary Nazi – '*Silence*! It is *I* who vill ask ze qvestions!' – so that he took on a life of his own. The future actor was beginning to find his voices. One ex-trooper, 80-year-old Ernie Skidmore, told me that 'Arthur was short, already bald, had ginger hair and wore specs, but he appeared to be acting all the time,' and Nobby Hewitt said: 'He used to imitate officers' voices and mannerisms, and he'd say "now gather round, men," just the way he did in *Dad's Army*.' One of Arthur's victims was Sergeant Jack Ashworth, who once heard an officer's voice bark 'Sergeant Ashworth to the Squadron Office!' and obeyed the order at the double, only to find Arthur sitting there alone and po-faced. His mimicry of the officers was so perfect that his comrades would often hear an officer's voice and leap to attention – then see Arthur grinning at them. 'He also used to take off the crooners like Jack Plant who sang with the big-name bands we listened to on the radio before the war,' said Hewitt. 'Then he would collapse helpless with laughter.'

The military shambles of the Dukes provided perfect comic material. 'Yes, the regiment *was* a bit like *Dad's Army*,' Ernie Skidmore told me.

> They took all our good gear from us because we were cavalry and completely out of date for modern war. Then they found a lot of our blokes weren't fit to go out to Palestine, so they sent the Cheshire Yeomanry instead and they took all our best equipment, our super lined cavalry greatcoats, even our rifles. We got some Canadian rifles instead. They needed the better stuff for the people who were doing the fighting, I suppose. We even had some 1914–18 men there, men over 40, so they were naturally *Dad's Army*, weren't they?

When the horses eventually arrived the regiment endured long hours of training on horseback, lectures on horsemanship and how to kill a man with a sword while mounted, and how to use a rifle and machine gun. Many of these 'cavalrymen' were youngsters straight out of the

Lancashire mines and cotton mills who had never been on a horse before. Not surprisingly it was decided at the end of November that the regiment should lose its horses and become instead a mechanised unit of the Royal Artillery, a decision that appalled Arthur, since he had joined it in the first place only because he wanted to ride. It then took another two months for the necessary artillery training instructors and manuals to arrive, and because none of the Dukes knew the first thing about gunnery they had to kick their heels for several weeks looking after the horses they were no longer going to keep and continuing to undertake pointless cavalry training. Eventually, at the end of January, a gunnery instructor, Major Arnold Forster, arrived along with a pile of *Artillery Training* manuals, so that at least some theoretical training could begin even though there was still no sign of any guns. Then many of the Dukes' redundant horses were transferred to a Royal Artillery battery that had just been ordered to change from being mechanised to being cavalry – and 9 out of 10 of *those* men had never been on horseback. Only the War Office in London could possibly understand the logic of turning a cavalry regiment into an artillery regiment at the same time that it was turning a group of artillery-men into cavalrymen. While they marked time Arthur found himself doing a stocktaking job as a clerk in the Quartermaster's stores. 'He was pompous all the time,' said Skidmore, 'but a nice sort of pompous, and he was acting a little bit, so he was popular.'

By early April 1940 the Dukes had lost all their horses and even though they still had no guns they were sent by rail to Llanion barracks at Pembroke Dock in South Wales. Gunner Lowe was by now in A Troop of A Battery – which was about to be renamed the 77th (DLOY) Medium Regiment Royal Artillery (TA) – and he wore the RA gun badge on his cap and the rose of Lancaster on his collar. Promoted to Bombardier, he was put in charge of the motor transport office and the drivers' work sheets. More instructors arrived and artillery training began in earnest, though Hitler would doubtless have howled with laughter had he known how amateurish the whole operation was. 'We had a six-inch howitzer which had probably been used in the Boer War,' I was told in 2000 by 83-year-old ex-Bombardier Harry Hartill, a signals instructor who taught Arthur semaphore and Morse code.

The howitzer had a plaque on it which said 'Property of Birmingham

Parks', and we had a flat-back lorry, a fruiterer's lorry, with a huge board behind the driver's head which said 'Persil'. And just as *Dad's Army* had a butcher's van, we had a furniture van with 'W. E. Evans' on the side, the name of the owner of the furniture firm – and that came to grief underneath a low bridge when they took the top off it! We really were expecting the Germans to invade us, and when they reported that parachutists were landing we used to jump into this furniture van, armed with sticks, and go off into the night to round them up. It was exactly the same as *Dad's Army*.

As for Arthur himself, 'he was quick and learned semaphore and Morse easily,' said Hartill. 'He was full of life and funny voices, and used to march up and down and pull faces. He was very popular because he was very funny.'

In June, as the brave young pilots of the RAF fought desperately in the skies over southern England to win the Battle of Britain and prevent a Nazi invasion, the Dukes sat around in Pembroke waiting for something to happen. In August it did: the men regularly had to bolt down into their air-raid shelters when the Luftwaffe launched several heavy bombing raids against Pembroke Dock and the oil refinery at nearby Milford Haven, the worst of which, on 19 August, started a fire that burned for three weeks. There were more raids in September, during one of which a bomb fell near the officers' mess and killed one soldier, Gunner P. Jenkinson. In another raid Arthur was very nearly killed when a heavy stick of bombs fell nearby one night and his billet was strewn with shattered glass. In the morning he discovered outside his window an enormous 500-pound bomb that had still not exploded, with its fins sticking up. He got out fast.

Even though the Dukes had by now officially been an artillery regiment for 10 months, its only defence was still just one Lewis gun on a tripod. This never managed to damage even one German plane, though it did succeed in shooting several holes in a Blenheim from a nearby RAF station. The RAF commander was forced to write to the Dukes' commanding officer, Lieutenant Colonel Musgrave-Hoyle, to ask him to 'please confine your firing to enemy planes only.'

In the meantime the Secretary for War, Anthony Eden, had made a national radio appeal for civilian men who had not been called up to form platoons of Local Defence Volunteers to guard important areas, keep a lookout for German parachutists, and to train and prepare to act as a back-up should there be a German invasion – a real threat that was taken highly seriously. A quarter of a million men throughout Britain volunteered within the first 24 hours and soon 2 million had joined the LDV, which Churchill insisted in July should be renamed the Home Guard. At first it was an embarrassingly amateurish and shambolic operation. There were no uniforms, ranks or proper structure, and the only available weapons were shotguns, pitchforks, pick-axe handles, kitchen knives and broomsticks. Typical of the Home Guard then was this instruction that appeared in the standing orders of the Buckinghamshire LDV: 'In the event of observing German parachutists landing, telephone High Wycombe 26.' Matters were equally ludicrous back in Levenshulme, where a Home Guard committee had been set up in June and was now squabbling in classic *Dad's Army* fashion over the distribution of sandbags, first-aid boxes and 100 stirrup pumps. On 1 August there was a letter to the committee from a disgruntled citizen in Gloucester Avenue who claimed to have been victimised by the committee, which ordered the secretary to reply refuting the allegations. In vain. The row escalated. At the end of August, according to the Levenshulme Local Defence Committee Minute Book for 1940, the secretary 'resented the letters from Area 9 suggesting that the Executive Committee were not doing sufficient to distribute pumps.' In September several Home Guard area controllers sulkily refused to send in summaries of what they had achieved so far, and there was yet another long argument about the allocation of stirrup pumps, during which the seriously overheated secretary now argued 'strenuously' that if the pumps were distributed to the wrong people, they 'may be a liability instead of an asset'. After some vociferous debate the secretary was outvoted.

Sadly Manchester was going to need something more than a few stirrup pumps to put out the huge fires that raged through the city three months later. On the nights of 22 and 23 December 1940 the Luftwaffe's Christmas blitz devastated 30 acres of the city centre, destroying 520 buildings, damaging more than 1,000 others, and starting more than 600 fires, so that 400 extra fire engines and 3,400 firemen had to be drafted into the city from outside. One of the buildings completely destroyed was the magnificent Free Trade Hall, and parts of Manchester cathedral were badly damaged. London Road railway station was unharmed, but two others, Exchange and Victoria, were badly hit. Arthur's parents, now aged 55 and 52 and living in Heaton, decided that it was time to leave Manchester and return to the comparative safety of rural Hayfield, where they moved into a tiny cottage at 3 Fishers Lane. It was a wise move: five months later Manchester suffered another vicious blitz.

In October 1940 Arthur went off to camps at Pontypridd and Sennybridge to practise live firing, and at the end of November was sent to Gosford Castle in Northern Ireland, where he was a clerk in the battery office. Despite being given promotion, he still had a streak of rebelliousness in him. His son, Stephen, wrote in his book:

> I remember Dad saying he used to put a row of pens in his battledress top pocket because their officer thought one pen was smart but more was unsoldierly. When I watch the start of the *Dad's Army* film … I note that Pike gets told off about the pens in his top pocket. I bet that's a bit of business Arthur devised.

Not so, in fact. 'A similar thing happened to me,' *Dad's Army* creator Jimmy Perry told me. 'Arthur didn't devise much in *Dad's Army*.' By now Lieutenant-Colonel Musgrave-Hoyle had been replaced by a regular Royal Artillery commander, Lieutenant-Colonel F. H. C. Rogers, who put the men through some really serious artillery training on local firing ranges and in the Mountains of Mourne as well as giving them training courses on wireless, driving, and vehicle maintenance. 'But it was still just like *Dad's Army*,' Harry Hartill told me. 'Even when the CO wanted an electric alarm bell put at the entrance to Gosford Castle, they installed it and then couldn't get it to stop ringing.'

Arthur's skill as a mimic was now so polished that when one of the men in the signals unit, Ray Wade, decided to produce a concert party, Arthur – for some reason calling himself Fred Lowe – went along to audition for it. He was turned down, not because he was no good but because Wade had already taken on an impressionist.

Arthur's poor eyesight had already kept him out of the merchant navy and now it was to keep him out of any real danger for the rest of the war. He was medically regraded, took a three-day wireless course in Coventry, trained in radar, transferred to the Royal Ordnance Corps, and worked on searchlights in Lincolnshire before being sent out to Egypt in 1942 with thousands of other soldiers on the Cunard liner *Queen Mary*. 'The outward voyage in the "Mary" made a great impression on Arthur,' wrote Stephen.

He reminisced about it often. The great liners down to the most pathetic rusty coaster stirred his blood. He held precious a romantic image in his mind's eye of the stoical, calculating Captain pitting his wits against the forces of nature. Judging the run of the tide. Dealing mischievously with bent port agents. Being father to his men. He held a love of the sea, or rather a love of his vision of the sea, close to his heart all his life.

In Egypt Arthur remained at first with the Royal Ordnance Corps, working on and repairing searchlights, but before long he was transferred to the newly formed REME, the Royal Electrical and Mechanical Engineers. The REME's unwritten rule was 'a soldier first and a trades-man second,' said Joe Roberts, a REME private who arrived in Egypt at the same time as Arthur, in his memoir *With Spanners Descending*.

We very soon discovered that North Africa isn't the most comfortable place to be during the month of June, its humidity being particularly dreadful. You only had to take a drink of water for the sweat to come pouring out of you. To make matters worse, the infantry training was still taking place – even in the heat of midday, when all other units in the Division were taking rest breaks. The Infantry lads themselves, camped close by, thought we were raving lunatics. As a result, because we were so cheesed off with having to combine Workshops duties with military training, morale dropped like a stone.

Throughout his three years in the Middle East, Arthur was stationed a long way behind the fighting lines and far from any danger, and he never saw any action. While the British armies were fighting a desperate, doomed rearguard action against the German general Rommel at Tobruk in Libya, Arthur was sent to the Suez Canal zone 500 miles away, to El Qassâsîn, 50 miles north-west of Cairo and 40 from the canal itself. When the war came much closer to Cairo as General Montgomery drove the Germans back at the Second Battle of El Alamein, Arthur was posted even further east to a big ordnance depot at Rafah, near the coast of Palestine, in the Gaza Strip, where the summers are immensely hot and arid, the humidity averages 74 per cent, and the springs and autumns are scorched by the dry khamsin winds and battered now and then by torrential rain. Here, on the northern edge of the Sinai Desert, he joined a captain, a sergeant and nine craftsmen at the REME's 15th Radio Repair Workshops, where he lived amid the sand dunes in a tent that was pitched in a three-foot-deep hole so as to offer some protection against the icy desert nights. Here he was supposed to help to maintain and repair the radar that controlled the searchlights and anti-aircraft guns, yet although he was promoted to Acting Sergeant and graded Radio Mechanic Class I, 'he was useless as a radar mechanic,' I was told by 81-year-old Norman Littlechild, a radar engineer at Rafah who became a friend of his. 'He had no experience. At least I'd repaired radios.' Arthur was third in command of the unit after the captain and the sergeant, but 'he wasn't mechanical at all and he never worked on radio or radar units unless he had to,' said Littlechild.

He was always busy doing paperwork. That was just like everything during the war: our officer, Captain Macmillan, was a brilliant professor from Aberdeen University, but he hadn't got a clue as far as anything military or to do with radio was concerned. He even lost his revolver one day. Our sergeant was the same – absolutely useless – and he wasn't military either. It was a shambles. We weren't soldiers, we were technical people, and we didn't have a lot to do. We saw no action at all and the only enemy I saw were prisoners of war. I even went on strike three times in the army and got away with it. We didn't even do guard duty: they got African soldiers to do it, though they were a menace because if you went down to the workshops at night in the dark you'd hear 'Halt, who goes there?' – *click* – and if you didn't say 'friend' quickly, you'd had it. Many a time we marched down in the mornings to the workshops and would find the body of an Arab lying on the side of the road. They'd blown his head off.

In those days an Arab's lot was not a happy one.

We were always given to understand that if you were driving a truck in Egypt and you knocked an Arab down, you went back and made sure you'd killed him, because it was cheaper to bury him and pay compensation than it was to pay compensation if he was alive. But the Arabs used to nick stuff off our lorries like nobody's business. We woke up one morning and the tent had gone: the Arabs had been in the night and took the lot. They decided we'd have to do guard duty at night, so some of the blokes put a rifle on a tripod and connected it to a truck headlight and battery so that it would automatically shoot any intruders, but the death rate in Arabs went up so strongly that they issued an order that said if you killed an Arab you had to bury him yourself, so that stopped that racket.

Arthur lived in the sergeants' mess in another camp, but at 7 a.m. each day, after breakfast, his men would shoulder their rifles and he would take the parade on the parade ground and then march them to the workshops a mile down the road. 'He was very pompous as a corporal, the pukka job,' Littlechild said.

He took himself seriously and strutted about. He was just like Captain Mainwaring: that was Arthur to a T. *Dad's Army* was Arthur Lowe playing Arthur Lowe. But being pompous didn't get him very far, because we weren't that sort of unit. He was just an ordinary bloke and we called him Arthur, not corporal.

He was also hardly an intimidating figure: a skinny little man balding fast and wearing small, round army spectacles, a bushy black Groucho Marx moustache, khaki shirt and shorts, and a long, thin 'cheesecutter' hat that perched on the side of his head. Even so, 'if you upset him, he could get very stroppy,' recalled Littlechild. 'One day we put on the wrong uniforms and Arthur went *berserk*. But it didn't do any good. That didn't cut any ice with anyone.'

In the workshop, with the help of an American lease-lend truck equipped with lathes, drills, avometers and other tools, the men would work all morning repairing radar, searchlights, and two-way radios. 'It was a mucky job sometimes,' said Littlechild. 'After the Alamein battle they parked a lot of tanks near the workshops so we could take the radios out, and there was blood and bits of flesh all over the place.' At midday Arthur would march them with their rifles back to the camp for lunch in the cookhouse with about 50 men from the other units. 'The food was terrible but you got used to it,' Littlechild recalled. 'We used to have camel sausages and the bread had always got weevils in it, but you either ate that or you went without. Arthur would eat up at the sergeants' mess: they didn't have better food, it was just the class system again.' After lunch Arthur would march the men back to the workshops and then at 5 p.m. back to the camp, after which they could do what they liked. Arthur would repair to the sergeants' mess and the men would go down to the NAAFI Nissen hut and drink a Stella beer – 'horrible Egyptian stuff' – or play darts. In the evenings they would change into their rough, khaki serge uniforms and wander half a mile across the desert to watch a film in the makeshift open-air cinema, which consisted of a screen, a few hard benches, some rush matting hung around the sides to keep the wind off, and an old projector that kept breaking down, at which point the men would hurl their beer bottles at the screen in frustration. It was here, in the desert, that Arthur first saw the films of the American actor who was to inspire his own career: W. C. Fields. Fields was a jowly, 63-year-old, ex-vaudeville, ex-silent movie comedian, whose nose was even bigger than Arthur's and whose voice was just as deep, and who had built himself a screen image as a boozy, child-hating grouch that made him internationally famous in the 1930s and early 1940s with films such as *It's a Gift*, *The Bank Dick*, *My Little Chickadee* and *Never Give a Sucker an Even Break*. He was also renowned for his off-the-wall remarks: 'Some weasel took the cork out of my lunch'; 'Anybody who hates children and dogs can't be all bad'; 'If at first you don't succeed, try again. Then quit. No use being a damn fool about it.' When asked why he never drank water, Fields growled: 'Fish fuck in it.' His offbeat, misanthropic sense of humour appealed to something deep in Arthur's soul, and after Fields died in 1946 Arthur often acknowledged his influence on his career.

On weekend afternoons in the desert the men might have a kick-about game of football but there was no organised sport, and for month after month they were dreadfully bored. Arthur did manage to borrow a horse and gallop it across the desert dunes, standing up in the stirrups – 'He was a good horseman,' Littlechild said – and he had a crack at riding a camel. He also learned to speak Arabic surprisingly well. But there was little to do except to get drunk every night. To stave off the boredom Arthur tried to organise a dance in the sergeants' mess and arranged for a truckload of girls to be shipped in from Gaza, but they never turned up, and he and several other men proceeded to get drunk as usual, boozing until they passed out in the early hours. More successfully he started an amateur dramatics group. 'It was sheer bloody boredom that did it,' he said later, 'and after that I was hooked.' He was already performing in a small way every evening: after some Arabs stole all the men's wireless sets one night Arthur began listening to the BBC news on the radio in the ordnance shop and then reading it out over the camp's Tannoy system at 6 p.m. He would play his signature tune, 'At Last' by Glenn Miller, bang a dinner gong to simulate the sound of Big Ben striking the hour, and read the news in a variety of accents, sometimes in Churchill's voice. 'He was very good at it,' said Littlechild, 'and he'd got a lovely sense of humour.' Years later Arthur confessed that he felt quite nostalgic whenever he heard the Glenn Miller orchestra playing 'At Last'.

He ordered a couple of one-act plays from Cairo and in January 1943 he called a meeting to form the REME No. 1 Welfare Club Dramatic Society. Eight men turned up, including Norman Littlechild, and agreed to stage a production of *The Monkey's Paw*. 'From the day we met we both clicked,' said Littlechild.

I used to carry a picture of my youngest sister, who was about 16 or 17, and I showed it to him one day and we seemed to get on like a house on fire after that. I think he probably fancied my sister, though he didn't seem to be interested in women at all.

The Monkey's Paw is a wildly melodramatic, old-fashioned play in three scenes, with five characters, that was dramatised from a famous horror story by W. W. Jacobs. It tells of an old couple, the Whites, who buy a magical monkey's paw that grants them three wishes, but with horrendous results. The play ends with a resurrected corpse at the door: '*A flood of moonlight. Emptiness. The old man sways in prayer on his knees. The old woman lies half swooning, wailing against the door-post.* CURTAIN.' It was strong stuff to perform on the sands of Araby under a desert moon, and Arthur and his fellow amateur thespians threw themselves into the production with gusto. He was only 28, but right from the start he seemed destined to play grumpy old men and cast himself in the lead role of sometimes-curmudgeonly old Mr White. Littlechild was

31

stage manager and prompter. 'Arthur was the only bloke who was any good,' he said. 'He was a born actor: it was obvious right from the start, and he had a well-spoken, resonant voice without any trace of a Derbyshire or Manchester accent.'

The men built a stage at one end of the NAAFI hut and scrounged props all over the camp. Private Thomas Thomas, playing Mrs White, needed a wig, so they persuaded one of the craftsmen in the instrument workshops to give them some raw cotton wool, which they then persuaded another member of the unit, an ex-hairdresser, to make into a wig. 'It was the most beautiful wig you've ever seen,' said Littlechild, 'and we even used a real monkey's paw.' For incidental music they played a couple of records, one of them *Fingal's Cave*, and one of the group hand-painted a striking poster in red and purple showing a monkey and a couple of paw prints – 'ADMISSION BY TICKET ONLY'. At 7.30 p.m. on Monday, 8 February 1943 the doors of the NAAFI theatre opened for Arthur Lowe's first adult appearance on a stage. Thirty or 40 bored soldiers turned up to watch, the curtain went up at eight o'clock, and the men roared with agreement when the character of the Sergeant Major remarked in Scene 1: ''ardship is the soldier's lot. Starvation, fever, and get yourself shot.' The actors were so nervous and amateurish that they rushed their lines and the play ran for no more than half an hour. That was too quick for Arthur, who persuaded the rest of the cast to slow down for the second and final performance the following night so that it lasted nearly an hour. He already showed the instincts of a professional actor.

Perhaps because of this initiative Arthur was promoted to the rank of sergeant. The unit was briefly posted 90 miles north of Rafah to the important industrial and petrol refinery centre and deep-water port of Haifa in northern Palestine. On 16 May – four days after the surrender of the German army in North Africa – Arthur took a day off to visit Nazareth, 20 miles away. By now he and Norman Littlechild had become friends despite the difference in their ranks – 'He didn't have any other special friends,' Littlechild said – and that summer they took a week's leave with another of Littlechild's friends, a Liverpudlian called Ron, to visit Jerusalem. There they stayed in a small hotel, enjoyed a visit to a proper, air-conditioned cinema, saw the Church of the Holy Sepulchre, the Mount of Olives, the Garden of Gethsemane, and passed through the seven stages of the Cross, although Arthur was never particularly religious. From Jerusalem they went by bus to Bethlehem and Jericho, and tried to swim in the Dead Sea: 'You just jumped in and bobbed up like a cork.' One particular scene in a Jerusalem tearoom fixed itself vividly in Littlechild's memory. A waiter brought cups and saucers. There was a slight crack in Arthur's cup, so he pointed it out to the waiter. The waiter shrugged. 'Arthur picked it up and just smashed it on the table. He didn't say anything, nor did the waiter, who just looked and brought another cup.' Arthur was becoming a perfectionist determined to have his own way.

W. C. Fields would have been amused by the unit's next posting: the men were sent for several weeks into a remote part of the desert to kid Hitler's overflying pilots into thinking that they had a large camp there by constructing mock aeroplanes, buildings and guns out of wood and hessian. They slept on palliasses, were each allowed only a quart of water a day, and washed their clothes in petrol, partly to save water, partly because petrol was extremely cheap, and partly to deter lice. For shaving they drained the water from a truck's radiator and poured it back afterwards.

Now that the shooting war had moved out of North Africa and on to Sicily and Italy they were posted hundreds of miles to the west, more than 500 miles beyond Cairo, to the captured and devastated Italian port of Derna on the Mediterranean cost of Libya, just beyond Tobruk, where they joined a Royal Artillery anti-aircraft unit. By now Arthur was itching to put on another play and he chose one that matched his love of the sea: *Bound East for Cardiff* by Eugene O'Neill, a one-act play with 11 characters. Set at night in the forecastle on a British tramp steamer, with a set consisting of bunks, portholes and sea chests and littered with oilskins and sea boots, it tells of an American sailor who is dying in his bunk after suffering a bad fall in one of the holds, and of how his ship-mates react. Much of the dialogue, which is in various accents ranging from Cockney to Norwegian to Irish, is barely comprehensible – 'How cud ye doubt ut, Oleson? A quane av the naygurs she musta been surely.' Arthur, with his talent for impersonation, could doubtless have played all 11 parts, but he restricted himself to that of the Norwegian, Oleson, and must have relished the chance to swill all those fat Scandinavian vowels around his tongue. He turned a room in an empty Derna hotel into a theatre, tracked down some sound equipment, and for scenery 'went up onto the plateau where a lot of aircraft had crashed, cut away the aircraft frames, and brought them back to the workshops,' said Littlechild. 'Some of the blokes made up frames, covered them with hessian, and painted them for the scenery.' After only a few weeks in Derna, while they were rehearsing the play, the men were ordered back to Rafah and the production had to be aborted. By now the theatre had become more than just a hobby for Arthur. He organised a regular play-reading group and in Rafah produced a third play, *Recall*, in which, another soldier, 'Chalky' White, told Stephen Lowe, an Indian sat cross-legged at the back of the stage playing the pipes and Arthur 'broke his dentures eating a goat sandwich, and had to do the performance with his top set held together with chewing gum.'

The war had moved far away into Europe and there was little to be done in Egypt except wait impatiently for the end. From Rafah Arthur's unit was posted back to the big base depot at Tel-el-Kebir, 45 miles north-east of Cairo, and there he organised an old-time variety and music-hall Christmas revue at the Young Women's Christian Association (YWCA) hostel. 'He was the leading light,' Littlechild told me.

It was all little sketches, bits and pieces. In one of them one of the women from the YWCA was lying on a bed and Arthur comes in wearing a Russian-type uniform and he kneels by the bed and says, 'Little mother, little mother, Napoleon's army is at the city gates, we must get up and go.' And she says, 'My son, my son, I am too ill.' And so off he goes, and the curtain comes down and we do another sketch, and then back he comes again and does the same sketch – 'Little mother, little mother, Napoleon's got through the gates, we've got to flee' – and she says, 'My son, my son, I am too ill.' And the third time he comes on and he does the same thing, but before his mother says a thing he stands up and walks to the front of the stage and says, 'Ladies and gentlemen, I'm sorry, we can't continue with this sketch. It's my mother. She's too ill.' Everybody just doubled up. It brought the house down. It was the way he said it, his presentation and timing. He never said he was going to be an actor after the war but he was so good that it didn't surprise me when he became successful. He was a natural. He was born to it.

Nor was Arthur simply comical. He also had a magic touch with sketches that were poignant or sentimental. 'In the closing scene of the Christmas revue,' recalled Littlechild,

a tall young woman from the YWCA wore a long blue robe and a beautiful pair of wings – made by Italian prisoners of war – which came from her shoulders almost down to her knees. The backcloth was dark blue with silver stars on it, and as we sang a carol she stood at the back of the stage and I put the spotlight on her, and all the people in the audience were given candles and they did a procession round the hall to end the show. That effect was brilliant.

It required courage to put on this sort of show for an audience of bored, restless soldiers. In his book Joe Roberts tells of a REME concert party elsewhere that ended in a riotous punch-up when the drunks in the audience started heckling the performers. 'It was generally agreed ... that the free-for-all was infinitely more entertaining than anything the concert party lot could have put on,' reported Roberts, though his tough commanding officer, Major Carrick, was so incensed by the brawl that he went into every tent afterwards and threatened to beat up anyone who was still spoiling for a fight. Arthur's audiences, however, appear to have behaved impeccably, which says a great deal for the quality of his productions. His troupe put on a second successful performance of the Christmas revue at a local hospital, and Arthur, by now completely hooked on the theatre, approached the famous actor–soldier Captain Torin Thatcher, who was in Cairo and about to set up three army Field Entertainment Units that would go into remote parts of the desert in trucks to encourage soldiers to put on their own plays and concert parties.

At first Arthur was seconded to work with a drama group of soldiers and civilians in Cairo, where he helped to produce a George Bernard Shaw festival and did some radio work for the Forces Broadcasting Unit and the Egyptian State Broadcasting Company. Cairo was a crowded, vibrant, frenetic city, the largest in Africa. British yet Egyptian, its elegant colonial mansions, clubs and hotels jostled with crowded Arab slums, crooked lanes, bazaars, mosques, and the stench of heat, spices and desperate poverty. It was renowned for its sophisticated social life and louche nightlife as a raffish place where anything and everything was available at a price. Arthur had little time to revel in this sudden civilization: he was offered a job with Thatcher's No. 2 Field Entertainment Unit, promoted to sergeant major, and posted to Almaza, outside Cairo. The Field Entertainment Unit consisted of an officer (Captain Kenneth Fraser), a senior NCO (Arthur), another NCO, a driver called Hurst, and a dogsbody private. Sergeant Major Lowe was soon helping outlying units to produce their own shows, finding scripts and musical instruments for them, and giving them tips about making costumes and props and building scenery. Among the soldiers whose talents were unearthed and encouraged by one of the Field Entertainment Units in Egypt was the young comedian Tommy Cooper, whose amateur performance then was little different from the professional one that was to make him famous years later. He was already appearing in the red fez, which he had picked up in the desert, doing conjuring tricks that always went wrong, and laughing the same big infectious laugh. Cooper 'was a bastard to be with as an officer', FEU officer John Arnatt told Richard Fawkes for his history of wartime armed services' entertainment, *Fighting for a Laugh*, 'because he delighted in getting you up on the stage to help him out and then he would take the mickey out of you something terrible. He had the entire audience on his side and if you weren't careful you came out of it looking none too dignified.'

Arthur's new job took him all over the Middle East. In Beirut, in the Lebanon, Captain Fraser was replaced by 27-year-old Captain Martin Benson, who had been a professional actor before the war with a repertory company in Tavistock, Devon. In 1944 Benson and Arthur were posted to Egypt's second city, Alexandria, a stylish banking and commercial centre on the shore of the Mediterranean just over 100 miles northwest of Cairo. It had been badly bombarded by the Germans and Italians during the war but was settling back into its privileged peacetime lifestyle. Arthur could hardly have chosen a more attractive place to be stationed in North Africa. Not nearly as hot as the hinterland, Alexandria was a notoriously stylish, cosmopolitan city: part Arab, part European; part ancient, part modern. About 100,000 of its residents – 10 per cent – were foreigners, and there were large, rich and snobbish British, Greek and French enclaves, and a strong whiff of French elegance, architecture and *joie de vivre*. The city had excellent museums, public parks, botanical gardens, beaches, British and French newspapers, and French restaurants and nightlife, as well as royal Arab palaces and belly dancers. It even had a posh English magazine called the *Sphere*, which took as its model the

London society magazine the *Tatler*. But Alexandria did not have a theatre, so Captain Benson decided that he, Arthur and No. 2 Field Entertainment Unit would start one.

As soon as they arrived in the city at the end of August with a truck and a few bits of equipment Benson commandeered a large, empty, first-floor space above the army's Pay Corps office at 8 Rue Nubar Pasha, off Mohamed Aly Square. With the help of £100 from army funds, several enthusiastic civilians, and some military volunteers – including women from the ATS and WRNS – he and Arthur converted the space into a 100-seat theatre, which Benson named the Mercury. Despite the great heat and humidity of Alexandria in August, the city's hottest month, when the average temperature is 87°F, they built the stage in six weeks, installed curtains and lighting, fitted out a green room, rehearsal rooms and a bar, and painted the scenery. 'Arthur painted sets, hunted around trying to find costumes, and rehearsed the actors, all of them amateurs,' I was told by Benson, 82 and a veteran of 83 films, in 2000. 'Originally, the Mercury was set up for the troops, but the audiences became more and more the local intelligentsia and less and less the troops, who didn't want too much of this intellectual stuff.'

From the beginning of October Benson and Arthur alternately produced new plays every week or two. Benson had at least had some experience in weekly rep, but with very little experience Arthur suddenly became a full-time producer. 'Well, he had to start at some point,' said Benson, 'and he was a good director.' Despite being a sergeant major Arthur had by now escaped all connection with the army, Benson explained:

> We were a very oddball unit and away from the mainstream of army discipline we had nobody supervising us. We didn't live in barracks – Arthur lived in one room, as I did – and we wore uniform only because it gave you admission to the various clubs and discount shops. We weren't really aware of the war at all. Alexandria was by then virtually untouched by the war and there was no bombing or rationing. It was a holiday place.

They worked seven days a week, starting at 10 o'clock in the morning and rehearsing until late at night. 'We virtually lived in that little theatre,' Arthur told John Graven Hughes, and Benson told me: 'We didn't really have any leisure. The work was the leisure. Luckily we all got on well.' As for the quality of the acting itself, Benson reckoned it was 'a pretty mixed standard. One or two people went on to become professionals, like Arthur, myself, and Henry Manning. The actors were not quite as good as amateur companies current in England at the time, but judged by standards in the Middle East we were the best there was.'

Entrance to the theatre was free for any man or woman in the services, and each could bring one civilian free as well. Performances were at 8 p.m. on Tuesdays, Thursdays, Saturdays and Sundays, and the programmes carried the following request: 'In view of the small size of the auditorium, please refrain from smoking. This theatre has been sprayed with D.D.T.' To attract potential actors and helpers this note was also printed in the programmes:

FORWARD PLEASE

You may be a lance corporal in your camp but in the MERCURY THEATRE you can be a knight in shining armour one week and a flashing pirate the next. You've always wanted to act, haven't you? Come and try. We also need technicians and dressmakers – in fact everyone from a chimney sweep to a tea taster.

Although Benson says he got on well with Arthur he found him an odd character:

He was very quiet, almost dour. You didn't get much of a laugh out of him. He wasn't in the slightest the life and soul of the party, and he didn't seem to have much sense of humour, which is strange in the light of what he went on to do. He was Mainwaring and Mainwaring was him: a little pompous, but you can't be too pompous in the army. He was a neutral man, neither likeable nor unlikeable. He was subdued and unobtrusive, and struck me as being a typical engineer type, and he looked a little funny in his long shorts, and he was on the way to being completely bald. I don't think he had any girlfriends. There were lots of pretty girls around at the Mercury but I don't think Arthur was interested. He was just rather dull: a quiet, slightly introverted man who lived a secret life in his head, and no one would have known what that secret life was. I had no inkling that he might become famous.

Benson was not all that popular himself, according to Anne Ferguson, one of the Wrens who acted with the company. She told Stephen Lowe that during rehearsals at the Mercury, Benson would sit at the back of the stalls and shout at her 'as she moved woodenly around the stage, trying her best'. Another actor, Richard Leech, told me that Benson was also unpopular with the rest of the cast when they and Arthur were in the same repertory company in Hereford in 1947. And 20 years later another member of the Mercury company, Ernest Holmwood, remembered fondly that Arthur was always trying to encourage his amateur actors and helpers by telling them kindly: 'Keep it up, lad, you're doing a grand job.' So Benson's less than glowing memories of Arthur's character were not shared by everyone.

Benson was, however, sufficiently generous to let Arthur direct the first play they put on at the Mercury just six weeks after they started building it. *Without the Prince*, by Philip King, was a three-act comedy about a company of amateur English country actors who are trying to put on a production of *Hamlet*. Set in the living room of Hill-Top Farm in the village of Upper Netherwick, it had a cast of six men and four women and opened at the Mercury at 8 p.m. on 9 October. 'Arthur Lowe has put on a play which will certainly give much needed entertainment to the Services and their friends,' reported the local English newspaper, the *Gazette*, in the first review he ever received. *Without the Prince* ran for a week before it was replaced by the second production, *They Came to a City* by J. B. Priestley, which Benson directed. *Without the Prince* then returned for a second week and was reviewed as 'a truly excellent performance'. Ernest Holmwood produced the third play, *Gin and It*; Henry Manning the fourth, *Musical Chairs*; and Arthur the fifth, *The Wind and the Rain* by Merton Hodge, a comedy about medical students in Edinburgh, which earned him another rave review in the local rag by none other than David Scott Daniell, a former drama critic of the *Manchester Guardian*. Daniell enthused that the play was 'charming, unsophisticated and very wholesome … It will fill the theatre and send the people away happy. Everything connected with this venture has an inherent freshness, born of the enthusiasm behind it.' Arthur must have been delighted to receive such a warm accolade from a professional reviewer for such a distinguished newspaper in his own home town.

The press was extremely supportive of the Mercury. 'All those who act and work at the theatre are infected with an amazing enthusiasm,' *The Sphinx* reported in November, and the spirit which pervades the place has to be seen to be believed. Professionals and amateurs, men and women from all Services, and civilians work in complete accord, and Martin Benson says that he has never experienced such *espirit de corps* in any theatre before ... It is fascinating to go into the theatre any evening, when you are likely to find a performance in progress and in other rooms behind the stage two other plays in rehearsal. There have been times when actors have come off the stage, popped into the rehearsal room to do a scene for the next play – still in make-up and costume – and then gone back onto the stage again to finish the performance. ... Audiences continue to be surprised at the exceptionally high standard attained in these productions ... This theatre, with its true repertory flavour, is more representative of the British drama than anything yet seen in Egypt.

Strangely Arthur never appeared on stage at the Mercury, though Benson often did before he returned to England at the end of the war and the theatre closed in 1946. Perhaps Arthur still preferred to be in control behind the scenes, or maybe he was not yet sufficiently confident of his ability as an actor. However, when the war ended and he returned to Britain in November 1945 he was determined to become an actor even though he was already 30.

Arthur's army record reports that his military conduct throughout the war was 'exemplary', and Benson gave him a glowing testimonial that read: 'Arthur Lowe has been found to possess initiative, imagination, and complete reliability. He has a good knowledge of all theatrical matters, including production and management. I have no hesitation in recommending him to any civilian management.' Arthur said later: 'On the whole I wasn't unhappy during the war. I rather liked it in the army' – so much so that he joined the Duke of Lancaster's Own Yeomanry regimental association, attended several of its reunions, and kept its rule book and membership card until the end of his life. He had certainly had one of the wackiest, least military army careers ever – a perfect back-ground for an actor who was to run a shambolic, amateurish platoon in *Dad's Army* 23 years later. Undoubtedly it was in Wales, Egypt and Palestine that Captain Mainwaring was born.

CHAPTER 4

Rep

(1945–1950)

Arthur was not officially demobbed until March 1946, but he went home to Hayfield, where his parents were living in a cottage at 3 Fisher's Lane. Big Arthur was commuting into Manchester by train every day to work for the LNER at London Road station, where his job now was to organise special outings and excursions in the Midlands and the north of England, including the special private trains that moved entire circuses, theatre companies, props and scenery from one town to another. He urged Little Arthur to go back to a steady job at Fairey Aviation and build a career there as an engineer or draughtsman, but Little Arthur was determined to try his luck in the theatre even though acting was a gamble. He seemed to know in his bones that he was going to be a huge success. 'You come into this business to be rich and famous,' he told Reginald Brace of the *Yorkshire Post* 32 years later. Big Arthur thought he was daft but agreed to help on the understanding that Arthur would give himself five years to succeed as an actor and that if he failed he would settle down in a steady job.

Because of Big Arthur's connection with the theatrical trains he arranged for Little Arthur to be auditioned by Eric Norman, the general manager and producer of the Frank H. Fortescue Famous Players repertory company, which was appearing at the Hulme Hippodrome. 'Frank Fortescue was the cheaper type of more humble rep,' I was told in 2001 by Jimmy Perry, the creator of *Dad's Army*. In those weeks immediately after the war theatrical managements were crying out for male performers – even if they were only 5ft 4in short, weighed just 124 lb, and were skinny, bald, bespectacled, ugly sergeant majors. At the end of 1945

Arthur went to the Hippodrome for an audition and was immediately offered a trial appearance the week before Christmas in *Bedtime Story*, a light three-act comedy by Walter Ellis.

The Hulme Hippodrome was a squat, seedy-looking building in Preston Street, Hulme, a suburb of Manchester, which put on a different play each week, twice nightly at 6.30 and 8.30. With 3,000 seats, it must have been a daunting experience to appear twice a night without any proper training. Nor was Arthur's trial role simply a small one. Incredibly he was given the remarkably meaty part of Dickson, a sad-looking, 55-year-old manservant, who has 64 lines and is on stage throughout Act 2. Right from that very first part Arthur was cast not only as a man much older than himself, as he was to be so often throughout his career, but also as the pompous, moralising sort of little man that he was to play so often in numerous theatre plays and TV performances.

On that first of all Arthur's many first nights, 17 December 1945, his first line on the professional stage was 'Hullo'. He was answering a telephone. 'Hullo,' he said. 'Hullo? Yes, Sir John. Pardon? No, no one has called, sir.' Throughout Act 2 Dickson is the perfect valet: 'Sir John has just telephoned, Madam, saying your arrival was imminent'; 'The pictorial papers are over there, and – er – may I take your bag?' When the lady asks whether Sir John is pleased about her arrival, Dickson replies mournfully: 'Quite overjoyed.' Later he remarks miserably: 'We are all happy if we only count our blessings.' Arthur was the born comedian. 'I reckoned I was a world-beater,' he joked many years later.

Bedtime Story is in fact a corny, unlikely, whimsical confection that depends on ludicrous misunderstandings and mistaken identity, and it has a silly 'happy ending', but it launched Arthur on the professional stage at last. His baldness, myopia, and talent for mimicry had already made him so good at impersonating older characters that he had little trouble playing the middle-aged butler even though he was only 31. Indeed, he played it so well that he was immediately offered a job as a character at £5 a week, the equivalent of about £112 today. To be paid at all was a coup: many other fledgling actors in the 1940s were expected to pay repertory companies as much as £50 to be taken on, the equivalent of £1,120 now, and in addition they were expected to provide all their own costumes unless they were appearing in a period play.

There were no reviews of Arthur's first performance. The Manchester press concentrated instead, understandably, on reviewing Donald Wolfit, who was appearing that week as Hamlet at the Opera House in a Shakespeare season during which he also played King Lear and Falstaff. The *Manchester Guardian* rarely reviewed any theatre at all and was far too snooty to mention a jobbing, downmarket rep company like Frank Fortescue's Famous Players, and it never once mentioned a play at the Hulme Hippodrome in the year that Arthur was there. The *Manchester Evening News*, where George Orwell was regularly reviewing books, also ignored the Fortescue company almost completely even though the paper published a weekly Saturday theatre column and reported on 15 January that a group of Hayfield children had just performed three plays in a barn that they had converted into a theatre. To be upstaged by a bunch of country yokels' kids must have seemed deeply humiliating to the Frank H. Fortescue Famous Players. Even the *Evening Chronicle* considered them to be unworthy of its notice, though it is true that the newspapers had more exciting topics to cover that week: on the Tuesday the traitor William Joyce, the Nazi broadcaster 'Lord Haw-Haw', lost his House of Lords appeal against the death sentence for treason; and Winston Churchill's son, Major Randolph Churchill, was divorced by his wife, Pamela, for desertion on the grounds that he 'seemed to prefer a bachelor's existence … He preferred the company of his friends to being at home' and 'was often rude to her in public'. On the Wednesday another traitor, John Amery, was hanged for high treason at Wandsworth Prison by the sinister 33-year-old executioner Albert Pierrepoint; Joyce followed him to the gallows a few days later.

Arthur returned to Hayfield for Christmas with his parents while Tom Brennan and Joan Simms played for a week in *Cinderella* at the Hulme Hippodrome. He did not appear in any of the three January pantos that followed, each of which ran for a week, but he helped with stage management and jobs behind the scenes and started rehearsing for his next part, in *Flare Path* by Terence Rattigan, which was due to open on 21 January 1946.

Weekly rep was still immensely popular. Each play was produced in a frantic rush, the acting and direction were often amateurish, and the programme depended on a staple diet of second- and third-rate comedies and 'thrillers' that would never have made it to the West End stage, but in cities all over Britain the local companies built up an unsophisticated but loyal audience that loved to spend a predictable evening at the theatre watching the same group of actors week after week in different plays in the company of the same familiar faces in the audience and often in the same seats on the same nights of every week. It was like the regular meetings of a cosy social or old folks' bingo club, and whenever a particularly favourite actor made his or her entrance in the next play, the audience would applaud wildly.

For the actors at the Hulme Hippodrome it was an incredibly hard life. Each week they appeared twice nightly on stage after spending each day rehearsing the play they were due to perform the following week and starting to learn their lines for the play that was scheduled for the week after that. In addition to learning their lines and finding their own costumes and props, often begging or borrowing them from local shops, the minor actors like Arthur were expected to help behind the scenes with the stage management, sound effects, painting scenery, prompting, and performing as general dogsbodies whether that involved manning the switchboard or box office, operating the curtains, sweeping the stage or making the tea. They would produce the sound of thunder by shaking a big sheet of metal, or the sound of wind by rotating a ribbed wooden drum against a strip of canvas. In fact the actors spent more time dealing with the no-nonsense practical difficulties of producing a new play every week than they did on any high-falutin' creative details or artistic interpretation. 'There was no read-through as such, no discussion of the play's meaning or the characters,' said the actor and playwright Henry Livings in his engaging theatrical memoir of his early years in rep, *The Rough Side of the Boards*, and 'nobody had read more than was needed to underline their own role.' They underlined their lines in pencil because when each play was over the pencil marks had to be rubbed out and the scripts returned to Samuel French, the theatrical publishers in London, who rented them out.

They rarely had any free time. 'The prospect of all the work we did renders me speechless,' Richard Briers told Kate Dunn for her book about the great days of rep, *Exit Through the Fireplace*. 'You didn't want to leave the theatre, you wanted to sleep under the stage. We lived in it and for it.' Derek Fowlds agreed: 'There was a feeling that no other life existed outside the stage door.' Merely learning all those lines week after week was a major feat. 'With only two weeks' rehearsal there was hardly any time to learn the play,' Tom Conti told Ms Dunn. 'People sat with their books at lunchtime, they went home with their books at night and did an hour, an hour and a half after the show.' Not surprisingly actors often forgot their lines and dried on stage, or suddenly started spouting lines from the previous play or the next one. Timothy West told Ms Dunn of one old rep actor who finally landed a part in a long-running West End play but still had to keep mugging up his lines every weekend even after four months in the show. Asked why, he explained plaintively, 'I've trained myself all my life to forget a play a week.' And Tenniel Evans remembered a production of *The Merchant of Venice* at Northampton rep where the assistant stage manager had to come on and ask 'What news from the Rialto?' but said instead 'What's on at the Tivoli?' Most reps had a prompter somewhere in the wings or under the stage, at least for the first couple of nights of each play, but Maurice Denham told Kate Dunn that when one actor dried on stage and whispered at the prompter 'What's the line?' the prompter replied, 'What's the play?'

Actors also kept forgetting who they and the other actors were meant to be. 'One week you were Sir Henry, then you were Charles, and the next week you were Geoffrey or whatever,' Shaun Sutton told Ms Dunn.

Gwen Watford and I were playing husband and wife in a play at Buxton and I was accusing her of adultery and she was hotly denying it [and I said] 'It's no use trying to deny it, I happen to know you've been unfaithful with Max.' There was a pause and Gwen said, 'You mean John', having just spend a whole scene denying it! And I said, 'Yes, yes, yes, yes, with John', then I put on a sneer and said, 'I see, you've been unfaithful with Max *and* John!' and Gwen, who was getting fed up with this, whispered, 'Shut up about Max, *you're* Max!'

Yet for all the hard work and pitfalls weekly rep was widely considered to be a vital part of any actor's early education. In later years Arthur always swore that his time in weekly rep had given him invaluable training that he could never have had at any drama school, and he regretted that younger actors were no longer able to learn their trade properly in this way. 'It was a splendid introduction to the theatre,' Alec McCowen told George Rowell and Anthony Jackson for their history, *The Repertory Movement*. 'The director taught me everything from tying a cleat to mascaring my eye-lashes.' Raw young actors learned a great deal from watching and listening to more experienced actors and Liza Goddard told Kate Dunn, 'Rep helps you understand how everything works. I understand the problems of the costume department, the props department, stage management, from having to turn my hand to everything. It gives me more tolerance if things go wrong now.' Lionel Jeffries added that the negative lessons of working in rep were just as valuable as the positive ones:

I learned what not to do. I learnt what an audience would not accept. I learnt what I wasn't good at. So I played character men. At the age of twenty-one, twenty-two, I actually got the grounding for what made my living once I left – a series of old farts, funny people.

Arthur learned quickly that he was best at playing funny old farts too. His next role was as another old fart of 55, Squadron Leader Swanson, far and away the oldest character in *Flare Path*. The play is a story of adultery, loyalty, cowardice and courage during the Second World War that has a wonderfully nostalgic period feel to it now – characters who say 'bung-ho' and 'tinkerty-tonk', and an alcoholic woman who is always having 'a little dinky' – but in 1946 it was extremely modern, set only a few years earlier in the residents' lounge of a hotel near an RAF airfield in Lincolnshire. The main theme of the play is whether a 25-year-old actress can bring herself to tell her heroic husband, a 20-year-old pilot who has won the Distinguished Flying Cross, that she is about to leave him for an American actor with whom she has been having an affair for more than a year.

Perhaps the play's lusty atmosphere heightened the sexual tension of the cast, because it was while Arthur was rehearsing for *Flare Path* that January that he met his future wife, the blonde, bubbly, 23-year-old, married actress Joan Cooper. Their son, Stephen, claims in his book that they met on a train, but in fact they met as they sat together on a sofa during rehearsals at the Hulme Hippodrome. In later years Joan liked to claim that she was a leading lady at the Hippodrome and earning nearly twice as much as Arthur, but in all of 1946 her name never appeared in any of the theatre's many newspaper advertisements and it seems that she was in fact just one of several actresses in the company. It was a bitter morning when they met, so cold after Egypt that Arthur was wearing riding breeches and his army greatcoat but was still freezing. 'Right from the start our love was an instantaneous attraction of opposites,' Joan told Gill Preece of the *Sunday Mirror* 36 years later, '...this very cold little man shivering inside his army greatcoat.' Through chattering teeth he told her about North Africa and the Mercury and 'it didn't take long to see that Arthur Lowe had real talent'. She loved his deep voice, and years later told Bill Pertwee that although Arthur was short, bald and very thin,

> even then there was something about his presence on stage, and when he was rehearsing he made you watch him even if he was only playing a small part. He was the sort of actor you watched even when he wasn't doing anything. It was what he *didn't* do that made you watch him.

It is possible that at first Joan had a rival for Arthur's affections, for his tiny, yellow 1946 diary lists regular telephone calls and meetings with a woman called Edith in February and March, often in the evening. In March he telephoned or met her on the 2nd, 3rd, 4th and 6th, remembered her birthday on the 14th, and visited her again on the 21st, 28th and 31st. But after 4 April, by which time Arthur and Joan's affair was probably common knowledge at the Hippodrome, he never mentioned Edith again in his diary. From then until the day he died he had eyes only for Joan.

She was the daughter of two musicians who lived in a stone mansion near Chesterfield, 40 miles south-east of Hayfield. Her father, Reginald Cooper, was the organist and choirmaster at a church in Chesterfield, and her mother, Winifred, a piano and singing teacher. 'Our childhood was very privileged although we weren't rich, not in the sense of having servants and holidays overseas,' Joan's younger sister, Margaret Stapleton, told me in 2001.

> Yes, we lived in lovely houses, beautifully furnished, and were quite well off, but it was all money that was earned through hard work. Daddy was very ill for a long time when I was a child – he had rheumatic fever that left his heart in a bad condition – and in about 1929 Mother was told he would never walk again. But she nursed him back to health, at the same time giving singing lessons and concerts to make ends meet. After Daddy was well again it was constant work – teaching, choirs, conducting, church services – and at the same time he was studying, first for his

Bachelor of Music degree and then his Doctor of Music. And Mother kept on teaching along with cooking, cleaning, sewing, and knitting. We were surrounded by music. I could never sleep on Sunday nights because every other night of the week there were two pianos playing: my father would be teaching in one room and my mother would be teaching in another, but on Sunday nights everybody was quiet and we couldn't sleep. They were always teaching. My father would be teaching up till half past 10 at night.

Joan was five years older than Margaret. They attended small private day schools where 'Joan did very well and got her matriculation,' Mrs Stapleton told me.

She was the clever one, I was the dunce! She was a quiet, very serious, studious, well-behaved girl, clever and musical, all the things I wasn't. She never seemed to get into scrapes or get dirty and she never had pets or went riding like I did. But she was a bit of a dreamer, highly strung, and inclined to hysteria at times. She wasn't at all sporty – we're not a sporty family – but she played the piano very well and passed a lot of music exams, whereas I took just one. And she was the pretty one: she was very good-looking. But she wasn't very strong: I was always stronger, more down-to-earth and practical.

Joan's temperamental nervousness and insecurity must have been deepened by having to listen to her parents' constant rows. According to Mrs Stapleton,

It was a stormy marriage. Our parents were both quick tempered. Mother was strong and steadfast but Daddy was sentimental and spiritual, and he did have an affair that I know of, and maybe there were others. I can imagine women would find him good company because he was sociable and fun. But it was Mother he came back to. Of course there were tears and rages, but then there always had been. All through my childhood I was never sure, coming home from school, what the atmosphere would be like at home. Maybe that was one reason Joan and I both married so young. I loved both my parents, and Joan, dearly, but she was Mother's girl and I was Daddy's.

48

As a girl Joan chose to be an actress rather than a musician, and at the age of 14 joined the Randle-Ayrton drama school in Stratford-upon-Avon. 'That's when she started smoking and drinking, which upset my mother,' said her sister. Two years later Joan joined Donald Wolfit's Shakespeare Company at the Theatre Royal in Brighton, so in Manchester that winter of 1945/6 she would undoubtedly have popped over once or twice to see Wolfit on stage at the Opera House. After Brighton she joined the Colchester Repertory Company as an assistant stage manager and bit-part player, but at the end of 1940, just after her eighteenth birthday, she had a fling with a 26-year-old Canadian actor, Richard Gatehouse, and became pregnant. They were married hurriedly but poshly four months later, in March 1941, by the Archdeacon of Richmond, Donald Bartlett, in the Cathedral Church of Ripon in Yorkshire. 'My parents accepted it,' said Mrs Stapleton. 'My mother was really quite ahead of her time and she accepted things that perhaps other women wouldn't have done in those days.' On the marriage certificate Joan claimed to be 22, not 18, and five months after the wedding, a fortnight after her nineteenth birthday, her son David was born at her parents' mansion, Penmore House at Hasland, Chesterfield. Her husband, whom she called Richie, joined the Royal Navy Volunteer Reserve and they were posted first to the Shetland Islands and then to Grimsby, where they were struck by tragedy: Joan's second child, Jane, was born at her parents' house in November 1943 but died just four months later in her cot at home in Grimsby. The death certificate records that a post-mortem was carried out and that the baby had contracted subacute bronchitis and had died after inhaling vomit. This would inevitably have made Joan blame herself and made her even more highly strung than she was already. 'It was extremely traumatic for Joan when Jane died,' Mrs Stapleton told me.

> I think it did something to Joan that she never really got over, and I think it was then that the marriage ended. It really made her very ill, partly because her husband wouldn't allow the baby to be spoken about and I think Joan needed to grieve, to cry and to talk about Jane. I think it affected her life permanently afterwards. She became very sad. It left the seeds of depression.

At the beginning of 1946 Joan, Richie and four-year-old David were living together in Manchester. Richie, who was working 30 miles away as a naval welfare officer in Liverpool, took to Arthur as soon as Joan introduced them. 'The three of us used to pal around Manchester together all the time,' Richie Gatehouse told me.

Arthur was a very pleasant man, very slim and presentable, didn't have a north country accent, and was more educated than most of them in the company. He liked everything old-fashioned, as I did, like a mahogany wardrobe, real wood instead of the modern phoney equivalent, and that was our main point of contact. I liked him because I liked his taste in things. He didn't like the modern world much.

They also had a similar taste in women. Richie, who was now 31, was posted 200 miles south to work as a naval welfare officer in Portsmouth Dockyard, and there he became involved with the composer Sir Arthur Bliss's 19-year-old daughter Barbara, another actress, who was a Wren in the navy and who helped him start a naval company of actors. Richie returned to Manchester regularly at weekends but Joan and Arthur, thrown together day after night in the theatre, were becoming increasingly fond of each other. 'Joan was very pretty,' Gatehouse told me, 'very loving, affectionate and attractive, with a nice figure. She was ebullient, very bright and clever, and very well-spoken.' As for what Joan saw in Arthur, who was hardly handsome, 'he was a very *solid* character,' suggested Barbara Gatehouse.

'Oh, yes,' said her husband. 'An honest man.'

'And thoroughly *dependable*. A good person.'

'Yes, and very presentable. Very nice.'

'I think she fell for Arthur because he was a contrast to Richie,' Margaret Stapleton told me.

I don't think Richie was very good for Joan because he was as temperamental as she was, and Arthur was a bit more placid. Perhaps he suited Joan's temperament more. But to be honest I never liked Arthur. He wasn't somebody that I could have got fond of. I was fonder of Richie, really, and I'm not particularly proud that Arthur Lowe was my brother-in-law.

Arthur must at first have felt guilty about his feelings for a friend's wife, a highly strung woman who had a four-year-old child and was particularly vulnerable after the recent death of her baby, but the affair progressed swiftly and he kept track of their early courting in a series of brief entries in his diary. Joan is first mentioned on 1 March with the single word 'Joan's'. On 5 March he wrote 'Joan's for tea', on 15 March 'Police ball and Joan's for tea', on 29 March 'Joan's for tea' again. They first kissed in Manchester's Piccadilly and like most new lovers they had 'their' tune, Glenn Miller's languid, lilting melody 'At Last', all gentle, sentimental strings and brass, which Arthur had adopted as his theme tune when reading the news in Egypt:

> *My love has come along*
> *My lonely days are over*
> *And life is like a song.*
> *At last*
> *The skies above are blue*
> *My heart was wrapped up in clover*
> *The night I looked at you.*
> *I found a dream that I could speak to,*
> *A dream that I can call my own.*
> *I found a thrill to press my cheek to*
> *A thrill that I have never known.*
> *Oh, you smiled...*
> *You smiled and then the spell was cast*
> *Now here we are in heaven*
> *For you are mine at last.*

Not only were Arthur and Joan falling in love but she also saved him from being sacked. The Hippodrome was such a big theatre that during the run of *Flare Path* he had difficulty projecting his voice up to the gods, and the management warned him that unless he improved they would have to let him go. Joan taught him to hold his head up and speak out, and persuaded the management to give him another chance. He was left out of the next four plays and must have wondered whether his acting career was over already, but he appeared again on stage in *Uncle Harry* at the end of February, and from then on almost every week: in March in *The*

Whispering Gallery, The Wrong Number and *The Fake*; in April in *It Happened at Blackpool, The Letter* and *Smiling Through*. His professional career was truly launched at last and he appeared in 25 more plays – among them *Jane Eyre, Trilby* and *Arms and the Man* – before Fortescue's hired an entirely new cast in October. In eight months he appeared in 33 plays and gave 396 performances. After such a ferocious baptism he could probably tackle anything.

Arthur was still living with his parents in their tiny cottage in Hayfield and commuting into Manchester every day. He and Joan did most of their courting in the theatre since they were far too busy working to meet anywhere else except on Sundays, and even then they were learning lines and preparing for the next week's play. It was not, in any case, a season for strolling hand-in-hand down sunlit country lanes or rolling in haystacks: the summer of 1946 was the wettest and gloomiest for 43 years. He called her Joanie at first and later Pony, partly, according to Bill Pertwee's theory, because it rhymed with Joanie and partly because he thought she was a smart filly. Joan's pet names for Arthur were Tim and Timmy because, Phyllis Bateman told me, Timmy was the name of one of the earliest characters he played at the Hippodrome. However, Arthur's parents' young friend Ann Middleton joked that Joan called Arthur Tim 'because he was tiny' and he called her Pony 'because she was a good ride'! In May Arthur succumbed to vanity and bought himself a toupée and on 5 June he wrote to Richie to tell him that he loved Joan and wanted to marry her. Richie took the news remarkably casually. A week later Arthur took Joan to Hayfield to meet his parents – he was appearing appropriately in a play called *Almost a Honeymoon* – and they slept together for the first time on 13 June. On the following day he wrote in his diary: 'Richie agreed to divorce Joanie. We became engaged.' The next day 'Richie sent Joanie £30' – the equivalent of about £700 today, a remarkably generous gesture considering she had just cuckolded him with one of his friends. Arthur and Joan certainly needed the money. He never had more than £18 10*s* in his bank account that year, the equivalent of about £400 today, and by becoming engaged to Joan he was also assuming part responsibility for David.

'When it became obvious that Arthur wanted to marry Joan it was quite amicable, because I had met Barbara,' Richie Gatehouse told me. 'In fact it was a godsend to everybody concerned, except poor little David, of course. I used to worry about him. But no one was jealous and there was no confrontation.' The following week Richie wrote to Joan and Arthur giving them his blessing, and on the Saturday they went to Hayfield again to tell his parents that they intended to get married and, according to Arthur's diary, 'received their approval'. In fact his mother was shocked and disapproved strongly not only of adultery and divorce but also of Joan, who was far too posh, well spoken and actressy for Nan. The women's dislike was mutual and enduring, but Joan and Big Arthur eventually grew fond of each other.

The excitement was all too much for Joan and she suffered an attack of angina that sent her to bed for two days. The following week she and Arthur met Richie for lunch to talk about the divorce and they agreed that David should be raised partly by Joan and Arthur and partly by her parents, who were soon to move to Hexham in Northumberland, where her father was about to become the organist at Hexham Abbey. On Sunday, 21 July Arthur wrote in his diary 'Slept with Joanie', and on the following Friday 'I tell Father I shall leave home and live with Joanie.' On he Saturday 'Home hunting began'. The strangest diary entry of all appears under the date 30 July, when Arthur wrote 'Married Joanie'. This must have been some sort of symbolic marriage, since they did not actually get married legally until 17 months later, in January 1948. 'Perhaps they exchanged rings,' suggested Richie Gatehouse. 'Or perhaps it was like they do in Hawaii, where a man and a girl stand in front of a church and declare their love, and they're married. Joan was very fey like that.' In the front of Arthur's diary he listed her telephone number, WEL 3973, under the name Joanie Lowe, as if they really were married, and on 1 August he wrote: 'Left home to live with my wife Joanie. Sussex Hotel.' They were to live together for 35 years.

Given the uncertain nature of their lives in the theatre, they were extremely lucky that Joan's parents were prepared to raise David and that they were rich enough to do so. 'I suppose it *was* self-sacrificing of them,' admitted Gatehouse, 'but I think it added interest to their lives.'

In September Arthur recorded his first radio broadcast, for a Northern BBC *Children's Hour* programme called 'Know Your County', but in October he and Joan found themselves out of work when their Fortescue contracts expired. It was in fact a good thing that they had to move on, since neither was going to become famous at the Hippodrome. The newspapers were still ignoring them and to add insult to frustration the *Manchester Evening News* had just started reviewing local amateur theatre but was still shunning the Fortescue professionals. It must have been a worry to be out of work, especially since Joan had to go into hospital for five days for an operation in November, but there were four other theatres in the same street as the Hippodrome and Arthur picked up a few casual roles by dropping into Cox's Bar, where they pinned up a list of acting jobs each week. It was only a few weeks before both he and Joan were signed up for a year by another rep company. Martin Benson had become a producer for the impresario Derek Salberg and hired them to join Salberg's new repertory company at Hereford, Arthur as a supporting character actor on £10 a week – twice what he had earned at the Hippodrome – and Joan as a stage manager who would occasionally also play small roles. She must have loved Arthur very much to have accepted such a demotion. Relieved to be in regular work again, they spent Christmas with Arthur's parents in Hayfield, travelled to Hereford on 30 December, and moved into wonderfully convenient digs in The Lamb pub at 42 Berrington Street, the same street as the theatre, right in the centre of town and just 300 yards from the cathedral.

Hereford is a pretty little market town that sits astride the River Wye a dozen miles from the Welsh border. In 1947 its chief glories were a beautiful eleventh-century cathedral with a chained library of 1,400 books and a unique 600-year-old map of the world, the Mappa Mundi; a bishop and his palace; and a castle, racecourse, professional football club, annual regatta and music festival, and several museums. Whichever way you turned there was another ruin, ancient alleyway or timbered building soaked in history, some of it theatrical. Here in a hovel in Pipewell Lane, now Gwynne Street, King Charles II's actress mistress Nell Gwynne is said to have been born in 1650, and here too the actor David Garrick was born in 1717.

Derek Salberg and his brother Reggie ran several repertory theatres across the country, most notably the Alexandra in Birmingham. With Martin Benson's help Derek assembled a remarkably talented company of actors at the County Theatre, some of them experienced performers borrowed from his theatres in Birmingham and Wolverhampton. Several of the younger actors, like Arthur, were to become extremely successful, among them Geoffrey Bond, Richard Leech, Nancy Roberts and Helen

Uttley. Bond, who later changed his name to Christopher because there was another actor called Geoffrey, was to become an award-winning scriptwriter, editor, producer and director of hundreds of films, plays and TV episodes. Nancy Roberts was later one of the first stars of television as the toothless Grandma Grove in the BBC's first TV soap, *The Grove Family*. Richard Leech, a 25-year-old doctor who had just given up medicine after a year as a house surgeon, went on to play in 20 West End productions and to enjoy several major theatrical triumphs, most notably when he created the part of Henry VIII in *A Man For All Seasons* with Paul Scofield. Leech's wife, Helen Uttley, went on to be the leading lady for years at the Sheffield Playhouse. Even Joan's pale, pretty assistant stage manager, 22-year-old Mary Brenchley, was to become incredibly rich and successful as the wife and co-author of the jockey–thriller writer Dick Francis. 'Most of us were at the start of our careers, brimming with enthusiasm and burning to get the war behind us and start a new life.' Christopher Bond told me in 2000, 'and rough hewn though it was, the burgeoning talent of that company was remarkable.' It was also a very happy company and many of the actors were to keep in touch for the rest of their lives. Once Arthur had become successful in London he and Joan used to throw an annual New Year party to which almost all of the Hereford company were invited. 'When Joan got very poorly, towards the end of her life, she spoke more of the time at Hereford than of any other,' Stephen wrote in his book.

The County Theatre, which is now the Gala bingo hall, had 580 seats and a stage just 14 feet deep. The company was expected to perform only once rather than twice nightly, with matinées on Wednesday and Saturdays. Even so the pressure was still terrific, with a new play to be learned, rehearsed and staged every week. 'On Tuesday morning you'd go in and plot the play with Martin Benson,' Leech told me.

You'd usually have the Samuel French edition of the play and you'd do what Samuel French said unless Benson told you something different. By that evening you'd learned your moves for all three acts. On Wednesday morning you went in and did Act 1 without the book and you went through Acts 2 and 3 with the book. Thursday morning was free for study and on Thursday afternoon you went through the whole play without the book. And every evening you were appearing on stage in the previous play. We thought nothing of it. Extraordinary. There was one week when Helen and I did a two-handed play and I remember there was a fair in Hereford and we were going round on the carousel saying the words. That went on all the time. You'd go anywhere and just say the words. I couldn't possibly do it now.

'You'd got three scripts running through your head all the time,' said Christopher Bond,

but it worked. Arthur was a great asset to the company because we were all just at the beginning of our careers, very much so, and he had some experience in twice-nightly rep. We didn't realise how little experience he had in fact had, but he'd obviously learned extremely quickly and we all turned to him for advice. This twice-nightly business teaches you very fast, and if you make a mistake in the first house performance you put it right in the second. And he had absolutely clear diction. He didn't have to shout but he made absolutely certain that you could hear the words.

Arthur's deep, rounded voice was in fact a joy to hear. 'He was a small little fellow,' I was told by Michael Morris, a semi-professional actor who appeared now and then at Hereford, 'but he had a very good speaking voice. Out of this very small frame came these lovely, mellifluous tones.' Arthur 'was totally professional already,' Leech told me.

I felt he was a man when I was a boy. It was typical of Arthur that he didn't tell any of us that he had been acting for only one year. He was a magnificent character actor. I cannot recall him ever being bad, and his range was fantastic. He did have a toupée, which he glued on for the rare occasions when he played his own age, but normally he left it off and gave us his bishops and gaffers. He knew how to hold an audience even if there was only one person in it, and his timing was extraordinarily brilliant. He could get two exit lines out of one exit. Supposing the exit line is 'That wasn't a lady, that was my wife': he'd split it by hesitating in the middle.

As for Joan's job as stage manager, it was incredibly demanding: she was expected to be onstage constantly throughout rehearsals as well as to find all the props. 'She was very efficient, pretty and blonde, and she worked every hour there was,' Leech told me, and Bond said:

She was a very good stage manager and designer, but Hereford was a comedown for her. Nobody wanted to be a stage manager because if you were any good at it they wouldn't let you change to being an actor. However, she accepted and realised this was a way that she and Arthur could stay together and she could do some acting. She really, really wanted to be an actress but she wasn't star quality, as he was, and she didn't have natural timing, as he did. But she had tremendous personality, she had steel in her, and she was well read and well educated. And she knew he was going to be a star. Even though he was a rather odd-looking man, I think it was a sexy marriage in the early years. It's said that women are always attracted to men who make them laugh, and Arthur was permanently funny and naturally witty, very seldom down. It was the way he said things. He was just a funny man. He only had to put his face round the door and the audience started laughing.

This did not help Joan's own acting since she was a terrible 'corpser', who often dissolved into a fit of the giggles, even when she was onstage. 'I remember her standing at the edge of the stage, tapping a rolling pin in her hand, because she was supposed to be furious with Arthur and was going to whack him over the head with it, and she couldn't keep a straight face,' recalled Christopher Bond's wife, Peggy, who was the company manager's secretary.

Since Arthur and Joan were living together the rest of the cast assumed they were married. 'She was sweet and he worshipped her,' Peggy Bond told me, and her husband agreed. 'They fell in love and stayed in love,' he said, 'and I doubt that he ever looked at another woman. Mind you, it wasn't as though the actresses were making eyes at him. He was quite odd-looking, so he was fairly safe.' Despite the happy atmosphere at the County Theatre, away from work Arthur and Joan tended to keep themselves to themselves. 'They didn't socialise much,' said Bond, although Leech remembered that Salberg would give the cast a party every Saturday night and that Arthur would sometimes do a brilliant crooning act imitating the Ink Spots, the black vocal harmony pop group of the 1930s and 1940s whose romantic ballads included 'If I Didn't Care', 'My

Prayer' and 'When the Swallows Come Back to Capistrano'. 'It was a marvellous act,' said Leech.

He sounded exactly like them. And I remember him singing 'Why do you whisper, green grass?' He really could do it. And another wonderful number he did was 'I wonder who's buying the wine/For those lips that I used to call mine?' It was perfectly tuneful but also managed to be a wonderful send-up of crooners.

But even on Saturdays

there wasn't a lot of drinking and sometimes Arthur didn't stay even for that. I guess he went home. He must have been exhausted. You don't know how hard it was, weekly rep. We didn't go and have a drink after the show, we went home and learned the words for next week. But he got quite keen on home movies after we had a party when we showed a movie we had made called *The Witch's Kitten*.

Not that there was much to do out of doors in Hereford, for that winter was the worst for several decades and February was the coldest since 1895, with an average temperature of 28.7°F. Ferocious blizzards swept the country and the days were dark, gloomy and short, the streets gripped by ice and smothered by snow. Major roads were closed, trains cancelled, and there were frequent coal shortages and power cuts. But nothing would keep the townsfolk away from the new company's first play, J. B. Priestley's *How Are They At Home?*, which opened on Monday, 6 January 1947. It had to compete with the town's three cinemas, the Kemble, Odeon and Ritz, but the theatre was packed with an audience that included the local Member of Parliament, A. E. Baldwin, and several civic dignitaries. 'Martin Benson, the producer, is to be congratulated on the team-work which was displayed by a cast that had met but a week previously,' said the weekly *Hereford Citizen and Bulletin*. The following week the company did Noël Coward's *Blithe Spirit*, in which Arthur played Dr Brodman, but it was not until the third production, *Pink String and Sealing Wax* by Roland Pertwee, a play in which Arthur had acted at the Hulme Hippodrome just three months previously, that he received his first review after more than a year as a professional actor: 'The parts of the Irish doctor and his barrister son were excellently done by Arthur Lowe and Richard Leech,' reported the *Hereford Times*.

The following week Arthur played a Free French officer in *While the Sun Shines* by Terence Rattigan, and the *Citizen and Bulletin* said of his performance that 'the "hot passion" burning in the breast of Arthur Lowe … reduced us to a state of helpless laughter.' The week after that the difficulty of learning a new part every week finally caught up with him when he was playing Engstrand in Ibsen's *Ghosts* and forgot his lines several times in the first scene. Many years later Derek Salberg told Stephen Lowe that Arthur never knew his lines at Hereford, and he was to find it difficult to learn a script properly all his life. The following week, however, the *Citizen and Bulletin* raved once again over Arthur's 'fine performance' in *Worm's Eye View* by R. F. Delderfield. And so it went on for the rest of the year: Arthur was 'superb', 'extremely good', 'superb'. At last he was earning praise and wild applause as well as money for doing what he loved.

Arthur was also able to indulge the mischievous side of his nature. John Hodges, then a 16-year-old bit-part actor, told me that during one performance of *Worm's Eye View* Arthur had to dive out of a stage window and land on a mattress behind the scenes, but some joker had removed the mattress and put a sheet of corrugated iron there instead. 'It made a hell of a racket,' said Hodges, 'but Arthur came back on stage with his usual aplomb and said very drily "That was a hot tin roof." He'd got a wicked sense of humour.' Leech remembered that when Arthur was playing the very small part of a Welsh caretaker in *The Corn is Green*, by Emlyn Williams, he was supposed to stick his head round a door and wish Leech good luck in Welsh: 'It was all Arthur had to do that week but when it came to the dress rehearsal he put his head round the door and said in a Welsh accent "A mouthful of Welsh, boyo!" But of course he had it right for the evening performance.'

During that year in Hereford Arthur appeared in 42 plays – among them *Flare Path* again, *Ten Little Niggers*, *The Importance of Being Earnest*, *This Happy Breed*, *Wuthering Heights* and *Arsenic and Old Lace* – and by some strange quirk of coincidence the last was *The Ghost Train* by Arnold Ridley, who was to play the incontinent Private Godfrey in *Dad's Army* more than 20 years later. Another odd coincidence was that when Arthur and Joan moved out of their digs in Hereford at the end of 1947 the 25-year-old actor who moved in after them was David Croft, the future director of *Dad's Army*.

Despite earning all those excellent reviews as well as the respect of his fellow actors, nobody then ever dreamed that Arthur would one day become a star. 'Absolutely not!' Michael Morris told me. 'The people you thought would become household names were the tall, good-looking leading men and the beautiful girls, not a fellow with ginger hair, like Arthur.' Richard Leech agreed: 'I knew he was a bloody good character actor – he was a *miraculous* actor – but there was only one star in that company. Me!' And Christopher Bond told me: 'In those days stars were not character men, they were leading men or leading juveniles. We didn't think he'd achieve what he did.' Martin Benson was one of the few of Arthur's contemporaries who did not rate him very highly as an actor. 'He didn't have a lot of vocal skill,' he told me, 'and I don't think he had after-wards, either. He delivered the lines but he was no Olivier. A lot of his success came from this strange, oddball personality that he had and the fact that later in his career he had some very good writers.'

Richard Leech once asked the company's manager, Tony Rutter, if there was anyone in the Hereford company who had star quality, hoping that Rutter would say 'Yes, Richard, you'. 'It's awfully difficult to tell,' replied Rutter, 'but you can tell somebody who *hasn't* got it. There's one person you could guarantee won't be a star, and that's Arthur Lowe.'

At the end of 1947, when their contracts at Hereford expired, Arthur and Joan decided that if they were ever to make it to the big-time theatres in London's West End they would have to move to London and try their luck with the various rep companies that were scattered around in suburbs like Bromley, Penge and Croydon. Arthur was 32, Joan 25, and if they did not make it soon they never would. Then Joan discovered to her horror that she was pregnant. It was only three years since her baby Jane had died, and she simply could not face the prospect of having another baby and risking another tragedy like that. It would ruin her career and Arthur's too, since he did not need to be saddled with an infant as well as an expensive London flat. She drank a lot of gin, lay in a hot bath for ages, and induced a miscarriage.

In November Joan's decree nisi came through at last. Richie cited Arthur as co-respondent, and when the decree absolute was finalised two days before Christmas both couples remarried within a few days of each other, Joan and Arthur almost furtively in London on 10 January 1948 in a register office in Robert Adam Street, just off Baker Street. Even in 2001 Joan's sister, Margaret, had no idea where they were married. Strangely they invited no guests or family witnesses, not even their parents nor any of the lifelong friends that they had made in Hereford. Instead, just before the ceremony they asked two strangers passing in the street, J. B. Howe and S. Barton, to be their witnesses. Afterwards they went to a Lyon's Corner House and ate welsh rarebit. Obviously they could not afford an expensive reception, and life in post-war England was still constrained by rationing, but it seems a cold way to wed. Even so they were sufficiently sentimental that Stephen says in his book that 'whenever they wanted to remember that day in later years Joanie made them welsh rarebit. And after Arthur died Joan never ate it again.' Thirty years later Joan told the *TV Times* poignantly that back at their flat after the wedding she had cooked Arthur 'a special meal ... canned soup' – yet she also said that on the way to the register office they had stopped at a post office and had each withdrawn £3 from the savings to pay 'for the celebrations', which would have given them their current equivalent of £125, certainly quite enough to buy a couple of rounds of drinks for a few close friends rather than just two bits of cheese on toast and a tin of soup. These two canny northerners were beginning to show a decidedly careful streak when it came to spending money, even on their wedding day.

They rented a room in Knightsbridge at 11 Trevor Street, an elegant little Georgian terrace of 17 three-storey houses patrolled by old-fashioned Victorian street lamps and guarded by trim iron railings. Among their neighbours were Viscount and Viscountess French at No. 14 and Lady Constance Howard at No. 7. Hyde Park was just across the road, there was a leafy little private garden a few yards away in Trevor Square, and Knightsbridge Underground station and smart department stores like Harrods were a short stroll away. It was a surprisingly upmarket area for a couple of hard-up, unemployed provincial actors to live in.

'It was a case of grabbing any part I could,' Arthur told Jack Foster of the *Birmingham Evening Mail* 30 years later.

Bromley would have a season and then say, 'Sorry, Arthur, nothing for you here next week.' So I'd go to Penge. 'Anything next week?' 'Yes,

£12.' You never asked what the play was, just accepted the £12. My God, it was the rent. You had to tout for work.

On the other hand there were so many theatres in those days that 'you picked up work anywhere you could and there was always plenty,' he told Jenny Campbell of the *Radio Times* in 1971. 'You could live the year round on "special weeks". Theatres would know you and pass you round. I played just about everything.' Many other actors did not find it nearly so easy, even though there were about 200 repertory companies all over the country. 'We would have a contract for six months but you could be fired in the middle of it,' I was told in 2000 by 80-year-old John Barron, who appeared many times on stage with Arthur in Penge and Croydon and went on to play several memorable parts in major TV series, notably C. J. in *The Rise and Fall of Reginald Perrin*, the vicar in the later Arthur Lowe series *Potter*, and the Chief Inspector in the police series *Softly, Softly*. 'It was pretty dodgy,' said Barron, 'a bit of a scramble. There were more actors than jobs and the stress in rep was unbelievable. It was staggeringly hard work.' To start Arthur off in London, Derek Salberg recommended him to his brother Reggie, who ran two rep companies that alternated between a week at the Empire Theatre in Penge and a week four miles away at the Grand in Croydon. Both theatres were big, with 700 or 800 red plush seats each, and ornately decorated with pillars and gilded cornices. 'The Penge Empire was beautiful,' said Barron, 'a magnificent variety house from the great days of Victorian and Edwardian variety.' Sadly both theatres have been demolished.

Each day Arthur would walk or catch a bus from Knightsbridge to Victoria station a mile away, take a train for the eight, 10 or 12 miles south to Penge, Croydon or Bromley, and walk to the theatre to begin again the gruelling business of appearing at 7.30 night after night in another new play every week or fortnight, with afternoon matinées as well at 2.30 p.m. on Wednesdays and 5 p.m. on Saturdays. Another actor who appeared regularly with him in those days was 'the most distinguished actor of us all', according to Barron: Alec McCowen, who went on to become hugely successful on the West End stage, particularly in *Hadrian VII* and *Equus*. 'The average day was crazy,' McCowen told me.

The journey from London to the theatres was horrendous, and I don't know how we managed to get plays on in a week, sometimes difficult plays like *The School for Scandal*. God knows how we did that schedule. Sometimes we would start a play not having done the dress rehearsal because you hadn't time to get to it or to change the set. Quite often I was sick on the first night with nerves, and I'd leave the stage and vomit into a bucket in the wings. It was quite usual to have buckets in the wings because you were so nervous. But I can't remember Arthur vomiting: he was a consummate bloody actor.

Arthur became convinced that rep was a vital part of any actor's education. 'The sad thing is that young actors now have no one with time to teach them,' he said. John Barron believed that Arthur's great strength in those days,

when we were all desperate for work every week, was that although he was only five years older than I was he looked 45 years older if he wanted to. In *The Linden Tree* I played his son! I was the conventional juvenile lead and he was particularly ugly in a funny sort of way, but he was the character man and could play Dad, so he was never out of work.

As Arthur once said to Christopher Bond, patting his bald head, 'That will be my fortune' – 'And he was right,' said Bond, 'because he was forever the character actor.' Arthur was utterly convincing as a much older man. In *The Linden Tree* Professor Linden has reached the age of retirement, 65, but is reluctant to stop working. After hearing a beautiful Elgar cello concerto from the next room he delivers a long, nostalgic speech mourning the long-lost summer afternoons of his youth and asks: 'Where are the bumblebees?' Arthur was still only 32 but he knew instinctively how it would feel to be 65. 'Arthur Lowe gives a delightful portrait of Professor Linden,' reported the local Croydon newspaper, 'warm, human, wholly likeable, and speaks through him for all the older generation who feel they can still give something to the modern world.' McCowen remembered that although Arthur was only 10 years older than he was,

he was always playing my father. He was only 32 but he looked 52. I knew straight away that he was a wonderful actor as soon as he read a play. He never said a line wrong, never put a foot wrong, and I never remember any director giving him notes. I thought 'I wish I could act like that.' Salberg, or whoever was directing, quite soon knew what a good actor he was, so even if he didn't look right for a bigger part they often cast him in one.

Arthur himself saw a huge advantage in being a character actor rather than a leading man. 'As a leading man you have to learn thousands of lines,' he said years later, 'and as a character actor you're always in work and you just come on for a couple of scenes and steal the show.'

Even then he was a perfectionist and became easily irritated with actors who were less professional than he was. 'A bad or selfish actor or an ignorant director could upset him,' recalled McCowen,

and he could get a little bad tempered if people took advantage of him. He would flush quite obviously and you knew he was getting a bit cross. He was red-haired and often they *are* short and fiery. Most of the time he was very good humoured, but he didn't like ignorance.

But Arthur could also be hilarious in the privacy of his dressing room, which he and McCowen often shared. They discovered that they also shared a love of old-time music hall, and as they put on their make-up they enjoyed talking about old music-hall stars, making up jokes, sketches and songs, inventing funny voices – '*Hall-oo!*' – and mimicking old cross-talk double-acts such as Murray and Mooney or Bennett and Williams. 'With Murray and Mooney, for instance,' said McCowen,

one would say 'I can't do it, you can't do it, my wife can't do it.' '*Do what?*' 'Milk chocolate.' It was so stupid! And we imitated Bennett and Williams's musical instruments, and that comedian who played a one-stringed fiddle, and Stainless Stephen, who ran all his lines together. Arthur was superb at it and made me laugh so much. His knowledge of the music hall was huge. We both *loved* Sid Field, who was unbelievably funny and the greatest comedian I've ever seen and who was performing in London at that time.

Arthur had a good voice and loved singing, especially if he could impersonate some well-known singer or group, and when Richard Leech invited him and Joan to a riotous St Patrick's night party in his little basement flat in Chelsea, Arthur and Richard Burton ended up singing the rousing Welsh rugby anthem 'Bread of Heaven', with Arthur doing the descant in a broad Welsh accent. Otherwise he was still pretty unsociable and after each night's performance never stayed on for a drink with the other actors. 'It was a great pleasure acting with him and we got on very well,' said Barron,

> but he seemed very private and there was no man quicker out of the theatre after the curtain was down. One would come off the stage slowly, thinking about half a pint of beer in the pub and gossiping on the way to the dressing room, by which time Arthur was already on his way to the station. I've never seen a man move so quickly. We never had a drink, meal or real chat together. I don't think he was standoffish, just slightly shy. He was a bit of an outsider in the company, a bit different from us. It may be that he had a great plan about how his career was going to go.

Or maybe he simply wanted to get back as soon as possible to his beloved Joan, whom he saw now only early in the morning, at midnight, and on Sundays. Perhaps he also wanted to avoid the ignominy of travelling back to London on a later train, which might mean he would be standing on the platform at Croydon while the posh West End actors' late-night train from London passed through the station going the other way to Brighton. Barron said,

> It was always rather amusing at Croydon station when we were all going back home to London after the show and coming down on the other line, on their way to their luxury homes in Brighton, were the West End actors being served supper in the beautiful cream and brown Pullman car, bowing graciously to the struggling repertory actors waiting to go the other way. I remember Robert Eddison, who was big in the Forties, graciously waving to the poor repertory hacks.

Nobody dreamed that one day this little, bald, weird-looking character actor, Arthur Lowe, would one day be better known than even Robert Eddison. 'It didn't occur to me that he would become famous,' said Barron, 'but I think Arthur had a plan, whereas I didn't. He was ambitious and single-minded.' Alec McCowen agreed:

It's a very difficult profession and I thought Arthur wouldn't be able to last in it. He looked rather small and did not have a good face for films or for anything but small character parts, so I didn't imagine him having the wonderful career he did have. It was sheer talent on his part that he gradually became a hugely popular leading actor and that in later years people like Olivier and Gielgud were very happy and honoured to work with him. As an actor I'd put him on the highest level because although he mainly did comedy, which is the easiest thing to get wrong, he never *acted* funny, so as a bank manager you could really believe he *was* a bank manager. His comic timing was fabulous. I thought he was a great actor and an astonishing man, and I learned a lot from working with him.

It was not only in South London rep that Arthur found work in 1948. In February he went north to Suffolk to play in *Dear Brutus* at the Ipswich Arts Theatre. In March he landed his first film part, a fleeting appearance (in a scene with Richard Attenborough) as a strap-hanging London Underground commuter wearing a hat and rimless spectacles and reading the *Evening News* on a Tube train in the highly praised black-and-white murder comedy-drama *London Belongs to Me*, which starred Alastair Sim. In April, May and June he was in Birmingham at the Alexandra Theatre and in Brighton at the Theatre Royal playing Crabtree in Basil Dean's production of *The School for Scandal* with Evelyn Laye, Peter Sallis, and his own Joanie, who had managed to squeeze into the same company as assistant stage manager and was also playing the small part of 'A Lady'. In October they were together again at the Theatre Royal in Bolton, where Arthur played Alfred Lockhart in *The Linden Tree* and Joan was again the assistant stage manager. She was finding it very difficult to land any acting jobs and was working only now and then as assistant stage manager at the Arts Theatre, and although Arthur was glad to be constantly in work he hated being separated from Joan for more than a few days. When she went north to stay with her mother and David in Hexham that summer he wrote to her lovingly in a letter that started 'Darling Pony': 'It was such a relief to hear your voice on the phone last night darling – I was frightened of your going on such a big journey on your own.' He added 'come home soon, soon, please!' and reassured her 'I am getting plenty of food. This morning the butcher gave me enough stewing steak to last a week + 6d corned beef, so I'm O.K.' And he concluded: 'Bye bye, sweetheart, I'll ring Wed. night about 8.30 p.m. Bless you, all my love Tim. Love to Mummy and David.'

Arthur was earning enough to keep them both, though hardly in luxury. In July he recorded a radio programme called *Adventure Unlimited* for the BBC. In August and October he was at the Mask Theatre in London in *The Linden Tree* again. In September he made a film documentary, *The Personal Touch*. In November he was on BBC radio again as a golf club steward in the hugely popular, long-running serial *Mrs Dale's Diary*. In December he was at the Pinewood film studios shooting a small part in his second film, another black-and-white movie, *Floodtide*, starring Gordon Jackson and Rona Anderson – a 'boring inspirational drama', according to *Halliwell's Film and Video Guide*, in which Arthur played a pianist and his future *Dad's Army* colleague John Laurie also had a part – and then he was back on BBC radio as 'Second Voice' in *Mrs Dale's Diary*. And so it went on throughout 1949 and 1950. He was becoming a workaholic, prepared to take on any job, anywhere, so long as there was money in it, and although he had an agent he hustled most of his work for himself by spending a couple of hours every morning telephoning theatres and producers.

In January 1949 he spent three days at Ealing Studios shooting his first film speaking role when he played the one-line part of a reptilian reporter at the very end of the black-and-white comedy *Kind Hearts and Coronets*, in which Dennis Price plays the Duke of Chalfont and is sentenced to hang for murdering eight members of the d'Ascoyne family, all played by Alec Guinness. Considered by many to be a classic, the film seems dreary and stilted to me today, but Arthur's toad-like appearance in the final 30 seconds is irresistibly slimy. As the murderous Duke is unjustly freed from prison, Arthur, the seedy reporter, wearing what appears to be a grotesque false nose, sidles up to him outside the prison gates, raises his bowler hat, exposes his excessively bald head, and wheedles oleaginously in a lower-class accent: 'Your Grace, I represent the magazine *Titbits*, by whom I am commissioned to approach you about the publication rights of your memoirs.'

That year, in addition to all the plays in which he appeared in rep at Penge, Croydon and Bromley, Arthur also landed parts in eight radio plays after writing a letter to the BBC in which he boldly stated: 'Character acting is my line of country, all dialects, any age.' The BBC gave him two auditions, one in London and one in Manchester. The

London judges reported afterwards: 'Voice age – 40. Pitch – strong, with incisive bite. Accent – Derbyshire. Dialects – several, rather unconvincing. General remarks – Knows too many accents. Good for Derbyshire.' The Manchester judges were kinder about his accents, of which they reported: 'Irish – passable. Scottish – unintelligible. Broken English – good. American – not bad, good strong voice, pretty distinctive.' By contrast the BBC producer Reggie Smith, who hired him that year to play a cobbler in a radio programme called *Return to the Black Country*, was ecstatic about Arthur's performance. 'This man is a first-class dialectician,' he reported. 'He is a native to the Derbyshire/Nottingham border, but did for me in all actuality cast a wonderful Black Country role – and Black Country is an extremely difficult accent, as you know. He has a keen sense of character and carries quiet but thorough conviction.'

In 1949 Arthur appeared in six more films, though all of them were poor and his parts were very small. In those early years he prided himself on never turning down any job, no matter how humdrum. 'I travelled a lot, took everything that was going, played whatever had to be played,' he told Sheridan Morley for an article in *The Times* in 1974. 'How can you say you're an actor if you're not acting? An actor who can't support his family shouldn't be an actor. There's nothing so special about being an actor, nothing which allows you to be out of work any more often than a bus-driver.' He made a similar remark in 1971 when he told Barry Norman of the *Daily Mail*: 'Success too soon has ruined many promising young actors. What you need when you're young is work. You shouldn't be feather-bedded. You should work and really earn your money, then if you get rich later on you've got the sense to enjoy it properly.' Unlike most other actors he worked so hard that he was never out of work and 'resting'. 'I've never been on the bread line,' he told Norman. 'I've always managed to make a living and for that I'm grateful. Failure can never be of any benefit to anybody. Poverty is as damaging as getting too much too soon.'

At the end of 1949 all his hard work and networking gave him his first important breakthrough: he landed his first part in a play in the West End of London. It came just in time, for a few months later he would have reached the five-year deadline that he and his father had agreed he should give himself to make it as an actor. A few months more and he might have had to face the awful prospect of returning to work in a Manchester factory.

CHAPTER 5

The West End

(1950–1958)

The play that brought Arthur to the West End in 1950 was *Larger Than Life* by Guy Bolton, a comedy about two famous West End actors, Michael and Julia Gosselyn, who are living together in Hampstead even though they have been divorced for years. Based on the Somerset Maugham novel *Theatre*, it is a light-hearted confection of social banter, theatrical chit-chat, gossip and flirtation, which opened at the Duke of York's Theatre in St Martin's Lane on 7 February with Reginald Denny and Jessie Royce Landis in the leading roles and Laurence Naismith playing their butler, Wilson. After two and a half months Arthur replaced Naismith and made his first West End appearance on 27 April.

He was only 34 but had again been cast as an old man, this time a silver-haired 70-year-old. Described in the play as 'the perfect stage butler', Wilson is a retired small-part actor who has played stage butlers throughout his career so well that he has become a real butler. Arthur must have relished the absurdity of being a real actor playing a stage actor playing a stage butler playing a real butler. The role was perfect for him, and it is difficult to read the play without hearing the fruity voice of Captain Mainwaring as Wilson opens the first scene at the Gosselyns' front door and says 'Good afternoon, Sir Charles' and 'I'll tell Mrs Gosselyn you're here', and proceeds later to rumble with perfect enunciation, 'Pardon me, madam', 'The young man is here with the photographs', and 'Shall I put the lights on, Master Roger?' Wilson delivers lines that could well have represented Arthur's own thoughts about the theatre. 'I don't suppose any of us who have ever been on the stage ever quite become like ordinary people,' he tells the Gosselyns' son,

Roger, who remarks that even offstage his mother is always acting and thinks of everyone as her audience. 'That's the way they *all* think,' replies Wilson:

They're a race apart, actors. I shall never forget old Brotherton Kemble … he was an actor. The day after his wife died he walked into the theatre with his hands full of newspapers. 'I've had a cruel loss,' he says, 'one I shall not get over – but I must say they've given the old girl some damned good notices.'

When Mrs Gosselyn asks him what makes a star, Wilson replies:

I'd say the two main ingredients are a little magic and a lot of guts. It's courage, but it's more than that. It's a kind of bigness, a feeling that you're just a little larger than life-size. You believe in yourself, you *must*. That's why the big people in the profession can ride over illness or sorrow or anything. Look at Sir Henry Irving. I was with him, in his company, I mean, the night he died – at Bradford. I was standing by the stage door when he came in. He looked very pale, and stopped as though he were out of breath, and put his hand to his heart. I went over to see if I could help him. I was only the assistant stage manager at the time, but he was always very gracious and friendly to all of us. I said, 'Good evening, Sir Henry – you're looking very tired, don't you think you'd be better off at home?' He just looked at me, and he said, 'Thank you, Mr Wilson, but I *am* at home, and I'm expecting a large company of my friends. I should hate to disappoint them.'

It was an attitude that was to rule the rest of Arthur's life: the show must go on, no matter what.

Joan sent him a loving telegram which was delivered to his dressing room – 'I HAVE BEEN SINGING OUR TUNE ALL MY LOVE = JOAN +++' – and in the audience too that night were Arthur's father and his girlfriend, Margaret, who were enjoying an illicit trip to London and staying at the Cora Hotel. That night Big Arthur wrote to Little Arthur:

Margaret and I decided to come to the theatre to-day and witness your debut on the West End stage. One word covers your performance:-

'Delightful'. Every word came over; your gestures were perfectly timed and the 'character' was always present. I cannot tell you how delighted and proud I feel that you have so soon obtained the break you sought. May it bring you more and more good luck and more engagements in the West End. (Please do not tell Mother I was there … Will be able to clear all this very soon. M goes over-seas.)
Love, Dad.

Big Arthur and Nan had recently moved from 3 Fisher's Lane in Hayfield to yet another tiny one-up, one-down cottage just around the corner, 'The Cottage' at 3 Chapel Road, otherwise known to the villagers as Rhubarb Square. It was a dark, poky little terraced house with an outside privy, almost a hovel and hardly an appropriate home for a 61-year-old railway clerk at London Road station who had been promoted yet again and had just been elected chairman of Hayfield cricket club. Big Arthur's job now was to buy food for the LNER trains and buffet restaurants early every morning at Manchester's Smithfield market. He had a free first-class rail pass and would have been earning a good wage for a man with no children or grandchildren to support, but if Big Arthur were secretly spending money on a mistress and naughty trips to London it is understandable that he could not afford a bigger house. Women certainly found him attractive. 'Big Arthur was absolutely lovely,' said Ann Middleton, whose parents ran the Railway Inn (now the Kinder Lodge), one of two pubs in the village, where Big Arthur drank numerous halves of heavy draught bitter every evening with a gang of cronies at 6 p.m. on his way home from the station and then again each night from 10 p.m. 'until they threw him out' at midnight.

He was a charming man with a gorgeous voice, very deep. You could feel it up your legs. It vibrated through the floor. And he spoke nicely. Big Arthur was sexy, the way he talked, and he used to tell me a few tales about his journeys abroad. Oh yeah, he had a very nice time! 'Don't tell Nan,' he said. He went to Amsterdam and he'd got a girlfriend. 'Never tell Nan,' he said.

Big Arthur's main vice, apart from cavorting with other women, seems to have been that he was notoriously tight-fisted and always accepted a drink in the pub but never bought a round if he could avoid it. Nan would join him in the pub three or four nights a week to sup gin and tonic, and Bill Higginbottom told me: 'They used to sit together, Big Arthur a really big fellow and this tiny wife who was growing smaller and smaller by the day. It seemed to be a happy marriage, but she liked to give advice and never said no to a drink.' Ann Middleton, however, told me:

> Nan wasn't liked in the village because she was a greedy little woman, very greedy, very tight. She didn't part with anything. She was tiny, like a little bird, and she was always ailing, she was always 'so ill'. She'd had every illness there was: if you'd got it, she'd had it. So me mother said 'Have you had VD?' and she nearly collapsed!

Little Arthur obviously inherited much of his character from his father, for they had a great deal in common: the love of alcohol, cricket and the music hall; the carefulness with money; the sense of humour; the conservatism and self-control; the touch of bossiness and pomposity; the respect in which they were generally held. Their less than handsome looks too were remarkably similar despite the difference in their sizes. 'Little Arthur was the dead spit of Big Arthur,' George Cooper told me, and Mary Miller, Hayfield's church organist, told me: 'It was so funny to see them walking together through the village – Big Arthur, Little Arthur, and tiny Nan – and Big Arthur and Little Arthur walked just the same, just like Captain Mainwaring.' And their deep voices and educated diction were remarkably similar.

Arthur had only three weeks in *Larger Than Life*, during which old Queen Mary was in the audience one night. When the play closed on 20 May he sank back into the obscurity of weekly and fortnightly rep for eight months, appearing again in dozens of plays in Bromley, Penge and Croydon – as the waiter in *You Never Can Tell* by George Bernard Shaw, as Hardcastle in Goldsmith's *She Stoops to Conquer* – and it was to be nearly a year before he landed another role in the West End. But the vital breakthrough had been made. He had shown that he could handle a substantial part in a major London theatre, and in the meantime he built on his experience by accepting everything that came his way including commercials, voice-overs and small parts in two more mediocre black-and-white films: *Cage of Gold* and *Mystery Street*. 'He was a workaholic,'

Richard Leech told me. 'He pretended he was greedy for money, but he wasn't; he was terrified of being out of work. And he loved being on stage, the applause. What we actors really love is getting it across, feeling you've got 'em *there*. It's power.'

Life for the Lowes was still chancy but they were bolstered by the closeness of their marriage. They adored each other and built a cosy domestic cocoon in which they needed no one else. Joan's unfaltering belief that he was a great actor led her to sacrifice her career for his, and in turn drove him on to prove himself worthy of her sacrifice. 'I resolved that because Timmy was such a good actor his career must come first,' she said many years later.

'Joan used to make fun of him a bit,' said Leech.

She'd call him 'little bald man', but she was very fond of him and he adored her. He was funny in private but she was more vivacious than him and gayer at a party. I never saw them having a row and I'd have said it was a tremendously good marriage.

Margaret Stapleton and David Gatehouse agreed. 'Arthur was a very good husband to my mother,' Gatehouse told me. 'A lot of actors would hang around after the show and go off to pubs and go over the minutiae, but I don't believe Arthur ever did that for five or ten minutes. He wanted to be at home.' The Lowes were of course extremely lucky that Joan's parents were still happy to raise David, who was nine in 1950, a pupil at Hexham County primary school, and beginning to show the interest in music that was eventually to give him a brilliant musical career. Reg and Winnie Cooper were incredibly selfless and had also taken in to their music-filled mansion in Hexham their daughter Margaret and her three children after her marriage broke up. 'My mother was an amazing woman,' Margaret Stapleton told me. David Gatehouse agreed:

Joan's mother was really quite wonderful. She was as tough as boots, taught singing and piano till nine o'clock at night, and cooked, cleaned this whole huge house, and brought up me and three cousins without batting an eyelid. I had a happy childhood and didn't feel ignored or neglected in the least, and I never thought it was strange that I was brought up by my grandparents. The reason for it justified it: Joan and

Arthur were absolutely broke at that time and had to be in a position to tour, and they had to be able to go around acting.

It seems odd that Joan was happy to let her mother raise her only child so far away and to see him so rarely, but she was not at all maternal. All she wanted were Arthur and acting, and luckily David seemed happy with that. 'Arthur was very nice and treated me just as if I was his son,' he said. 'The family all got on very well and my father seemed perfectly at home with them and there was never any fuss. I grew up completely unaware of the divorce.' Richard Gatehouse was also impressed by Arthur's kindness. 'He was a very good stepfather,' he told me, 'and we would meet whenever David needed something like a new pair of pants or a new suit. We shared the expenses and would halve the cost of his clothes and that sort of thing. Arthur was very generous.'

At the beginning of 1951 Arthur landed another part in a London theatre, the Lyric, Hammersmith, where he enjoyed a six-week run as a pompous charity worker in *The Silver Box*, a comedy by John Galsworthy about the theft of a rich Liberal MP's silver box and the huge gap between rich and poor in England at the turn of the century. Two months later he and Joan were both back in the West End at the Cambridge Theatre in James Elroy Flecker's *Hassan*, a musical about a fat, ugly, middle-aged, Baghdad confectioner who falls in love with a beautiful girl called Yasmin. Arthur played no fewer than three roles. His first was as a greedy porter who delivers Hassan's sweets to Yasmin along with lines such as these: 'From my hands, O dispenser of bounty', 'Curses on the fat sugar cook and his love-sick eyes. Allah be praised, his confectionery is better than his countenance!' and '*Ya Hawaja, v'aleikum assalam!*' His second part, as a calligraphist at the caliph's court, was a silent one, but his third, in the final scene, once again as an old man, allowed him to quaver in rhyming verse:

> 'Have you not girls and garlands in your homes,
> Eunuchs and Syrian boys at your command?
> Seek not excess: God hateth him who roams!'

– to which the assembled merchants of Baghdad replied in chorus: 'We take the Golden Road to Samarkand.' With Flecker's poetry and the music of Delius, *Hassan* was 'the most beautiful musical I was ever in,' Arthur said many years later, but although it starred Laurence Harvey as Rafi, the King of the Beggars, and Elizabeth Sellars as Yasmin – and Joan landed the job of assistant stage manager – the show ran for only 29 performances.

For the next nine months Arthur had to struggle once again to earn a decent living in rep in Bromley, Penge and Croydon in plays such as *A Streetcar Named Desire*, *Charley's Aunt* and *The Barretts of Wimpole Street*. He joined touring companies that travelled all over the country, taking Joan with him whenever possible and living out of suitcases in a series of theatrical digs from Eastbourne to Llandudno: with Mrs Jones in Cardiff, Mrs Holyoake in Birmingham, Mrs Bell in Southsea, Mrs Savage in Blackpool, Mrs Walsh in Liverpool, Mrs Hill in Brighton. Some landladies, like Mrs Lee in Eastbourne, failed to please him and he crossed their names ferociously out of his little blue notebook before trying someone else. He made a radio programme entitled *The Young and Ancient Man*, appeared in a passable Western film called *New Mexico*, and made his first three TV programmes (historical documentaries in a series called *I Made News*), and three TV commercial voice-overs, one of them for a car-hire company. He was flirting at last with the despised medium that was eventually to make him famous.

Then in 1952 all his years of persistence brought him at last the West End success of which he had dreamed for so long. The dance-band leader and impresario Jack Hylton was casting for the London production of a big new award-winning American stage musical by Irving Berlin, *Call Me Madam*, which he was about to put on at the Coliseum in London. Arthur went nervously along to be auditioned and sang 'Bye Bye, Blackbird' so well that he landed the juicy part of a randy American senator, Jim Brockbank. The London production of *Call Me Madam*, which starred Billie Worth (in the role made famous by Ethel Merman in the original New York production), Anton Walbrook, Shani Wallis and Jeff Warren, had a brief out-of-town run in Oxford before opening in the West End on 15 March. It was to run for 16 months and 485 performances, and to give Arthur at last the boost that he needed to move his career up into third gear.

Call Me Madam was loosely based on the story of the Washington socialite Perle Mesta and tells of how Sally Adams, a rich but ignorant

American socialite, 'the hostess with the mostest', is sent to Europe as US ambassador to the small Grand Duchy of Lichtenburg. It was packed with memorable songs, among them 'The Hostess With the Mostes' 'On the Ball' and 'It's a Lovely Day Today'. Although Arthur had only 16 lines as the lustful, bald-headed Senator Brockbank, he was also called upon to flirt with one girl, to chase another across the stage, to goose a third, and to dance and join in singing three songs. One of his songs, which speculated about what was expected to be the forthcoming 1952 presidential election battle between President Harry Truman and General Dwight D. ('Ike') Eisenhower, 'They Like Ike', was a lively, staccato, rum-ti-tum-ti-tum number with words like 'wanna' and 'gonna' and a loud trumpet finale. Arthur sang alternate lines with Launce Maraschal, who played another senator, and Sidney Keith, who played a congress-man, and with an immaculate American accent he sang of 'squudders' rights' and 'a suck on the jar'. 'The people soon will choose their fav'rite son,' warbled Arthur in between lines from the other two. 'But Harry won't get out. They're in for plenty of fights … For nearly twenty years we've had the people's cheers. The Democrats continue to advance … But Harry won't consent. They'll get a sock on the jaw … Please don't do that to Harry.'

With Billie Worth and the others he also belted out a bouncy, tuneless song that developed into a big, noisy, orchestral number, the 'Washington Square Dance', during which he danced, capered, leapt about the stage with amazing energy, and sang these memorable lines:

> *Hi! hi! Do, do, do, do, do, do, do, do, do, do.*
> *Hi babe, waddya say*
> *Change your partners*
> *Square dance.*
> *Bow to your partners*
> *Bow to your corners*
> *Dance till your cheeks are red as a rose.*
> *But try not to step on your partner's toes – now*
> *Duck for the oyster*
> *Dig for the clam*
> *Duck for the oyster, dig for the clam.*
> *But do your diggin' for Uncle Sam – and*

One for the money
Two for the show
One for the money two for the show
And three to get ready for Uncle Joe.

David Gatehouse was 10 but already highly talented musically – he was later to win a music scholarship to Balliol College, Oxford – and he was deeply impressed by his stepfather's performance in *Call Me Madam*.

People say Arthur's great sudden breakthrough was in *Coronation Street*, and I suppose financially it may have been, but it wasn't the bloody great blazing spotlight that *Call Me Madam* was. When he landed the job he knew it could last for a year and a half, and he went out and bought their first bottle of wine. I was there and it cost 3/6*d*. I remember being taken down onto the stage at the Coliseum. It had a double revolve, for heaven's sake, in the middle of the stage, and a London bus up on a shelf backstage, and they put the house lights out and I stood on the stage and saw five circular shelves of seats above the stalls, and then all the boxes, and the impression was overwhelming. I was allowed to stand in the wings while this big show was going on, and it was a big chorus-girl production with these big, big dance numbers, and I stood in the wings with these chorus girls dancing off an inch from my nose. I was very proud of his very professional approach to his work. They had a big band in the pit, a *BIG* band – three trombones, four saxophones, all the drums, all the trumpets, *and* violins – and there were no microphones onstage at all. He had never sung onstage before and didn't consider himself any good, but I heard him not only from the wings but also from the gods, right up at the back, and there was no trouble hearing him, and it was a big, big band. He had quite a nice voice, no trouble projecting, no problem standing on stage and being heard. I was immensely proud of knowing anybody who was that good at it.

Arthur was earning £20 a week in *Call Me Madam* and a further steady income from the BBC for several television and radio jobs – among them three appearances in the new *Dan Dare* TV series, twice as a thug and once as an American – so when it became clear that the musical was set for a long run and that he was at last free of the humble grind of weekly rep, he and Joan felt secure enough to leave their rented room in Trevor Street and move into a fourth-floor flat three streets away at 45 Rutland Gate, a broad, quiet avenue of huge trees, imposing four- and five-storey pillared houses, and seven-storey blocks of mansion flats set around two private gardens and with immediate access to Hyde Park through a gate just across Kensington Road. At No. 45 the Lowes' new flat, number 5, one of six apartments, was perched at the top of the building with stunning views north over Rotten Row, the Serpentine and Hyde Park, to Regent's Park and Hampstead, and south as far as Battersea and Wandsworth. Although the flat was tiny, Rutland Gate was even more exclusive and salubrious than Trevor Street, housing as it did 23 titled residents, from Lord and Lady Hardinge of Penshurst, who lived next door in The Clock House, to the Earl of Cathcart, the Countess of Latham and Lord Wrenbury. Their immediate neighbours on the floor below, however, were not quite so upper class: a Polish couple, who Arthur and Joan joked were probably spies. The Lowes' flat was small, consisting of only a long corridor, sitting room, bathroom, kitchen, and one bedroom with a little balcony. It also contained a sitting tenant: a sofa that had been installed before the top floor had been converted and that was now too big ever to be removed along the narrow corridor. David Gatehouse thought that

it was very clever of them to find this flat on the top floor, and Arthur and I used to go into Hyde Park a lot and played cricket with a bat and a tree. But there were too many flights of steps up to the flat, especially when Joan discovered just a few weeks later that she was expecting Stephen.

Joan was appalled to be pregnant yet again. Having another child in such a small, inaccessible flat would probably destroy her faltering acting career for good. According to Peggy Bond she tried to get rid of this baby too – or babies, since it seems that she was pregnant with twins. 'She was so cross,' Mrs Bond told me.

She was pregnant with Stephen and a twin and decided to have an abortion, but they didn't realise she'd got twins and they aborted only one. It was Stephen's twin who was aborted, and she told me woman to woman: 'I went back to the hospital and I told them "You've only taken one baby away, and I've got another one, and I'm going to sue you." She was *absolutely* furious that the abortion hadn't worked.'

It is possible that Joan might have obtained a legal abortion safely in hospital because of her baby's cot death nine years earlier, but it seems extremely unlikely that any surgeon would remove one foetus without noticing another, or that even a back-street abortionist would induce one foetus to abort without the other. Nonetheless, Peggy Bond insisted more than once that the story was true, although she never mentioned it even to her husband. A leading British gynaecologist told me: 'Yes, non-identical twins can have two different sacs and two different placenta, and one can come away and the remaining one can survive.'

Arthur himself was certainly not at all furious and when Stephen was born at Queen Charlotte's Hospital in Hammersmith on 23 January 1953 he wrote proudly in his little black diary for that year: 'STEPHEN ARRIVED! 6pm 6lbs 12³/₄ ounces', and made at the back of his diary a careful list of the things that Joan needed: 'trousers, vest, nightie, 2 mat coats, boots, gloves, bonnets, shawls or blankets, nappies (2), clothes for Joan, pins, shoes'. Neither Joan nor Arthur was at all religious but two months later, on Palm Sunday, 29 March, Stephen was christened at Holy Trinity Church.

Call Me Madam closed at the Coliseum in May after a run of 14 months, but was kept alive for a further 3 months when it was transferred to London suburban theatres at Streatham Hill and Golders Green before it closed for good in August. Arthur's income, which he noted carefully in his diary, dropped dramatically. In January 1953 he had earned £118 10s 0d (including £29 from the BBC) and in May £146 12s 0d, but in September, October and November he made just £12 2s 0d, £27 3s 9d and £34 18s 0d. He was always such a hard worker that by December he was making reasonable money again, £79 14s 0d, but even so his total income that year, £920, was worth only £14,700 in modern terms. It was not much for a family man of 38, and Joan could no longer supplement his earnings since they had agreed that she should give up work to look after Stephen, at least for 10 or 11 years. Money was still so tight that when Joan fell in love with a beautiful carved wooden screen they could not afford to buy it even though it cost only £3, about £50 today.

'In the early days we were all enormously skint,' Christopher Bond told me.

Arthur did a lot of touring and had to maintain a home and pay for digs as well, so there wasn't much left. I think this is what turned him into a workaholic. He used to tell me 'Never turn down a job. All right, the next morning five better jobs will arrive through your letterbox, but that doesn't matter: you're working. That's more important than anything: to be working.' He felt insecure and worried that he might be poor in old age, and that drove him to be mean and to work. He had a list of people in management, films, and agents, and every morning he would get on the telephone and ring six of them, and he would ring six the next day, and six the day after that.

To keep afloat financially that year Arthur appeared in seven small plays, a revue, a couple of TV and radio programmes, and two bad films: *One Way Out* and *The Mirror and Markheim*. *One Way Out* was a good example of how Arthur would accept any work, no matter how pedestrian, for it is slow, dreary, utterly unbelievable and with a dreadful script and terrible leaden acting, although his own performance as a crooked cockney jeweller (yes, of course he says '*Give me a break, guv*') contains one glorious moment: when he stands in a doorway and does a little double-take and suddenly you glimpse the future Captain Mainwaring.

In the theatre, however, Arthur's star was rising, and six months after the closure of *Call Me Madam* Jack Hylton hired him again to play in the London revival of another lavish American musical, *Pal Joey*. This was a much more realistic and innovative musical than *Call Me Madam* – a tough, dark, cynical story of sex and blackmail so gritty that when it was first performed in New York in 1940 the *New York Times* critic Brooks Atkinson called it 'an odious story' and asked: 'Although it is expertly done, can you draw sweet water from a foul well?' The musical was based on a collection of sardonic *New Yorker* short stories by John O'Hara about Joey Evans, a handsome but selfish, swaggering cad: a lying, opportunistic, utterly amoral Chicago nightclub singer, dancer and gigolo, who dreams of owning a nightclub and heartlessly dumps his nice, naïve girlfriend for a rich older woman. The show's music was by Richard Rodgers, the lyrics by Lorenz Hart, and the songs included 'My Funny

Valentine', 'The Lady is a Tramp' and the evergreen 'Bewitched' ('I'm wild again, Beguiled again, A simpering, whimpering, child again, Bewitched, bothered and bewildered am I…') It opened at the Prince's Theatre in London's Shaftesbury Avenue in March 1954, another massive, big-band production, starring Harold Lang, Dick France and Carol Bruce. Arthur played the part of Mike, a tough-guy Chicago night-club owner who hires Joey as his MC. Also in the show, playing a delivery boy, was Lionel Blair. The London reviewers were impressed. *Pal Joey* was 'a biting, stinging piece of ginger among the barley sugar of musical comedies,' said *Picture Post*, and the *Sketch* called it 'a fast, funny and (above all) honest piece of entertainment … may become one of the classics of the genre'.

Arthur loved appearing in these musicals and later said that these were very happy years for him. Playing an American again allowed him to indulge his lifelong penchant for mimicry and impersonation, and it was fun to dress up each night as a spivvy Chicago South Side nightclub owner in a pinstripe suit and black moustache that made him look uncannily like James Beck would look 14 years later as the *Dad's Army* spiv, Private Walker. But even though he was again in a secure, long run and was onstage every night, he still worked as often as possible every morning making BBC radio broadcasts (including several history programmes for children), playing small TV parts (one of them in the six-part mini-series *The Three Musketeers*), and doing commercial voice-overs for products such as Sharp's toffee, Summer County margarine and Cadbury's chocolate. He also had parts in three more films: *Death Keeps a Date*, *Dangerous Money*, and *Final Appointment*, the latter a desperately poor murder mystery in which he played a solicitor's crooked head clerk.

Pal Joey ran in London for seven months before it closed on 30 October 1954, and for the next year Arthur worked very little in the theatre, making radio and television programmes, films and commercials instead. For BBC radio he made numerous educative schools programmes, and for television he appeared in two six-part mini-series for children: *Children of the New Forest* and *The Prince and the Pauper*. He also played small parts in four films in 1955: *The Reluctant Bride*, *Windfall*, *John Dark*, and *The Woman for Joe*, which must surely qualify as one of the worst movies ever made. It tells the story of an irritatingly bossy 19-year-old midget who takes over a travelling circus. Heading the cast were George Baker (as Joe), Diane Cilento (as the midget's girlfriend, a sort of poor man's Marlene Dietrich) and David Kossoff, but the acting was dreadfully wooden and Baker's accent veered alarmingly from Irish to Yorkshire to Irish again. Fortunately Arthur, who played the midget's agent – 'Shake hands with the shortest man in the world for thrippence a time' – appears for just 15 seconds and emerged from the experience relatively untainted.

The only straight theatre play in which he appeared that year was *Witness for the Prosecution* at Palmers Green in July, but then he landed a part in yet another American musical comedy, *The Pajama Game*, which Price Littler was about to stage at the London Coliseum. It had been a huge success in New York and the London production, which starred Max Wall, Joy Nichols, Edmund Hockridge and Elizabeth Seal, was to be massively popular too, running for 584 performances and keeping Arthur employed for almost a year and a half.

The Pajama Game was set in the Sleep-Tite Pajama Factory in a small Mid-western American town, Cedar Rapids in Iowa, where the workers demand a pay rise and stage a go-slow but are betrayed when their female union leader, Babe Williams, falls in love with the factory's new superintendent. It included a sheaf of songs that became hits – among them 'I'm Not At All In Love', 'Hernando's Hideaway', 'Steam Heat' and 'Hey, There':

> *Hey, there!*
> *You with the stars in your eyes,*
> *Love never made a fool of you,*
> *You used to be too wise! ...*

Among the factory workers is a pajama salesman, played by Arthur, who wears a white Panama hat, a fancy red bow tie, a yellow checked waistcoat with brass buttons, and a grey checked suit, and who is given to chanting slogans such as 'Wear Sleep-Tite for a Happy Home Life'. The salesman reports that someone is sabotaging the manufacture of the pajamas by not sewing the buttons on properly and he joins Babe, Prez and the Steam Heat Boys in dancing and singing 'The Pajama Game' song:

> *The Pajama Game is the game we're in,*

And we're proud to be in the Pajama Game.
We love it.
We can hardly wait to wake
And get to work at eight,
Nothing's quite the same
As the Pajama Game.

In the next scene the salesman joins the others in singing about the pay rise they are hoping for:

Seven-and-a-half cents doesn't buy a helluva lot,
Seven-and-a-half cents doesn't mean a thing,
But give it to me ev'ry hour
Forty hours ev'ry week
And that's enough for me to be
Livin' like a King!
Livin' like a King.

In the final scene Arthur came on stage wearing a white nightgown with red polka dots and a white nightcap. With his huge nose and bulbous eyes he must have looked hilarious.

The Pajama Game opened at the Coliseum in October 1955 and was an instant success. Max Wall, who played the leading part of Hines, a time-and-motion-study man, recalled 20 years later in his autobiography that although the Coliseum was a vast theatre the producers had insisted that there should be no sound amplification system, so that the actors were forced to develop perfect voice control, diction and delivery. Arthur enjoyed *The Pajama Game* so much that he and Joan were constantly singing the show's songs at home, and when he suffered severe stomach pains in April 1956 he tried to ignore them until his appendix burst and he had to be rushed to hospital, where he stayed for more than five weeks. 'Dearest, darling Timmy,' wrote Joan. 'We love you. You have now been away for five <u>weeks</u> … Poor darling, what a bore. Never mind, you will feel a new man after this – all that beastly indigestion will go away <u>and</u> your tiredness – these things develop for ages you know before they hurt.' A local shop assistant had offered to babysit Stephen so that Joan could visit the hospital without him, but she was nervous about upsetting

Stephen: 'I feel if I start off on the wrong foot with S he may be unhappy without you if he feels <u>I'm</u> disappearing too and leaving him with strangers.' Perhaps she had a premonition that in later life Stephen would indeed resent the closeness between her and Arthur. She added: 'I'm sorry I was so irritable this morning – I am <u>not</u> a nurse, I have a horror of illness, I'm sorry I can't cope with it, it frightens and annoys me.' And she concluded: 'See you on Sunday dearest one. I do love you and I <u>want</u> you, you silly old cuss. Pony and Steve xxxxxxxxxxxxx.' Attached to the letter was a childish scrawled drawing of a face that was signed shakily 'LOVE St*'

In reply Arthur wrote:

My Darling,
I'm very perky this morning and writing this letter sitting in a chair for the first time. My temperature is way down this morning and I have walked to the toilet (with success) and to the bathroom to wash and shave. Sister is well pleased and says I'll be home at the week-end. I think that as the fever has dropped and there is no additional pain it is fairly safe to assume the danger to be over. They are terribly sweet here but what harrowing places surgical wards are. It will always be a mystery to me why anyone takes up medicine – thank God they do, but if I thought I would ever come to be such a revolting, disgusting travesty of a man like these old men opposite, I would rather die young, and violently! I love you … I'll soon be on a Joanie diet again … Bye bye my darling – I do love you and want to be home – Give my little man a big hug.
Tim xxxxxxxxxx.

Underneath, for Stephen, he drew a face with a stethoscope and captioned it 'Doctor Golliwog'. Arthur was in hospital for so long and became so worried that his understudy might upstage him while he was away that he telephoned Richard Leech from a public telephone box and asked him to smuggle him out of the hospital through a side door.

Even though he was once again in secure employment, Arthur never let up on the amount of other work that he took on in 1956 and 1957: 14 radio programmes, mainly for schools and children; 6 TV programmes; 10 commercials, among them ads for Black and Decker, Bisto, Quaker Oats and Horlicks; and 10 films, all crime thrillers or comedies. One of the films was the comedian Benny Hill's big-screen debut, an Ealing comedy called *Who Done It?*, in which Hill played an ice-rink sweeper who becomes a private detective and tracks down a nest of spies. Another was *The Green Man*, about a politician stalked by a professional hit-man, a black comedy that was decidedly unfunny despite being stuffed with many of the big comic cinema actors of the 1950s: Alastair Sim, George Cole, Terry-Thomas, Dora Bryan, Raymond Huntley, Richard Wattis. Arthur makes just one five-second appearance, as an electronics shop salesman with a vulgar sarf-London accent.

The Pajama Game finally ended its long run on 9 March 1957. Almost immediately Arthur started rehearsals for the play that was at last to put up his name in West End lights and to bring him his first West End reviews, *A Dead Secret*, a murder melodrama by Rodney Ackland, in which the lead was played by the distinguished 35-year-old Shakespearean actor Paul Scofield, Megs Jenkins played Scofield's downtrodden wife, and Dinsdale Landen played his clerk. The play was based on the case of a real murderer, Frederick Seddon, who was hanged in 1911 for poisoning his middle-aged woman tenant with arsenic from boiled-down fly papers so that he could get his hands on her money. In *A Dead Secret* Scofield played Frederick Dyson, a brutal property owner who is thinking of murdering one of his tenants, a rich, fat, unpleasant old lady called Maria Lummus, so that he can steal her property, stocks and shares. Before he can do so, however, someone else beats him to it by poisoning her with arsenic from boiled-down fly papers, and Dyson becomes the main suspect even though he did not commit the murder. Miss Lummus's drunken cousin, Bert Vokes, played by Arthur, tells the police that he is convinced that Dyson has murdered her. Dyson is arrested and the case against him is so strong that as the play ends it seems inevitable that he will be hanged for a murder that he did not commit.

The role of angry, boozy Bert Vokes was a wonderfully meaty part for Arthur that was to earn him excellent reviews, but first there was a minor crisis when *A Dead Secret* opened at the Theatre Royal in Newcastle in May and the actress playing Maria Lummus was fired almost immediately. 'Bags of excitement!' Arthur wrote to Joan in London.

Olive Sloane got the sack last night after the second performance! It seems they've had her marked for over a fortnight ... Poor old duck. One

85

can't help feeling sorry, no matter who it happens to, and personally I don't think she's as bad as all that … Now, of course, we are rehearsing the understudy like mad to get her on by Friday. Apart from that the show is settling down nicely and Megs told me this morning that Binky is absolutely delighted with my performance so thank God for that!

The critics were complimentary when *A Dead Secret* went on to play in Brighton and then opened in the West End at the Piccadilly Theatre on 30 May. The raves were mainly for the play itself and the seedy, claustro-phobic set as well as for Scofield, whose portrait of the sinister, unctuous, pseudo-genteel Dyson was hailed as magnificent by the critics, but Arthur's performance, too, was 'excellent', 'flawless', 'memorable' and 'beautifully played'. But he was so disconcerted by the northern accent that Scofield adopted for the play that he summoned Richie Gatehouse to the theatre to listen to it one afternoon. Gatehouse told me:

Afterwards I went round to Arthur's dressing room and he opened the door, looked up and down the corridor, shut the door, and said in a low voice 'What do you think?' Great conspiratorial behaviour. I said I was surprised at his voice and north country accent. 'Yes!' said Arthur. Up to then Scofield had been Laurence Olivier's successor and spoke all lippy like Olivier, and Arthur told me 'The whole company is upset because it's not Scofield as they know him.' That's how interested Arthur was in acting. He had it out with Scofield, but understood eventually because Scofield was trying to improve his voice.

Scofield was himself deeply impressed by Arthur's acting in *A Dead Secret*. 'He was a seriously brilliant actor,' he told me.

He was immensely funny, of course, but that is only half the story. I was taken aback. I had never before encountered his work, and suddenly here was a fully-fledged master of his craft. I think it was his timing which set him apart – timing is an art which is difficult to define; it sounds merely technical, but it springs from a deep inner sense of rhythm, and rests on an innate truthfulness. When I watched him later on television, I felt strangely proud that I had worked with him, and had had a close-quarter knowledge of his rare talent.

Several letters that Joan and Arthur wrote to each other in 1957 have survived. In one he wrote: 'Darling, what a lovely surprise to hear your voice – this place was depressing me but that has cheered me up wonderfully … can't wait till morning for your letters … Bye bye darling, I do love you so.' While he was away in Newcastle Joan's nephew Andrew came to stay with her and Stephen in London, and she answered Arthur happily to say that Stephen had at last stopped wetting his bed ('I don't weejee him any more! Revolutionary'), that she had just taken both boys to the Tower of London and was about to take them to look around the junk shops in the Portobello Road, and that David, too, would soon be coming to stay. Her letter began 'Dearest Daddy! (Westminster Abbey! Steve says I must – it's such a good rhyme)' and went on:

Stephen (John the Cabin Boy) and I are sitting together in the zedbed having our morning tea – I have no idea what time it is as 'John' when he first looked at it this morning was afraid it was too late for tea in bed (as it was yesterday when no one woke until 9 a.m.) so he just put the clock back to 6 p.m! Very efficient!

Money was still tight, and she added that she was worried that she might not have enough to pay the local rates:

Took £5 out of the bank on Friday – which makes the overdraft £49, but I expect by now you will have paid in some money … You may run for a week or two I should think!?

She went on with sexual innuendo:

Oh darling, I do love you so. I've started dreaming about you now. It is rapidly becoming agony but I'm hanging on drinking far too much coffee and trying not to think about you too much. Not with your specs off anyway! It seems like a wonderful dream now that wonderful night just one long week ago – years and years ago to me.

She ended the letter with 32 Xs and 'I love you, I love you, I love you'. Her letters suggest that she was a loving mother who adored Stephen. During Andrew's stay she took the boys all over London and helped

Andrew to write in a notebook about everything they had seen and to illustrate it with photographs. Stephen, she said, was 'a joy': 'We had a lovely day yesterday at the round pond – Steve now <u>has</u> a boat! – he's so happy.' She called Steve 'Poopsy' and wrote to Arthur that as she was about to go to bed one midnight 'out walked Poopsy to weejee – so grown up, so nonchalant, we spoke and he went back, taking his pot with him. I followed him and found Sammy Whisker burning very cheerfully.' And she ended one letter: 'I wanted you <u>very</u> <u>badly</u> after lunch – is it really only a week? Dearest one, don't forget me. Pony. xxxxxxx.' In another she wrote:

> Bless you for your <u>gorgeous</u> <u>letters</u> – they are balm and nectar and see me through quite beautifully – I am <u>longing</u> to see you, but the time really is going quite quickly – for me!! I love you more than ever. I have always loved you desperately – ever since that first day we talked on the sofa at rehearsal of 'Flare Path' and I've been jibbering with love ever since you first kissed me in Piccadilly. I'm glad you understand now how I have felt all this time.
> Your very own Pony.

Ominously, though, in one letter she made a remark that boded ill for the future: 'I have to confess a little sin – a very small sin – I have a glass of sherry <u>every</u> night while Andy is bathing before supper – it certainly <u>does</u> help and I <u>never</u> miss my bath.'

A Dead Secret ran for six months and 212 performances, and was such a success that in 1958 Arthur felt confident enough about his future to move from the little flat in Rutland Gate into a larger apartment – albeit still rented – a quarter of a mile away, a couple of hundred yards from Knightsbridge tube station, at 33/35 Pavilion Road, which runs closely parallel to Sloane Street. Their new home, an empty, derelict, converted granary above a carpet warehouse, on the site of what is now the Millennium Hotel, consisted of two flats on two floors. The Lowes still had a few titled neighbours – the Earl and Countess of Cromer at No. 167, Lady Moira Combe at 150, Sir Robert Mackenzie at 95 – but Pavilion Road was a narrow, undistinguished little street, not nearly as smart as Rutland Gate, and it had a seedy atmosphere. The flat itself had once been a brothel, and Stephen Lowe suggests in his book that 'one of the girls had jumped to her death in the street below'. One advantage, however, was that the telephone number began with the snooty BEL prefix of the upmarket Belgravia telephone exchange, which would have fooled theatre managers and producers into thinking that Arthur was living somewhere immensely stylish. In fact the flat was dank, derelict and decidedly bizarre. To reach it you had to squeeze through a narrow front door and climb a steep flight of stone stairs while clutching a rope banister. 'It was like going up into the gods in the theatre,' chuckled Phyllis Bateman. 'Pavilion Road was a scream, a fun place. Once when they let us stay there for a week while they were away, they had to draw us a plan of all the switches because they just did not connect!' Richard Gatehouse agreed – 'it was a very strange place'. Stephen's childhood friend Ted Shine, the son of the Lowes' great actor friends Diana and Bill Shine, who lived nearby in Ennismore Gardens Mews, told me:

It was an odd place. On the first floor there was a nice big dining room with a lovely old wooden floor, but there was no proper kitchen, just a bit curtained off, and then you went onto the roof garden, which was the roof of somebody else's house, and up another flight of stairs to a living room with a piano, and Arthur and Joan's bedroom was off that, and they had a bath bang in the middle of their bedroom with a screen around it.

There was also a tiny lavatory and a separate, damp little two-room flat that Stephen was later to use as his own self-contained apartment. 'It was derelict and strange and entirely to my parents' liking,' said Stephen, but Christopher Bond was less impressed. 'It was a nothing place, another example of Arthur and Joan being careful with money,' he told me. 'Most people would have said it's nothing but a warehouse. They always rented. Their thinking was that if you bought a house it meant you were in debt.' At first Arthur relished the fact that the flat had once been a brothel, though he was less amused when furtive men kept ringing the doorbell late at night. One prospective customer was so persistent that Arthur had to go down to the front door to tell him to fuck off, and when the fellow objected to his language Arthur stepped out into the road and punched the intruder with a quick left and a right, said Stephen in his book: 'At breakfast the next morning he had plasters over his knuckles but he was puffed up with pride and Mum was unusually attentive. They were like two pigeons.'

'It wasn't an official brothel but there were girls there who were prostitutes,' David Gatehouse told me. 'The girls had maltreated the flat dreadfully and had even had a bonfire in the middle of the parquet flooring, which Arthur and Joan restored themselves, and very well too.' Surprisingly Arthur turned out to be a skilled do-it-yourself fanatic. 'He was very good with his hands and taught me how to put wallpaper on,' Richard Leech told me. 'He didn't have many hobbies – I don't remember him playing any games – but he did all the decorating.' With the help of builders, plumbers and electricians, the Lowes transformed the derelict rooms into a warm and welcoming home, with enough bedrooms for all of them, including David when he came to stay. In his book Stephen wrote that Joan

> devised extraordinary furnishings for the place which could never be forgotten by anyone who ever saw them. Dreary wooden pillars would be covered with marble-effect Contact and flutings painted in at their base, and from six feet away the result was convincing. Sheeshee [chichi] lampshades were stripped of their fabric, and the frames were woven with coarse string.

They installed two pianos, one a baby grand, and Joan turned the little lavatory into a sort of Chinese temple, though the low red light that was cast by the lampshade encouraged even more sex-starved potential customers to ring the doorbell. The result was that the Lowes created what Stephen called

> a lovely, rambling home for two boys – David was at home quite often at that time … – and with no neighbours it was a place where my Mum could breathe, and play the piano and sing, and David could practise at the piano at all hours, and I could have my railway set up properly on a big table.

There was only one drawback to the new flat: Joan was convinced it was haunted, possibly by the ghost of the prostitute who was said to have thrown herself out of the window. 'Joan would have said Pavilion Road was haunted even if it wasn't,' said David Gatehouse. 'She liked that sort of thing. I was with her once when she saw one in Hexham Abbey.'

David was now 16, a pupil at Queen Elizabeth Grammar School in Hexham, and such a brilliant organist that during a recital at Hexham Abbey in January he played five pieces by Bach, E. C. Bairstow, Karg-Elert and C. Franck in aid of the abbey's restoration fund. He was also remarkably well adjusted and seemed completely untroubled when his grandfather left his grandmother for another woman. Stephen, on the other hand, who was now five and attending a kindergarten in London, seems not to have had nearly as happy a childhood as David. In his book Stephen remembers nostalgically how Arthur would sit at home learning his lines and Joan would take the script and test him while he paced the room with his eyes screwed up, and how all three of them

> bathed in the early evening before Dad went to the theatre. Then he would set off, a little brown suitcase in his hand. It contained his make-up, just a few simple sticks, an eyebrow pencil and some powder for his shiny pate, an electric egg-boiler in which he brewed his tea, and a novel to read while he was waiting to be called. He was very fond of the W. W. Jacobs *Captain Kettle* stories and Para Handy. He travelled on the tube. Mum would say, 'Break a leg,' and they'd kiss … Then Mum and I would have our tea and listen to the wireless until it was time for bed … and I can remember the security of a familiar eiderdown and blanket. I used to hear my parents' voices late at night.

He gives the impression that when he was older his life was almost perfect:

> For a while our lives seemed charmed. This big bohemian flat, the roof garden so hot in summer that sweetcorn and tomatoes grew in tubs, Arthur in work, David at Oxford, me at a good school in Sussex, a happy circle of friends for parties and the bistro. On Saturday afternoons we met the Shines in the park and played cricket, on Sunday mornings we went to the pub before lunch.

And every year, on the Sunday after Christmas, Arthur and Joan would throw a Black Velvet party for their actor friends and children.

It all sounds cosy and idyllic, and when Stephen was five he was excited to be sent briefly to a drama school and to be given a part in a film, just like Daddy. In *A Night to Remember*, the 1959 movie written by Eric Ambler and based on Walter Lord's book about the sinking of the *Titanic*, starring Kenneth More as the First Officer, Stephen played Honor Blackman's son, Tom, a fat, ugly child who is woken by his father as the ship begins to sink. The film was a one-off and although Stephen was given two advertising roles as well – as an Ovaltiney and one of the Milky Bar Kid's gang – he did not enjoy acting and asked to be taken away from drama school. He went instead to a smart, local, private primary school, Gibbs.

Sadly his childhood was not as happy and secure as he pretended. Joan and Arthur were so wrapped up in their love for each other that Stephen came to feel excluded and to see himself as just an extra in their marriage. 'Arthur and Joan were very close,' Barbara Gatehouse told me, 'and maybe Stephen felt neglected.' Pam Cundell, who was to play Mrs Fox in *Dad's Army*, agreed. 'Joan and Arthur were so bound up with each other,' she said, 'and although she was quite proud of David, she never talked about Stephen. In a way the children were peripheral: it was always Arthur. The children were a kind of impediment.' Many years later, when Stephen was over 40, he told Deborah Ross of the *Daily Mail* that as a small child he rarely saw Arthur, though he was 'always friendly' and kissed him goodnight whenever he could. But it was always to be an uneasy, distant relationship. In later years, wrote Stephen in a brief contribution to Perry, Croft and Webber's *Dad's Army: The Complete Scripts*:

> If people asked me was Dad like Mainwaring at home, I would look at them as if to say 'Bugger off!' But maybe I was like that because he was, and I didn't want it to be that way. He was fixated by unimportant detail, had an inflated sense of his own importance, tripped over things and banged his head. But he was brave, too, and I saw him once put his fists up to a man half his height again.

He also remembered making home movies with Arthur, 'proper productions with clapper boards and everything', but otherwise he did not know him well. In fact, surprisingly for actors, who usually plaster their homes with dozens of photographs of themselves, not one picture survives of the Lowes as a family. Stephen and David both told me that they have no photographs at all of Arthur, 'and I've never had one of all four of us together,' said David. 'We weren't a picture-taking family and Arthur never owned a still camera, although he did play with a ciné camera for a while.'

Stephen told Deborah Ross that he had been much closer to his mother than his father. 'She was very strict,' he said, 'but very loving and affectionate. She gave lots of kisses and hugs and she was always very patient when I was very little. She always answered all my questions.' She could be great fun, gay and witty, and she and Arthur, said Stephen, both felt 'a deep undercurrent of love for each other'. At first sight Arthur might look pretty unsexy but at heart he was a great romantic, who never forgot a Valentine's Day, birthday or anniversary. He would give Joan soppy cards, bouquets of flowers, sugared almonds, and once, said Stephen, a diamond ring. 'He understood exactly how a woman longed to be treated,' Joan herself told Romany Bain of the *TV Times* in 1982. 'The passing years make little difference. He was the perfect present giver. Once it was a brass double bed with billowing net drapes. Then there was a porcelain egg in which to keep trinkets, and a framed Hearts and Flowers Valentine.' Unlike most husbands he was even able to buy her clothes that fitted perfectly and that she adored, on one occasion a fur coat from Harrods. But Joan admitted that he could be extremely intolerant and hated noise, especially from loud radios, which must have been a cause of regular dissention as Stephen grew up and started to play the trombone.

'Stephen and I were good friends when we were small,' said Ted Shine.

Our parents were very close friends because of the theatre – they would talk all night incessantly about the theatre – and Stephen and I used to play cowboys and Indians in Brompton Oratory churchyard, all dressed up, with wigwams. But our friendship wouldn't have lasted if it wasn't for our parents being so friendly. He was inclined to throw tantrums over nothing or if he didn't get what he wanted, and many a time he'd stamp his feet and whine, and he cried a lot. Arthur was never quite the father to Steve that my father was to me: he didn't play with him and he was a bit more aloof, and I never saw him sitting down for a chat or messing around with Steve, and I don't think he disciplined him much. Arthur never took him anywhere and he had no friends in London except for me, and he never seemed to have many toys. I don't think he had much fun. Joan was far more patient with him but she wasn't very maternal, and she smoked too bloody much, those Craven A Black Cat uncorked cigarettes, and she never stopped coughing and never ate. And she was the most useless cook; desperate. Whenever I went there it was beans on toast and more beans on toast. You might get a poached egg, but she was a disastrous cook and they ate out all the time. Stephen never looked particularly healthy. He always had this pale skin and his hair was very red, with a fringe. And he used to do this annoying thing when he was eating: he would hum, *mmmm-mmmm-mmmm-mmmm*, all through a meal. He was always eating and going *mmmmmm*. Later on they gave Steve one of the flats so that he didn't live with his parents but had a bedroom, bathroom and sitting room of his own. I think Stephen probably had a very unhappy childhood and was very lonely.

At the start of 1958 there was nothing to suggest that Arthur was on the brink of a huge change that was soon to make him a household name. It seemed in fact as if his career had almost stalled. He did not reach the West End stage at all that year and he made only three BBC radio programmes and four commercials, two of them for Wrigley's chewing gum. He did make three films, but none was particularly memorable: a crime thriller called *Dial 999*, *Stormy Crossing* and *The Boy and the Bridge*, a drama in which Bill Shine also had a part. Arthur played a bridge keeper on London's Tower Bridge, where a boy who thinks he is guilty of murder is hiding in the ramparts. There was, however, one significant development for Arthur's career that year: he started to appear increasingly in television series. First he was in two episodes of a crime series called *Murder Bag*; then he had a small part in an ABC-TV comedy series entitled *Time Out for Peggy*, in which Billie Whitelaw starred as a dotty boarding-house landlady; and in October he surfaced in a six-part BBC mini-series starring Mervyn Jones and Helen Cherry, *Leave it to Todhunter*, a macabre comedy thriller set in London with episodes entitled 'In Search of a Corpse' and 'Death on the Lawn', in which he played a gunsmith. Then ABC-TV offered Arthur his first starring role in a long-running adult television series, *All Aboard*. At last he had found a leading part in the medium that was to make him famous.

CHAPTER 6

Coronation Street and the Royal Court

(1958–1965)

All Aboard was screened for half an hour at 5.30 every Saturday evening for 26 weeks from December 1958 to May 1959. Although the first seven episodes were transmitted only in the Midlands and the north of England the programme quickly became so popular that from January it was networked nationally. Arthur played the part of Sydney Barker, a ship's steward aboard the transatlantic liner *Adriana*, as bald as a dolphin and dressed in a crisp, white, high-buttoned waiter's jacket with a dark pocket embroidered with a white anchor. 'Barker was a morally handicapped steward of the Sergeant Bilko persuasion, who worked every fiddle in the book,' I was told by the programme's co-writer Dick Sharples. 'His only friend was a female steward, played by Avril Angers, who mothered him and tried to protect him from himself, and Arthur played the part with a strong Scouse accent.' Tony Warren, who was about to create *Coronation Street*, was highly impressed by Arthur's performance as Barker. 'Oh, goodness, he was sinister!' Warren told me. 'He was *terribly* good.' The programme depicted life on board during four voyages between Liverpool and New York as well as a cruise in the Mediterranean, and apart from the regular cast – Avril Angers, Susan Shaw, Richard Coleman, Charles Morgan, Richard Thorp, John Gale and Peter Greenspan – there were guest appearances by Gordon Jackson, Richard O'Sullivan and Susannah York.

Making the series was almost as hectic as weekly rep, for rehearsals started only a fortnight before the first transmission and although some location scenes were recorded in advance each week – including those on board the ship, a New Zealand Shipping Company vessel called the

Rangitoto, which was berthed in London's King George V Docks – much of each episode was transmitted live from ATV's studios in Birmingham. Television was still such a luxury that the Lowes did not yet own a TV set, so Joan and Stephen watched each episode on the tiny green screen of the set in the Forge Café on the other side of Pavilion Road. Arthur still kept himself to himself. 'We got on very well,' Avril Angers told me, 'but we used to travel by train to Birmingham to do the programme and he always got into a carriage by himself. He wasn't like an actor at all. He seemed like a bank clerk – like Captain Mainwaring. I had no inkling that he'd become a star.'

The Stage found *All Aboard* 'most enjoyable … The characters talked and acted like real people,' and it praised Arthur and Avril Angers. *Punch* was less enthusiastic. Under the headline 'Hokum Afloat' its reviewer wrote:

What we have here is not life but melodramatic fantasy in an ocean liner … Thieves, stowaways, dope-smugglers, ship's officers and Mysterious Persons play out a confused and dreamy drama in the thrillingly confined space of the SS *Adriana*, with a cliff-hanger every Saturday and very acceptable performances by Arthur Lowe, Avril Angers and Susan Shaw.

Joan Lowe was even snootier than *Punch*. Stephen wrote:

My mother continued in her belief that television was a pernicious device, a poor corruption of the cinema and a prostitution of the actor's art. Reluctant to waste her money – as telly-visions were obviously going to be discontinued at any moment – it was some time before we acquired a set of our own. Even when we did, it was hidden away behind curtains. A weakness, of which we should be thoroughly ashamed.

Joan's contemptuous view of television was widely shared by actors in those early days, when it was called dismissively 'The Box' and considered vulgar and seriously inferior to the theatre. 'In those days we only did television if there was no other work,' Richard Leech told me. 'We all thought television was totally infra dig. None of the big stars did it at all. But Arthur didn't despise television. Arthur didn't despise anything that paid money. He had no time for piss-elegance about Art. His answer would probably have been "What's the salary?"' Christopher Bond agreed. 'We all thought we would be demeaning our talent by going into television,' he told me. 'It was considered ephemeral rubbish.' Yet it was to be the much despised television – not the theatre, not films – that was soon to bring Arthur fame and fortune. As Stephen says in his book, 'His subtle delivery and tricksy facial expressions were ideally suited to the new close-shot medium. He enjoyed the workplace of the studio floor, and he liked the factory feel of the television centres with their canteens and egalitarian style' – all perfectly understandable in a man who had once worked in an aviation factory in Manchester.

Arthur appeared next in the West End in another highly successful play, Wynyard Browne's *The Ring of Truth*, a genial comedy that opened in Glasgow in June 1959 and went on to Edinburgh and Manchester before its first night in London on 16 July, where it ran for seven months at the Savoy Theatre. A domestic farce based on Murphy's Law – if anything can go wrong, it will – *The Ring of Truth* tells of a married woman designer (played by Margaret Johnston) who loses her engagement ring and stumbles into one personal crisis after another as she tries to find it and to claim on her insurance policy. Arthur played a shifty insurance agent, Mr Filby, who sets the whole disaster running by telling her and her husband (played by David Tomlinson) that his company will pay for the ring only if she lies that it was stolen. He was on stage for no more than ten minutes but his performance earned him rave reviews. The Scottish critics called it 'an hilarious cameo', 'delightful', and 'a beautifully observed performance … than which I cannot remember much funnier'. The *Manchester Guardian* called it 'a perfect study', and in London it was described as 'very funny', 'a very distinguished piece of comedy acting', 'witty and incisive', 'outstanding' and 'impeccably observed'. *What's On* enthused that 'Arthur Lowe beautifully polishes a gem of a part', and the *Daily Herald* reckoned that although the play was utterly uninteresting, 'the only actor who emerges with any credit is Arthur Lowe: his insurance agent explaining the mysteries of claim fiddling is splendid.'

Such wonderful reviews (and the fact that the play was broadcast live on BBC TV on 15 September) attracted the attention of several television producers, including Stuart Latham, the first producer of *Coronation Street*. Arthur had another reason for feeling jubilant that summer: David, now 18, passed his A-level exams with distinction and won a scholarship first to the Royal College of Music and then to Balliol College, Oxford, where in due course he took a first-class degree in music. 'Arthur was very proud of me,' said David.

The Ring of Truth ran at the Savoy for 251 performances, finally closing in February 1960. During 1959 Arthur also had small parts in two movies: *Follow That Horse*, a spy comedy in which he played an auctioneer; and *The Day They Robbed the Bank of England* (with Peter O'Toole, Aldo Ray, Elizabeth Sellars and Hugh Griffith), in which he made a 15-second appearance as a Bank of England clerk and his future fellow *Dad's Army* banker, John le Mesurier, already a great deal more famous than Arthur, played a much bigger part as the deputy head of the bank's bullion vaults. Arthur also had a part in another TV serial, a six-episode teatime story called *The Diamond Bird*, and in 1960 he appeared on television in another 14 TV programmes, among them the Oscar Wilde story *Lord Arthur Savile's Crime*, an episode of the courtroom drama *Boyd QC*, the Harold Pinter play *A Night Out*, and the police series *No Hiding Place*.

Then came the television series that was to make him a star. On Stuart Latham's recommendation, Arthur was asked by the north-western company Granada TV to go to their Manchester studios to play the part of a pompous northern haberdasher and lay preacher, Leonard Swindley, in three episodes of their new twice-weekly soap opera, *Coronation Street*. The part was to make him a household name within a few months, yet he thought it was just another small bread-and-butter job that might pay a few bills. 'It didn't sound very exciting,' he said years later. 'Anyway, never one to turn work down, I agreed, believing that it would only be screened in the Manchester area and that not many people would see it.' He was not alone in his opinion: even Mike Scott, who directed several of the early episodes of *Coronation Street* and later became Granada's programme controller, felt that although it might do well in the north-west of England it would never succeed in the rest of the country. Granada was so uncertain about the programme that it planned to screen just 12 episodes and then, in a 13th, show the street being demolished. The small production team reckoned that at best it might run for six months.

Coronation Street was the idea of 23-year-old Tony Warren, a Granada promotions department writer who lived by extraordinary coincidence in

Little Hayfield, just a few hundred yards north of Arthur's birthplace. He persuaded Granada to commission him to write 12 half-hour episodes about the humdrum daily lives of a group of ordinary working-class northerners living in a grimy, terraced, crowded Manchester back street: a row of seven early-1900s back-to-back terraced houses with a pub, the Rovers Return, at one end, and Florrie Lindley's Corner Shop at the other. In the first few episodes the main characters were a bossy old battleaxe in a hairnet, the widow Ena Sharples, played by the scowling Violet Carson; a cantankerous old soldier, Albert Tatlock, played by 64-year-old Jack Howarth; the landlord of the Rovers Return, Jack Walter, played by Arthur Leslie, and his snobbish wife, Annie Walker, played by Doris Speed; a dull, serious, 21-year-old Manchester University student, Ken Barlow, played by William Roache; and the glamorous sexpot Elsie Tanner, played by Pat Phoenix, who by another remarkable coincidence also lived in Little Hayfield.

At first the actors were highly nervous because the first programme of each week was transmitted live, at 7 p.m. on Fridays, though the second was pre-recorded 15 minutes later to be broadcast the following Monday. The first episode went out in grainy black-and-white from Granada's studios in Manchester on Friday, 9 December 1960, and Arthur and Joan, who were visiting his parents in Hayfield that weekend, watched it on the set in the George Hotel. The first instalment began with the slow, nostalgic, soon-to-be-famous trumpet signature tune as two children played in the cobbled street outside the corner shop that Florrie Lindley had just bought in the fictional suburb of Weatherfield. Elsie Tanner made her first appearance having a row with her layabout son Dennis and telling him to get a job. Ken Barlow's father was berating him for wasting money on his new middle-class girlfriend by meeting her in an expensive hotel. In the Rovers Return Annie Walker was refusing to let Dennis Tanner buy a packet of fags on tick. And Ena Sharples' first line, as she introduced herself to Florrie Lindley in her new shop, was typically crisp: 'I'm Mrs Sharples. I'm a neighbour. Are you a widder woman?'

That first instalment did not impress the *Daily Mirror*'s television critic, Ken Irwin, even though the *Mirror* was a dedicatedly working-class newspaper that might have been expected to enthuse over such a determinedly working-class programme. 'The programme is doomed from the outset,' wrote Irwin, 'with its signature tune and grim scene of a row of terraced houses and smoking chimneys.' But other reviewers – even in upmarket papers such as *The Times*, the *Observer* and the *New Statesman* – were impressed. With remarkable perspicacity the *Manchester Guardian* prophesied that it would run for ever, and the programme was quickly taken up by other ITV regional companies such as Anglia and Southern, so that by the spring it was being networked nationally. After just three months *Coronation Street* entered the British top 10 TV chart in March as the fourth most popular programme, with regular viewing figures of 7½ million households. By the summer it was so popular and the cast so famous that they were asked to switch on the Blackpool illuminations, and in October 1961, 10 months after the programme was launched, it reached number one in the charts. Since then, for 40 years, it has never been out of the top 10 and is usually in the top 3. It has won numerous awards, inspired the American TV serial *Peyton Place*, become the world's longest-running TV series, and been screened all over the globe, even in Thailand and Zambia. For millions of ordinary viewers the programme became so convincing that soon they started believing that it depicted real characters rather than fictional ones, and would try to rent a house in the Street or to book the Rovers Return for parties. Even Laurence Olivier became an admirer of the programme and confessed that he would love to appear in the Rovers Return with Annie Walker. 'Olivier was desperate to appear in *Coronation Street*,' Tony Warren told me, 'and the producer, Bill Podmore, arranged for him to play an unspeakable tramp, but, unfortunately, he got a job in New York, so he couldn't do it.' Melvyn Bragg called the programme 'the most professional product of television this country has ever known', and by the time that it was going out at 7.30 p.m. on Mondays and Wednesdays the future Poet Laureate John Betjeman was fulsome in its praise:

Manchester produces what to me is the *Pickwick Papers*. That is to say, *Coronation Street*. Mondays and Wednesdays, I live for them. Thank God, half past seven tonight and I shall be in paradise … Not a word too many. Not a gesture needless. It is the best writing and acting I could wish to see.

Arthur joined the programme in the third episode. With his big, bulbous nose and deep, pseudo-posh voice, he was perfectly cast as Leonard

Swindley, the bossy, fussy, pompous, testy, teetotal, little chairman of the local Glad Tidings Mission Hall, who ran his own draper's shop in nearby Rosamund Street. He was brought into the programme as a foil for Ena Sharples, the resident caretaker at the mission hall, and made his debut in the snug bar of the Rovers Return, where he reproved her for drinking a glass of milk stout, accused her of intemperance, and upset her so much that she collapsed in the vestry with a stroke and had to be rushed to hospital.

Even though Tony Warren lived in Little Hayfield – 'an idyllic village; there were people there who had never been to Manchester,' he told me – he had never met Arthur before, although his father, a fruit importer, knew Arthur's father since they had both worked at Manchester's Smithfield market. 'Old Arthur was much taller than Young Arthur,' Warren told me,

and he considered everything before he replied, which Arthur did too in his work – those pauses and hesitations – and he was wonderfully polite, with excellent manners. So was Young Arthur, who was perfectly polite, perfectly pleasant, but very distant from the rest of us. He had this wonderful quality of touch-me-not. There was a little space all around him and woe betide anybody who went into it: this little circle of distance that people took for complacency but it wasn't. He came from a world where you didn't tell strangers too much. Firstly he was a country boy and secondly he was from the north of England. But he was well liked and as far as I was concerned he couldn't have been nicer. He had come up through the old hard school of rep, so he valued what he'd got and he paid due deference to the author, and the fact that I was 24 made no difference whatsoever. I was The Author, so he was very, very polite to me. But I don't think I knew him any better at the end of the show than I did at the beginning. He was never a friend. He was a wonderful lesson in distancing. He was never cold, but I don't think he was a man with any small talk. I never knew anybody being particularly friendly with Arthur, but he never looked lonely. He was just a very good actor who came and did his job and went home. The mystifying thing is that I can't remember any anecdotes about him: I can about everyone else, but he was happy to be private. After he'd become famous I saw him just once and he was exactly the same.

In those early months the programme settled into the steady rhythm of day-to-day trivia, heightened emotions and melodrama that has made it a winner all over the world. Albert Tatlock collapsed on his kitchen floor with high blood pressure. Elsie Tanner's sailor husband, Arnold, returned to ask for a divorce. A main gas pipe was found to be leaking, which forced all the residents to take refuge overnight in the mission hall despite Ena Sharples' objections. Ken Barlow jilted his new girlfriend because she was too posh. And so it went on, the minute examination of humdrum working-class lives twice a week, month after month, year after year.

When it became apparent early in 1961 that the series was going to be a huge success Arthur was asked to stay on. Joan tried to dissuade him. She believed that he was destined for greater things in the theatre and should not waste his talent by hanging around television studios for days on end to make brief appearances in trashy TV programmes, no matter how well he was paid. He was about to open in a new play in the West End, *Stop It Whoever You Are*, and if he was as good in that as she knew he would be, who knew where he might go next? The Royal Court, perhaps. The National Theatre. The Royal Shakespeare Company. The very top of the profession. But to do that he needed to be in London, in the straight theatre, not up in some hot, stuffy TV studio making humdrum soap opera for the ignorant masses back in dreary old provincial Manchester. They had both escaped from Manchester 13 years ago. Why return?

Arthur, however, had a new agent, Jimmy Lavall, who was keen that he should stay on in *Coronation Street*. It was good money and regular employment, and the programme could run for months, maybe even a year or two, and Arthur never turned down work if he could help it. Maybe Joan was biased because she did not want to be separated from him every week and yet she did not want to have to leave her wacky flat in London to go and live with him in digs in Manchester. 'I can remember heated arguments at home,' wrote Stephen, who was then nearly eight and came to believe that Joan was right and that Lavall 'could see only the money'. Arthur's decision to stay with *Coronation Street*, he said, was

a significant – if not disastrous – turning point in his life and career …
If [Joan] could have looked further ahead and seen how this would lead to *Turn Out the Lights*, *Potter* and *Bless Me, Father*, not to mention advertising Lyons' Pie Mix and Clearasil, she would certainly have

fought to the death to stop that move. If she had won the day and Arthur had stayed playing the London stage, his would have been a greater discipline, he would have been fitter, mentally and physically ... There is nothing quite so gut-wrenching as wasted opportunity.

Later in his book Stephen describes *Coronation Street* as 'just a self-gratifying, narcissistic replay of our daily lives ... The banality of it all could split your head.' Yet if Arthur had indeed shunned *Coronation Street* to concentrate on the theatre we would have been deprived of his unforgettable performances as Captain Mainwaring, which were surely worth any number of minor character parts in Shakespeare that he might have played instead at Stratford-on-Avon or in the West End.

Arthur's part as Leonard Swindley in *Coronation Street* had its full share of drama. In June he took on a nervy, strait-laced spinster, Emily Nugent, played by Eileen Derbyshire, as his partner in his draper's shop, and as the months passed she fell hopelessly in love with him without daring to declare it. In November he was threatened with bankruptcy and had to sell his shop to the Greek owner of Gamma Garments, Spiros Papagopolous. Once again he found Ena Sharples drinking stout and this time she resigned as caretaker at the mission hall and moved in with her gentle old widow friend, Minnie Caldwell – though she and Swindley made it up in February 1962 and she went back to live in the vestry. In September Swindley went into politics and launched the Property Owners and Small Traders Party, only to be mortified when he stood in the local elections and came last. In the most memorable episodes of all, in June 1964, Emily Nugent invited him to dinner and nervously proposed to him in a scene of unexpected poignancy. At first alarmed and horrified by her forwardness, Swindley eventually accepted her proposal – but Emily, now even more nervous and terrified, jilted him on their wedding day while he and their friends awaited her in the church. The dignified pathos that Arthur brought to Swindley's noble acceptance of his humiliation, and his loving concern for Emily, marked it as one of the high spots in the series and demonstrated how brilliant Arthur could be in this new medium that he was to make his own.

'He was enormously professional,' Tony Warren told me.

He was an established actor, he knew his value, he could see where television was going, and he was dead letter perfect. He'd say a line exactly as you'd written it, but he had the mark of the true star in that just occasionally he would sparkle a little and add something of his own, and that is star quality. He was a joy for a writer: a beautiful, polished actor. There was also a self-deprecating quality about him. He'd come out with the most terrible pompous line and then turn back and wink. I once saw him in a very drab, ordinary television play and suddenly he picked up a tennis racket and swung it up and down, and he turned that shit into Shakespeare!

Bill Roache, who was still in *Coronation Street* 40 years later, wrote in his autobiography, *Ken and Me*:

I used to love watching him work because he was so meticulous and very amusing … A great deal of the humour he generated in [*Dad's Army*] and as Mr Swindley, came from this thing of trying to stand on his dignity in undignified situations. And his timing was immaculate.

But, Roache added:

He was essentially quite shy and didn't like mixing outside work hours, or doing the personal appearances and so on that go with the *Street*. He wasn't easy to get to know … He wasn't someone who automatically or naturally became part of the team.

It is revealing that when *Coronation Street* won an award as Britain's best television show in 1963 Arthur did not appear with the rest of the cast in the celebratory photograph.

Two reasons for his standoffishness were that he was terrified of becoming typecast and contemptuous of many of the other *Coronation Street* actors, who seemed only too happy to sink into a rut where they did nothing but *Coronation Street*. He could not believe that so many of them had no wider horizon than that. Eight years later he told Lynda Lee-Potter of the *Daily Mail*: 'The rest of the cast … were quite different. They were bought body and soul. They were puppets on the ends of strings. I always wanted to be free to do other things.' Three years later, in 1972, he was astonished that many of the original *Coronation Street* cast were still there after 11 years. 'It's a wonder some of them aren't screaming with insanity,' he told Weston Taylor of the *News of the World*. 'It just goes on and on, grinding its way twice a week. The regulars might just as well be working in a bank.' When Taylor asked him if he ever saw Violet Carson, Pat Phoenix, or any others in the cast, Arthur said 'brusquely: "Not if I can help it".' Five years after that he told Pearson Phillips of the *Evening News*. 'I knew I would have to prevent myself being trapped up there. It was a peep into hell, that was. Imagine, cornered in a Manchester telly series for the rest of one's life!'

He escaped from the treadmill by persuading Granada to give him a contract under which he worked on the series for only six months a year, three months on and three months off, which allowed him to take on other work in the theatre and films in between. 'Managements in the theatre have been very good to me,' he told Sheridan Morley in 1974.

They all knew me before the TV series so they think of me as a character actor, not as a tele-star who can't do anything else. If there's anything I dread it's being a 'personality' – at Granada I always refused to sign autographs and open fêtes and they couldn't understand it but I think it's essential for an actor to be unknown off the stage: that way you can have a clean slate and you can draw a fresh character on it every time.

He admitted that Leonard Swindley was the part that made him famous at last, when he was 46 – late for an actor – and it may well have been Swindley too who taught him something of the pomposity and self-importance that he was going to need to interpret the character of Captain Mainwaring seven years later. But 'oddly enough it was never my ambition to be a star,' he told John Graven Hughes for his book *The Greasepaint War*. 'I simply wanted to be the best character actor going, but stardom obviously came through television. I don't think I'd have done it without television.' Yet he felt ambivalent about Swindley, whom he once described as a 'pompous, busy-bodying windbag'. On the one hand he was grateful to him and even admired him. 'He was everyone's little man, always taking on too much and coming unstuck,' he said. 'But he had the courage of all little people and always got through – even if he was left with a little egg on his face.' On the other hand the part swiftly made him so famous that people stared at him in the street, pointing, whispering, and nudging each other in shops. 'It got so bad that I couldn't throw back a pint or two without everyone in the pub crowding round me,' he said. Strangers would hail him jocularly as Len or Mr Swindley, and Joan as Mrs Swindley. 'This irritated the hell out of me,' said Arthur. 'I wanted to be recognised for *myself* and not one of the characters I created.' To Lynda Lee-Potter he complained: 'I loathe and detest being called Mr Swindley. The public are so stupid. If they've seen you on television, they seem to think in some extraordinary way that they have some right to talk to you, that you belong to them.' He told *Weekend*: 'For eight years it was like living with a Siamese twin. There seemed to be no escape from Swindley. Sometimes I loathed him … Swindley suddenly took over my life.' He refused to open bazaars and do personal appearances, he told Lee-Potter,

> because it's so disappointing, so dull, for fans to find that I'm just an ordinary little man who has the rent to pay and worries about his income tax. I don't want any relationship with the public. I think this 'hands across the footlights' thing is a load of rubbish.

In his book Stephen looked back on those days with sadness and regret. He and Arthur had started riding horses along Rotten Row, in Hyde Park, but now 'the cabbies leant out of their cabs, one arm on the window. "Blow me! It's Mr Swindley on a 'orse!" It was the end of our private lives together.' At the age of eight Stephen had lost his father to the goddess of Fame – and it did not help that at about the same time he was sent away to boarding school, Hurst Court, at Hastings in Sussex, which made him feel even more excluded than before. Arthur's success was 'the most dreadful trial when I was at school,' Stephen confessed to John Brunton of the *Nottingham Evening Post* in 1995, 'and I didn't deal with it very well. I felt pestered by the other boys, who used catchphrases from the show and generally took the mickey.'

A month after Arthur's first *Coronation Street* episode he was back on stage at the Arts Theatre in Great Newport Street playing a smug, pompous north-country alderman, Michael Oglethorpe, in 31-year-old Henry Livings' first play, *Stop It, Whoever You Are*, which opened on 15 February. It earned Arthur a clutch of magnificent reviews – the best of his career so far – from some of London's smartest critics. Some had their doubts about the play itself because of its general farcical vulgarity, four-letter words and lavatorial humour, but most agreed that it was very funny, original, and wonderfully irreverent, and that the humour had to be lavatorial since the play tells of a doddery, downtrodden, dirty-old-man lavatory attendant (played by Wilfred Brambell) in a northern factory who is nagged by his wife, beaten up by homosexuals, seduced by a 14-year-old nymphomaniac, and patronised by his conceited old school friend Alderman Oglethorpe, one of the visiting dignitaries who uses the lavatory during the ceremonial opening of a nearby municipal library. 'There is a man called Arthur Lowe,' Bernard Levin enthused in the *Daily Express*, 'whose performance is literally unbelievable. I think he really is a Manchester alderman who wandered on to the stage while looking for King's Cross.' In the *Evening Standard* Milton Shulman wrote: 'Arthur Lowe, self-satisfied and unctuous, is hilarious as the ambitious Alderman,' and in the *Observer* Kenneth Tynan said that Arthur's Oglethorpe was 'the smuggest provincial alderman outside Arnold Bennett.'

Such a brilliant performance must have eased Joan's fears about the direction of Arthur's career, but as the months slipped by *Coronation Street* did indeed dominate his life, to such an extent that it was more than two years before he appeared on stage again in the West End. By his own workaholic standards he was virtually unemployed during the rest of 1961 apart from *Coronation Street*. He had just one small part in a film, as a prison warder in *Go to Blazes*, a comedy about a gang of ex-convicts who become firemen so that they can use the fire engine for robberies. He had a small part in one episode of the television sitcom *Three Live Wires*, and he made two children's radio programmes and another commercial for Wrigley's chewing gum. Otherwise, nothing. But for the first time in his life, thanks to *Coronation Street*, he was making enough money to take a proper holiday, and he indulged his love of the sea by treating himself, Joan and Stephen to a voyage to Copenhagen, Aarhus and Odense aboard the 12-passenger Danish cargo boat *Freesia*. Joan loved the sea too, even though it was foggy most of the time, but Stephen was nervous and admits that he 'snivelled all the way':

Dad wore his habitual flat suede cap and jacket and let the sea air empty his overloaded head and refill it with a spirit of adventure. A man's man, he befriended Larson the bosun, and the two made a heart-warming sight for a frightened boy as they sat on the hatchboards and chattered away in pigeon English, my short father animated beside this gentle toothless giant. I was taken to my cabin early because in the saloon the jokes were getting blue, and the drink aboard a Danish ship is not allowed to rot in the bottles.

Back in England Joan and Stephen returned to Pavilion Road and Arthur to Manchester, where he spent each lonely week in digs, although in the evenings after work he often went to see his old army friend Bill Bateman, who was now an insurance company surveyor, and his wife Phyllis, a nurse, who were living in Manchester. Mrs Bateman told me:

Arthur was a very shy man and he didn't make friends easily, but I think we got on together because of our sense of humour. We never treated him as a star: he was just Arthur. He'd walk around our flat in his underwear and he'd find the wrong door and say 'Oh, I've gone into the bloody airing cupboard again' to make us laugh, and he was so natural. We became one of his very few friends. We weren't theatricals, we were just good friends, northerners, and Joan and I hit it off. But she used to get very depressed when she was in London and Arthur was on tour, and one of the reasons she started drinking was she was lonely.

Arthur would return to London by train each Friday night, but sometimes sudden changes to his *Coronation Street* schedule meant that he was unable to come home even at the weekend. In one of his letters to Joan, which was headed '<u>The Prescription</u> (To be taken when feeling low)', he wrote lovingly but with revealing deletions:

Darling Pony,
I really <u>do</u> understand how much you hate to be alone and I'm terribly sorry not to show it more. It's a rotten trick of Fate to have arranged my work this way and I would give anything for it not to be so. Please try not to fret too much – today will soon be over, then ~~I'll~~ you will be ~~home on Friday~~ with the children. We've had a much happier time these last few days – lets ~~have a~~ go on being happy! ~~weekend?~~
I love you very dearly.
Tim
xxxxxxxxxxx

To make matters worse, Joan was beginning to resent that she had sacrificed her career as an actress to look after Stephen. She also had a much stronger sexual appetite than Arthur and became highly frustrated when he was away. On 13 June 1961, the 15th anniversary of the first time they had made love, she gave him a cheeky little handwritten spoof certificate with a fake seal affirming his skill as a lover. He kept it all his life:

<u>University of Beds.</u>
We, the examining body,
having satisfied ourself of
the fitness and capability of
the candidate:-
<u>Arthur Lowe</u>
are pleased to grant him a
Doctorate in the subject of
<u>Husbandry</u> at the conclusion
of his course of study
which commenced on June 13th
in the year <u>1946</u>.

Signed this	Signed:-
day	Joan Cooper
June 13th 1961	(Examiner)

To dull the pain of Arthur's long absences Joan began to drink too much. In one letter headed 'B.B.C. <u>Dancing Club</u>!' she wrote:

Darling,
I am a clot – I forgot to tell you that I heard 'the tune' this afternoon – V. Sylvester – so what that is for we shall see. I love you. I'm watching this tosh while I drink a little brandy and think about you and our lovely weekend and fairly soon now I shall have to go to bed.

She ended the letter: 'Goodnight my own darling, I love you so very much, Pony.'

Both she and Arthur drank heavily when they were together. Each evening they would pour their first large glasses of gin at 7.15, the second at 7.45, and at dinner they would each have a glass of white wine with the first course, a bottle of red between them with the main course, and several brandies after the pudding. Arthur had become a foodie and had an excellent appetite, so that he was not at first unduly affected by this amount of alcohol, but Joan ate very little and quickly became drunk. Stephen remembered that when he was at home for the holidays she tended to push her food around her plate and would then cover it with a napkin. 'Mummy can't eat very much because Mummy's tummy shrank during the war,' she told him. Arthur would urge her to have breakfast, the full bacon-and-eggs, toast-and-chunky-marmalade meal in which he always revelled, but Joan cared more about booze and cigarettes than food. Perhaps she was anorexic – as an actress she dreaded the possibility of losing her slim figure, and she was openly rude about fat women – but when Arthur was away she started drinking at midday as well as in the evening. 'It's five to twelve,' she would tell the bewildered little boy. 'Only five minutes to go.' The drinking made her aggressive, and Stephen remembered that when Arthur returned home for the weekends their reunions were often marred by dreadful, foul-mouthed rows, often about sex. 'As you aren't fucking me, who *are* you fucking?' she would scream. 'You have other fucking lovers, don't you?' Arthur would try to avoid these confrontations – 'For God's sake!' he would mutter – but time and again she would grab her fur coat and storm out of the flat in Pavilion Road, scattering a trail of four-lettered expletives behind her. Little Stephen used to wail with fear whenever she walked out, but she always returned within an hour or so after walking off her rage. The best nights, said Stephen, were when she drank so much that she passed out before she could start a fight and Arthur could put her quietly to bed, but afterwards he would sit on his side of the bed, in his vest, with his head in his hands. His 'other lovers' did not exist. He was always faithful to his beloved Joanie, but according to Stephen Joan was sexy and Arthur was not and despite that spoof certificate he failed to satisfy her sexually.

Arthur tried to make her happier by moving her up to Manchester so that they could be together during the week as well, and they rented a big, detached furnished house in the southern suburb of Wilmslow for the six months each year that he had to be in Manchester. 'For him this was coming home,' said Stephen. 'It was local boy makes good, and he thoroughly enjoyed being there.' Even then Joan was not satisfied, despite the fact that the house came with a gardener and the living room had a bar: 'She and Arthur had some stinking rows in that house,' said Stephen, but at least she now had her friend Phyllis Bateman to confide in. 'We were very fond of each other,' Mrs Bateman told me:

Joan was very friendly, chatty, lovable, kind, and generous, and we had some good laughs together. But she was stagestruck and I think she resented being a mum. I didn't know Stephen very well, because he was always away at school and I didn't see much of him, though we met him occasionally during the holidays. Maybe he did have an unhappy childhood. Arthur was such a busy man and he wouldn't have had much time to give to Stephen. It's very sad.

Yet Christopher Bond was puzzled by Stephen's unhappiness:

It's weird, this, because he had the best of everything, but there was a streak in Stephen which was a bit bolshie and resentful. He would much rather have been just an ordinary boy at an ordinary school, and because he had no brothers or sisters of his age, perhaps he felt left out.

In 1962 Joan must have begun seriously to worry about Arthur's theatre career for he did not appear on the stage at all, though he did land parts in six TV programmes apart from *Coronation Street* – among them one episode of the police series *Z Cars*, in which he played a scrofulous Lancashire crook called Jakey Ramsden; one episode of the French-detective series *Maigret*, in which he played a Monsieur Triboulet; and, along with Michael Caine, as one of the boarding-house landlady Thora Hird's ne'er-do-well residents in a sentimental, tear-jerker play called *So Many Children*. He also made seven radio programmes, mainly for schools. Thanks to *Coronation Street*, however, the Lowes no longer had to worry about money, and Joan told Diana Shine that he was earning £10,000 a year – more than £120,000 in current terms. Never again would Arthur be short of money. Socially, though, he was bored with Manchester, and in a letter to Diana and Bill Shine he wrote: 'Our greatest privation is, of course, civilized company. We tried one or two local dinner parties, but gave up in despair at the paucity of conversation and waste of good food and wines – pearls before little piggywigs and

God knows we are no scintillating socialities!'

Thanks to his new wealth Arthur could indulge his taste for good food and fine wines, and when in London he relished regular visits to the food departments of Harrods just around the corner from Pavilion Road, and revelled in the myriad delicacies that would eventually make him grossly obese. Stephen reports in his book that Arthur's conversations with the food counter assistants were worthy of a good sitcom script:

'Tell me, how much is the salmon a pound?'
'Five shillings, Mr Lowe.'
'Five shillings?'
'Come all the way from Scotland, ennit?'
'Well, it must have travelled first class.'

Although there were no parts on the stage that year, 1962 was to prove important for Arthur's film career, for it was then that the iconoclastic, left-wing, 38-year-old Royal Court theatre director Lindsay Anderson gave him a part in his first full-length feature film: the movie of ex-coal miner David Storey's bleak novel of the working class, *This Sporting Life*. Today the film seems dated and dreary to me, but then it was hailed as highly original and passionate. Rough, rude, gritty and sexually explicit for those times, *This Sporting Life* starred the hard-drinking, hell-raising young Irish actor Richard Harris, who had recently played *The Ginger Man* in the theatre and appeared in the film *The Mutiny on the Bounty* with Marlon Brando and Trevor Howard. Playing Harris's widowed land-lady and mistress was Rachel Roberts, fresh from *Saturday Night and Sunday Morning*. The film also had among its distinguished cast Alan Badel, William Hartnell, Colin Blakely, Leonard Rossiter and Frank Windsor, and it told the tragic story of an aggressive, arrogant and over-bearing, yet unexpectedly sensitive and vulnerable, northern rugby player, Frank Machin, and his violent, doomed affair with his landlady, the fussy, tightly repressed Mrs Hammond.

Anderson, who had directed actors of the calibre of Peter O'Toole, Robert Shaw, Tom Bell, Albert Finney and Mary Ure at the Royal Court, but whose films so far had been only short documentaries, had been a great admirer of Arthur ever since seeing him a year earlier as Alderman Oglethorpe in *Stop It, Whoever You Are*. 'He played an incredibly pompous north countryman quite superbly,' Anderson told Bill Pertwee. 'It was really acting. It wasn't a caricature at all.' In *This Sporting Life* he offered Arthur the part of another well-heeled, influential north country-man, a gruff, no-nonsense local businessman called Slomer, who is one of the directors of the rugby team that has Machin as one of its players. Slomer dislikes Machin and disapproves of his foul play, but eventually it is only Slomer who keeps Machin in the team. The film was shot at Beaconsfield Studios and when it was released in February 1963 the reviewers were stunned. '*This Sporting Life* is a major breakthrough, which opens the door to a new kind of film-making,' wrote Philip Oakes in the *Sunday Telegraph*, 'and to play down its importance would be like describing Picasso as a Sunday painter.' The critics raved about Richard Harris and Rachel Roberts, but tucked away in the small print there was high praise too for Arthur, whose immaculate performance Oakes described as that of a 'small-town Machiavelli brooding on plots like nest eggs … tough, true and excellent.' For Arthur the praise that mattered most was that of Anderson himself. Although Slomer was a very small part, Anderson told Pertwee: 'It wasn't a comic part and he played it tremendously well, and after *This Sporting Life* I knew that I never wanted to make a film without Arthur in it.'

Even so Arthur found himself once again scratching around for work away from *Coronation Street*. In the next three years he made no more films and appeared in only four television plays, one an adaptation of *The Pickwick Papers*, in which he played Mr Pickwick as though the part had been written just for him. He did make nine radio programmes, most of them broadcasts for schools, but only one commercial, and Joan must have begun seriously to question the direction of his career. His only West End appearance was at the Royal Court in Sloane Square with 26-year-old Nicol Williamson and 19-year-old Sarah Miles in another weird Henry Livings play, *Kelly's Eye*, which opened in June 1963. Arthur played the narrator who introduces each of the two acts, and The Eyeless Man, a blind, ingratiating, Scottish insurance salesman who is already dead after being murdered by his friend Kelly, the owner of a Liverpool timber yard and ex-Northern Ireland soldier. Williamson, who had just been acclaimed for his Hamlet and was generally considered to be the next Olivier or Gielgud, played Kelly, and Sarah Miles was his lover, Anna Brierly, but the play was doomed from the start because Miss Miles could not stand Williamson. Later, they were to become lovers in real life and to live together, but during the run of *Kelly's Eye* she disliked him intensely. 'He was the epitome of the angry young man,' she wrote in her autobiography. 'The chip on his shoulder was so vast it dug right down into a great inner cavern.' She accused him of confusing her hopelessly on the first night by introducing completely unrehearsed business into the play, and she ended the evening in tears in her dressing room. Arthur did what he could to help her but the reviews were not good, though they tended to blame the play rather than the actors. 'It was my first job at the Royal Court,' she told me in 2000,

and I was terribly young and having quite a lot of difficulty with Nicol Williamson. It was a horrible situation, but Arthur was very supportive of me, very gentle and sweet and kindly. He was just there, always around, a quiet little man. He'd keep himself quite a bit to himself but he wasn't at all standoffish and I found him absolutely enchanting. We got on very well and I liked him a lot.

Otherwise, amazingly for an actor of Arthur's calibre and experience, it was briefly back to weekly rep in Bromley, where he appeared in *The Tulip Tree* and quickly made it obvious that he should not really be there. One of the other actors, Derek Benfield, told me: 'He had an incredible natural comedy talent that set him apart from the rest of us. During rehearsals the rest of the cast would sit and watch him rather than chat amongst themselves or do the *Telegraph* crossword, as they did when we lesser mortals were practising.'

With such an excellent regular income from *Coronation Street*, Arthur bought himself a collectors'-item 1948 drop-head Daimler coupé even though he knew nothing about cars, and found himself spending almost as much time under the bonnet as in the driving seat. He called the car Henry and 'he could be pompous but he was also comical,' Tony Warren told me. 'He was Mr Toad of Toad Hall, quite definitely! In his Daimler his little head came just above the wheel and he leaned out and said to me "I'm mo-tor-ing down to London, taking the two days over it."' Thanks to *Coronation Street* too he could also afford to take a break and not to worry about not having much work. 'I am so glad to hear that Arthur spoils you,' Joan's mother wrote to her from Hexham in October 1963. 'It is so very pleasant for me to know you are "cared for" … please say to Arthur that I do appreciate that you are in good hands and am happy therefor [sic].' In the spring of 1964 the *Coronation Street* scriptwriters arranged for Swindley to have a nervous breakdown and the Lowes took another rare holiday, this time a month-long cruise in the Mediterranean on another 12-passenger cargo boat with Stephen, who was now 11, and his 12-year-old friend Ted Shine. They embarked at Hull and called in at Lisbon, Gibraltar, Genoa, Leghorn, Naples and Salerno before returning via Genoa again.

'Joan became obsessed with Italy and mad on Italian, and she started signing her letters Giovanetta,' Ted Shine told me.

Before we went on the cruise she told us that she had dreamed of a place in Italy called Poggibonsi, and when we got off at Leghorn she looked at the map and there was Poggibonsi! So we hired a taxi and it was like she had dreamed it was. Then Dinky Toys or Corgi brought out an Italian bus that had Poggibonsi on it!

'My dream-town Poggibonsi really is there,' Joan wrote ecstatically to Diana and Bill Shine in a letter headed 'Just off Elba. sabata, diecinova marzo',

a curious little town half ancient, half modern, rather 'industrial' in a vineyard, olive growing sort of way – and believe it or not it is the nearest railway station to where we should love to live – five miles away on a high hill – a walled Etruscan city – of such absolute beauty as to be unbelievable – San Giminiano [Gimignano] lovely red sandstone and uniform architecture – 1100 years old …

At lunch that day

we all shared a litre of the local brew Chianti – Poggibonsi is the centre of Chianti land – and the view from the huge picture window was more intoxicating than the wine – miles and miles of vines and olives in country that is more like Derbyshire than anything else I have ever seen. In fact I found the whole experience rather creepy – to dream of this curious little town and actually to find it in the heart of miles of my own kind of country – but with an Etruscan city, sunshine, grapes and olives and <u>happy</u> people seems so much like a prevision as to be frightening if it had not been so breathtaking.

Joan's dream now was to live in Italy. 'We could fly to Florence, get a train to Poggibonsi, pick up Henry … and be "home" quicker than getting to Newcastle!!' she wrote.

They hated Naples, which Joan wrote to the Shines was 'the biggest, busiest, noisiest, dirtiest bit of inhabited land that I have ever seen … seething and teeming with thousands of people and cars and motorcycles and buses and the NOISE was incredible'. They visited Capodimonte and took a train to Pompeii, where 'we went into a house – with a dining room, kitchen, bedrooms, courtyard garden, and a beautiful <u>painted</u> drawing room and the whole thing was 600 BC!!' They took the ferry to Capri – 'as beautiful as one has always heard – but, naturally, very commercialised' – and spent the following morning wandering around the markets of Naples, where Arthur revelled in all the fishmongers' stalls, with their huge variety of fish, octopus, starfish, cockles and mussels.

That trip both Arthur and Stephen indulged their latest craze, making home movies – 'Arthur is prowling round the ship with the camera,' Joan wrote – and they loved the complicated business of editing the films and synchronising the sound when they returned home. A lot more film was shot in a little seaside resort six miles from Genoa, Nervi – 'quite the loveliest place I have ever seen,' Joan wrote – where they picnicked on the seafront. 'The palms and the orange trees, still loaded with fruit, and the little quay at siesta time will always be like a dream to me.' In that letter Joan said that she now spoke 'quite reasonable Italian … we have spoken Italian all the time' and she ended it 'Sono multo sanco. Buona Noce, arriverderci,' and signed it 'Con amore, Giovanetta.'

Ted Shine particularly enjoyed that long voyage. 'Arthur *was* pompous,' he told me,

and he became Mainwaring more and more, but he was partly sending himself up. When he did Pickwick on television, he was perfect: he *was* Pickwick. I liked him. He was a nice man and not at all daunting because he was small and I was always taller than him.

Stephen, however, could still be tiresome and whiney.

He got into the habit of going for a walk with the engineer at six o'clock every evening, but one evening Stephen didn't go and I went walking with the engineer instead, and Stephen got very, very upset – that was one example of the tantrums – and he told me that I'd be left off at the next port of call and flown home. He was jealous. But Arthur didn't side with him at all.

Back in England Arthur climbed onto the *Coronation Street* treadmill again for three months, but in August he was back on stage, once again with Nicol Williamson, in John Osborne's play *Inadmissible Evidence*, which opened at the Theatre Royal in Brighton and transferred to the West End four weeks later, opening at the Royal Court Theatre on 9 September. Williamson played Bill Maitland, a solicitor who despises himself and whose whole world and personality are disintegrating as he alienates everyone close to him: his wife, ex-wife, children, mistress, girlfriends, managing clerk, secretaries, many of whom are preparing to leave him. It is a complex, wordy play – some of it realistic, some of it a dream in which Maitland finds himself on trial – in which several of the actors play two parts: a real part and a dream part. Arthur played Maitland's prissy managing clerk, Hudson, as well as the judge in his dream, and many of the critics and audiences were utterly baffled by it. Arthur himself admitted later that it was not a play he would have gone to see, and in the *Daily Telegraph* W. A. Darlington confessed that he could make neither head nor tail of it, but that 'Nicol Williamson gives a fine study of a likeable, weak man at the end of his tether' and 'Arthur Lowe gives a solidly good performance as the managing clerk'. Lindsay Anderson was impressed by Arthur's performance as the judge: he gave it 'a bite and an acidity, an edge, that I shouldn't think it has ever had again,' Anderson told Bill Pertwee.

I'll always remember when Nicol Williamson hesitated at the beginning and the judge came in with the single word … *mediocrity*, and this, spoken by Arthur, had an impact and a cutting edge that I don't think anybody else could do. If Arthur had a good part, nobody else would be better. He was one of our finest actors.

John Gielgud was one of many who found the play unbearably dreary and Osborne noted with amusement in his caustic and entertaining memoirs *Almost a Gentleman* that some time later he was invited to dinner by Gielgud, who remarked loudly during the meal, while discussing Nicol Williamson: 'That actor – oh dear me – young, Scottish, *most* unattractive … He was in that long, terribly dull, boring play. Oh, dear God, of course, you wrote it.'

Inadmissible Evidence went on to New York and Osborne and the play's director, Anthony Page, tried to persuade Arthur to go with it. 'I cannot imagine anyone playing Hudson after the marvellous way you created it, and … I am sure you would have an immense success,' Page wrote to him. But in the end, probably for financial reasons, Arthur decided to stay with *Coronation Street*: an Osborne play as obscure as this might not do well across the Atlantic, and Arthur had bills and school fees to pay, and a non-working wife. 'I can only say it seems very glum indeed to think of the play without you,' Osborne wrote. 'You brought such authority and sensibility with you that is so rare.' At the end of October Williamson, Arthur and Osborne, who was still an actor as well as a playwright, all appeared on stage together at the Royal Court in a month-long revival of Ben Travers' 1925 farce about adultery and divorce, *A Cuckoo in the Nest*, in which a couple who are married to other people are forced to spend an illicit but completely innocent night together in a hotel. The play had originally starred the celebrated Twenties and Thirties farceurs Tom Walls and Ralph Lynn, and Osborne described it in his diary as Travers' masterpiece. '*He* thinks we are all marvellous!' wrote Osborne. 'Arthur Lowe certainly is.' Arthur, who played the Tom Walls part, was described by Travers in his autobiography *A-Sitting on a Gate* as 'the uppermost of all up-and-uppers in the profession', and when Osborne introduced them in his dressing room, he told Travers: 'Here he is, better than Tom Walls – and cheaper.'

By now Arthur was thoroughly fed up with *Coronation Street* and when the Granada TV moguls decided to boost the serial's ratings by having one of the characters die of a heart attack in the snug of the Rovers Return, he was inspired to indulge in a piece of frivolous tomfoolery, which his playwright and actor friend Henry Livings described hilariously in his 1994 autobiography *The Rough Side of the Boards*. Livings had been cast to play Our Lily's Wilf at the funeral, and as the stars of the *Street* arrived at the chosen Manchester cemetery they were besieged for autographs by crowd of fans whom Arthur called 'the neck-less'. Wrote Livings: 'Arthur, his eyes baleful half-moons of malice, scribbled W. C. Fields, Gracie, or Henry Irving Bart, indiscriminately. "One of these days, Henry," he said, "I shall be assassinated by some enraged member of the Great Unwashed."' Arthur was particularly taken by the suggestion that one of the camera shots at the funeral should be from the bottom of the grave looking up, as though the deceased were witnessing her own funeral. 'Where are the crippled dwarfs and terminally diseased fallen women?' rumbled Arthur mischievously. 'This *is* a Bergman film we're doing here, I take it?' And when the mourners were all filmed trooping back along good old Coronation Street, said Livings, 'Arthur's gold-rimmed spectacles were to be seen gleaming from the set's GPO letterbox, and a small hand waved small cheerful Pickwickian gestures to passing colleagues.'

Arthur assumed too soon that filming was over for the week, sped off to catch the evening train to London, and was apprehended on board by two policemen, who brought him back to the studio to reshoot the final gloomy funeral scene in the vestry of the Glad Tidings Mission hall. 'They even had the gall to ask me for my autograph,' Arthur told Livings indignantly. Still, he had the last word as the mourners gathered in the vestry for the final take. He had always been a lover of jazz and now he approached Livings with a wicked gleam in his eye and said:

All right then, Henry, just a quick chorus, *Abide With Me*, I'll take the cornet, you're on trombone.' He jiggled his imaginary keys to be sure the valves were free, cocked a solemn eye to see if my slide was mobile and ready to play, opened and blew through his imaginary spit-valve, with a grave moue of apology for the pool of imaginary spit at my feet, pressed his imaginary instrument to his lips, blew out his cheeks like Dizzie Gilliespie, nodded, and we were off. Arthur's wavering, mournful, unwarmed-up cornet soared in B flat among the cobwebs, my extended fart of the harmony labouring up after it. The rump of the cast sat still at their places around the vestry table in the only real light, like a *Last Supper* painted by L. S. Lowry. There was a reverent silence as we finished, melancholy with long-cherished and now lost hope. Then the crew, who were on fat overtime, applauded warmly.

It was obviously time for Arthur to leave the show. He had by now become too big for it. 'I didn't care whether I stayed or not,' he told Lynda Lee-Potter in 1969, 'and because I didn't care, Granada gave me everything I asked for. Every clause I asked for, I got. They paid me more money when I asked for it. They leaned over backwards to accommodate me.' In December 1964 Granada agreed to give him his own 12-part comedy series in which he could continue to play Leonard Swindley but this time as the assistant manager of a department store. At last, after appearing in about 90 episodes of *Coronation Street* over four-and-a-half years, he would be in a television series in which he was the undisputed star. He had finally arrived.

CHAPTER 7

'The Unmatchable Arthur Lowe'
(1965–1968)

Arthur left *Coronation Street* on 31 May 1965 and the first episode of his new weekly series, *Pardon the Expression*, was screened two evenings later. Swindley was now the assistant manager of a department store, Dobson and Hawks, but in Arthur's own words he was still 'a pompous, busybodying windbag … If I ever had to deal with a man like Swindley, I'd bypass him and take my complaint straight to the top.' At times, however, he seemed fond of Swindley and once remarked: 'I think he has an almost Chaplinesque appeal. He is everybody's little man. He is always taking on a bit too much and coming unstuck.' The series showed the harassed old fusspot desperately trying to climb the social ladder at a golf club dance, entertaining foreign buyers, trying to charm a headmistress, and sucking up to the Chamber of Commerce. Unlike *Coronation Street*, *Pardon the Expression* was pre-recorded in front of an audience. 'Arthur liked having a live audience and responded to it immediately,' said Christopher Bond, who became one of the series' team of writers. There were three other regular characters: the store's manager, played in the first series by Paul Dawkins and in the second by Robert Dorning; the staff manageress, played by Joy Stewart; and the no-nonsense northern canteen manageress, played by Betty Driver. The first episode was greeted unenthusiastically by the reviewers – the *Daily Mail* sneered at 'a cut-price script of ineffable feebleness' – but the viewers loved it, and after just four episodes *Pardon the Expression* was the sixth most popular TV programme in Britain, behind *Coronation Street* and *No Hiding Place* but ahead of *Emergency – Ward 10* and *Front Page Story*. From then on it was regularly among the top five, the original 12 episodes stretched to 39, and it ran for more than a year, although Arthur still made Granada agree to six-monthly contracts so that he could appear on stage as well. 'For the first time in my life I was actually earning decent money,' he said.

Not everyone was uncritical of him. Betty Driver, who was later to appear for more than 30 years in *Coronation Street* as the Rovers Return barmaid Betty Turpin, admired his acting but not his character. 'He was brilliant in *Coronation Street*, wonderful in *Pardon the Expression*, and terrific in *Dad's Army*,' she told me,

but he was a very selfish actor, always made sure that he was in front of the camera, and didn't mind if he upstaged you. He had to be the centre of attraction all the time and if anyone else had a comedy line he'd have it removed. The first time we did a read-through of *Pardon the Expression* I had quite a lot of script because I was the second lead, but every time we came to a line that had any comedy in it he said 'Just a second. I do feel that I'd say that better than Betty.' At the end I put my script down and said to the producer, 'Well, I'm going. You've just cut all my lines out, so I might as well go home.' He said 'Oh no, we can't have that', and it was all rewritten again. Arthur was a devil like that and he did it with all the people on the show. He was a strange little man, really, a very odd little man, very solemn, very introverted. You didn't know where you stood with him and I never knew what made him tick. He used to come in and do his work and then just disappear. Those kind of people worry me a bit. He was so remote that he didn't have any real friends. He was very pompous, very like Mainwaring in *Dad's Army*, and he had a very strange, sarcastic sense of humour. And he didn't know his lines very well, but he was very short-tempered with people who didn't know *their* lines.

Whenever I spoke to a woman about Arthur while researching this book I always asked her if he had been at all sexy. Betty Driver exploded: 'Oh God, no! Oh blimey, no! Oh Christ, I've gone all hot! No! No way! No way! My God, nobody'd put up with him. Oh no no no. He was quite ugly.' Men tended to agree. 'He was very plain, completely unsexual, and didn't even have the charm of the *jolie laide*,' Derek Granger, who produced the second series of *Pardon the Expression*, told me in 2001:

He was very prickly and pernickety because fundamentally he didn't rate it as the kind of quality piece he should be in, and he was right. Everybody at Granada thought it was very low-class rubbish and I remember Arthur coming into rehearsal with a script, raising his eyes, and saying with a miserable face 'Is this the best you can do?' He resented the fact that he was cornered in an incredibly popular show and yet it was below his standard. In the end I admired him so much that the difficulties were fairly unimportant. He was terribly professional, always superb, and I can't remember any character actor who was so impeccable in delivery, with marvellous timing and an absolutely wonderful sense of where the joke was. He *was* a pain in the arse, but a pain in the arse whom you always forgave in the end. He was saying 'Look, I'm better than this material', and he was right.

Granger remembered that Arthur used to come to rehearsals wearing 'those little chequered shirts that are popular among old-fashioned, middle-class, county people, and a kind of discreet sports jacket, polished brogue shoes, and a trilby hat with a small brim.' Like so many others who worked with Arthur, Granger found him standoffish:

I never had a drink with him, nor did anyone else. He was completely unconvivial and didn't like the mass of people. He and Joan didn't have any social life at all and I doubt he had any friends. But you didn't really want to *be* with Arthur very much, since he had every kind of right-wing prejudice.

On one occasion Arthur behaved so badly that Granger positively disliked him. It occurred when the then-unknown actor Warren Mitchell, who was later to play Alf Garnett in the TV series *Till Death Us Do Part*, played a small comic role in *Pardon the Expression*. Granger told me:

Mitchell was marvellous, and Arthur absolutely hated it and was terribly denigratory about him. He was jealous. 'Who is this you're employing?' he asked me. 'What kind of actor is this? Is this a *professional* actor?' He was really very naughty, because Warren was a marvellous little actor. That is the one instance on which I remember Arthur being *genuinely* disagreeable, because a leading actor is *not* supposed to start criticising other actors in that mean way, and I told him it was mean.

Demonstrating yet again his independence of television and Granada, in September 1965 Arthur was back on the boards at the Arts Theatre in Cambridge playing the lead, Matthew Bellows, in Peter Whitbread's comedy *Foursome Reel* and later taking it on tour to several provincial and Scottish theatres. Stephen had just been packed off back to boarding school in Hastings, so Joan went with Arthur, wishing that she too was appearing on stage every night. She wrote nostalgically to the Shines from the University Arms Hotel in Cambridge one evening while Arthur was in the theatre: 'We have been behaving like touring actors in the pouring rain – draught Guinness and bread and cheese and then the cinema – two days running! … and then Bill's delight, tea and toast at the local cinema café. It's <u>almost</u> like old times.' She consoled herself by indulging her lifelong passion for buying antiques, this time bidding at an auction for a small chest of drawers, a wall mirror and a lacquer tea caddy, all for £2 5*s*. After going on with Arthur and *Foursome Reel* to Hull, Joan forced herself to go to Hexham to see her mother, who was still looking after several grandchildren, although David, now 24 and teaching music, had left home. 'I'm afraid I really must go,' Joan told the Shines reluctantly. 'My mother sounds quite exhausted – morally and mentally – and was so thrilled when I offered! Which, oh God, means that I shall probably not escape until Half Term … but I must do it – and after all it's a small contribution really.' She ended her letter: 'Must go, A should be in the lift and I'm dying of thirst!!! Lots of love, Giovanetta.'

In October Arthur returned to Salford to play the part of yet another pompous, self-important northerner, this time the smug, narrow-minded mayor in Lindsay Anderson's experimental film *The White Bus*, a weird, avant-garde, 45-minute 'documentary' by Shelagh Delaney in which a girl living in London returns to her northern home town and takes a conducted bus tour around it. Fantasy and reality are intertwined, and some scenes shot in colour, others in black and white. In one scene a group of people in a park suddenly become characters in paintings by Fragonard, Goya and Manet; in another the passengers in the bus turn into tailors' dummies as they watch a civil defence demonstration. The critics gave the film a loud, unanimous raspberry and it was never widely distributed. It seems surprising that Arthur – a firm, no-nonsense Tory, who despised any whiff of the pretentious or arty-farty – should have so much enjoyed appearing in so many strange, experimental films directed by a man who was a committed socialist and anti-Tory, yet he and Anderson were both mischievously anarchic by nature and they loved working together on these weird projects.

A second series of *Pardon the Expression* began in January 1966, but the critics were still unimpressed. 'Swindley is a rich character, and Arthur Lowe is an excellent comic actor. Yet somehow the show is never quite as funny as it could be,' wrote John Stevenson in the *Northern Daily Mail*. The viewers disagreed. An estimated 21 million watched it every week, which made it the most successful comedy programme of the time. The reasons for that, said Arthur, was that viewers were fond of Swindley because although he was pompous he was also human and they could see something of themselves in him. When the second series came to an end in the summer Granada decided to make the most of Arthur's and Bob Dorning's popularity as Swindley and Hunt by giving them a new series of six hour-long stories, *Turn Out the Lights*, in which they become ghost hunters and investigators of the occult and paranormal: poltergeists, mediums and weeping statues. But the reviewers savaged the first pro-gramme when it was screened in January 1967 and *Turn Out the Lights* lasted for only one series.

In the meantime Arthur, Joan and Stephen, who was now 13, treated themselves in August to another long cruise on a cargo ship, this time to the West Indies on a Geest Lines banana boat, the *Geestbay*. They ate at the captain's table and all three revelled in being at sea again and marvelled at the sight of the whales and hundreds of flying fish. 'Oh how fabulous the Atlantic is,' wrote Joan to the Shines. They called in at the Azores ('a delight'), and found the ship 'enormously comfortable' and the few other passengers 'a most congenial bunch'. As they neared the tropics they were stunned by the heat – 'The shade here … is hotter than any sunshine I have ever felt' – but luckily the ship was air conditioned and they would rise at 6 a.m. to make the most of the coolest part of the day. At night, wrote Joan, 'A and I sit on the deck – still in no sleeves – drinking pints of chilled Whitbread's keg beer – the beer has never tasted better.'

They called first at the island of Dominica, of which Joan wrote: 'Oh darlings, fabulous, fabulous … the most beautiful island emerged – I can't really begin to tell you <u>how</u> beautiful.' She enthused about the black pumice beaches, the forests, the primitive little shanty towns with their pale pastel houses, the street markets, the palm trees, flamboyants, and red, yellow and white hibiscus. 'It made me feel like a two year old on its first visit to a pantomime,' she wrote. 'But we took lots of film and hope to show it to you anon … Stephen was as excited as I was and obviously will never forget.' Joan was still signing her letters 'Giovanetta'.

They went on to Barbados – 'This is so exciting,' she enthused – an island that they found to be 'most unsophisticated' but 'a paradise of exotic flowers [and] humming birds, rowdy crickets, lizards, pretty little ones'. They photographed the statue of Nelson in Barbados' Trafalgar Square and found a 'luscious rattan screened hotel by the sea', where they enjoyed a 'most incredible buffet' lunch of breadfruit, mango, and

Mountain Chicken (a cultivated toad with tastes just like eel) [and] Pepper Pot, an earthenware stewpot with nothing recognizable in it which they guarantee has never been off the boil for seven years – there are some which families have had for tens of years, they are never emptied – just added to – and the curry! and the pudding! and the coffee! and the swinging couch under the hibiscus…

They did not, however, think much of their fellow diners, who were 'some of the horridest Europeans one can imagine … the bulging women in too tight shorts and the horrid old …'s with their "friends" in flowered shirts and all drinking themselves and eating themselves to death'. They watched part of a village cricket match, 'and the <u>children</u> – all quite exquisite in their Sunday white, off to Sunday school – with different hats, all so pretty, for the different churches.'

From Barbados they went on to Grenada, where they spent two days: 'pure jungle – we've got lots of film, and we drove through miles of bananas, coconuts, avocado pears, breadfruit, nutmegs and coffee trees for 6½ hours.' Then they called at St Vincent, of which Joan wrote to the Shines: 'This, so far anyway, is my island. It is so beautiful and <u>clean</u> and <u>pulled together</u> – the people are different; darker, better educated.' Just as she had done in Italy, she fantasised about living in St Vincent: 'There is an "hotel" for sale – <u>it started life as a theatre</u>! And once more I am enjoying pixilated dreams of owning "foreign" soil. Stark madness but why shouldn't I dream!'

Their final port of call was St Lucia:

The humidity here ... is immense and we have spent the evening on deck watching the women loading bananas by hand carrying them, of course, on their heads ... Oh! they are so fast and so happy, they giggle all the time, our youngest steward tells us that they have a rum or two before they start! The smallest 'hand' weighs 18lbs and they balance them and RUN with them – 3 cents ($1\frac{1}{2}d$) a go! – but they come round and round and so, I suppose, make a subsistent wage – not much jam on the bread I'm sure ... But they certainly sound HAPPY!!! I was longing to try and I was offered £20 to run the gauntlet but I swear that they would have torn me to shreds if I had tried.

That voyage was the most adventurous holiday of their lives and they all enjoyed themselves so much at sea that when they returned to England Arthur and Joan were determined to buy a ship of their own one day. Stephen, too, had been inspired by the trip and made up his mind to join the merchant navy when he left school unless he could find a job as a movie cameraman.

Arthur's career was able to survive occasional TV disasters such as *Turn Out the Lights* because of his outstanding performances elsewhere on stage and screen, and at the end of 1966 he was signed up to play the star part of the bewigged cuckold Sir Davy Dunce in Thomas Otway's bawdy, rollicking Restoration comedy *The Soldier's Fortune* when it opened at the Royal Court theatre on 12 January. But at Christmas Arthur suffered a shocking financial blow: his agent, Jimmy Lavall, a South African alcoholic who had once been a variety artist himself, absconded with about £2,000 of his fees for *Pardon the Expression* – the equivalent of £22,000 today – as well as several thousand that belonged to about 30 other actors who were on his books, among them Hermione Baddeley. Arthur was appalled by his loss but persuaded Lavall's assistant, Peter Campbell, to keep the agency going and lent him the money to do so.

Despite this setback Arthur gave a brilliant performance as Sir Davy Dunce. *The Soldier's Fortune* tells of two lecherous young officers who return from the war in Flanders in 1680 to enjoy the bawdy pleasures of

Charles II's London, and of how one of them makes every effort to seduce rich, fat, old Sir Davy's randy, frustrated young wife, who was played by Sheila Hancock. Sir Davy, according to his discontented wife, is 'an old, greasy, untoward, ill-natured, slovenly, tobacco-taking cuckold … a horse-load of diseases, a beastly, unsavoury, old, groaning, grunting, wheezing wretch that smells of the grave he's going to', and Arthur made the most of such a rich part. 'Mr Lowe gives him a pink pig's face between a King Charles II wig and a snuff-stained snuff-brown suit, and plays the part as freshly as if it were something from a very good current comedy,' wrote B. A. Young in the *Financial Times*, praising Arthur's 'tremendous comic style' and adding: 'Mr Lowe can speak the most insignificant line with such point that it gets a laugh; and at the end, where he is humiliated beyond all permissible bounds, his pathos is all the deeper for being expressed in comic terms. A marvellous performance.' In the *Sunday Telegraph* Alan Brien called him 'the unmatchable Arthur Lowe', and in *Plays and Players* Tom Stoppard wrote: 'Arthur Lowe brings to the part of Sir Davy a lightness of touch, a felicity, an innocence and a charm which is lacking everywhere else … and one long moment of brilliance in Mr Lowe's negligent awe at being invited to dine with the Lord Mayor.' Felix Barker reported that 'the evening's triumph is the delicious off-key performance by Mr Lowe', and Herbert Kretzmer said in the *Daily Express*: 'The play is worth seeing for him alone.'

His performance brought an ecstatic fan letter from Bernard Miles, the director of the Mermaid Theatre in London, who offered him a part in another bawdy comedy, this time a ribald musical, *Lock Up Your Daughters*. When it opened at the Mermaid, Arthur played the corrupt magistrate Mr Squeezum and song two solos, and when it went on tour Joan joined him with a small part as a maid, for which she also sang a song. After 15 years of motherhood off the stage Joan was determined to make a comeback, but it was the start of a sad attempt to rebuild her career by clutching at Arthur's coat tails as he became increasingly famous. 'She felt that she'd made a big sacrifice giving up her own career,' said Peter Campbell, 'and when Stephen was of an age she wanted very much to be back on the boards.' Unhappily 'Joan wasn't a great actress but she thought she was,' Ted Shine told me, 'and she had a weak voice that didn't carry much.' Barbara and Richie Gatehouse agreed, and Christopher Bond told me that Joan's acting had inevitably became rusty during her years out of the business while Arthur's skills had developed far beyond her abilities.

Joan didn't have natural timing. She was a quite competent actress but she wasn't star quality, and he was. I don't think she was at all jealous of his success: she was absolutely thrilled by it because even at second-hand it gave her the entrée everywhere, and Arthur never went anywhere without her. But she was also very forceful and would call a spade a spade.

The tour of *Lock Up Your Daughters* began with a fortnight in Sunderland and went on to Darlington, Bradford and Cambridge. Joan was excited by her return to the stage after so long. She wrote from Sunderland to the Shines:

I was very scared at the dress rehearsal, quite scared on the first night and not at all scared last night, and I would not have believed it possible that one could pick up exactly where one had left off after such a long time. Sally assures me that they can even hear every word of my number and I find the projecting bit so enlivening that I have developed a great appetite and I am eating like a horse. In fact, of course, I suppose that I have been like a fish out of water all these years and now I am back in the tank I have started to live again.

Since she was such a forthright woman she probably found it difficult to hide these sentiments from Stephen, who was now 14 and had become a boarder at Aldenham, a public school at Elstree, near Watford, in Hertfordshire; the fact that she felt so strongly that she had sacrificed her career for him and had been living a half-life cannot have made him any happier about his childhood. She added: 'Oh darlings I can't tell you how good it feels to have a "place" laid out, with the flowers, cards and telegrams etc and to be a part of a company again.' She signed the letter 'Gio'.

When Aldenham broke up for the Easter holidays Stephen joined his parents on the tour after the Shines met him in London and put him on the train north to Bradford. In a poignant, excruciatingly polite letter he wrote from the school to the Shines two months after his birthday:

I am sorry that I have not written before to give you information such as time of arrival I was meaning to do so a long time ago. My heart leapt yesterday when I thought I had forgotten to write thanking you for my stage cookery book, if I did forget, thank you very, very much indeed. I shall arrive p.m. if this is convenient for you, between 4 and 5. With almost no luggage, very little washing, which, thank you kindly dear, you need not trouble yourself with, but thank you very, very much indeed for offering, and myself.

I gather that you have my railway ticket.

This is extremely kind of you thank you very, very much. It will make the affair much more bearable. Thank you once again, thank you.

Love Steve

See you Thursday between 4 and 5 p.m.

Mr Gough has your address

It is the letter of a boy who was deeply insecure and would probably have much preferred to be at home in Pavilion Road for the holidays with all his familiar things around him rather than sitting in hotels while his parents were in the theatre every night, and it must have been difficult for him not to feel lonely and neglected as he began to face all the stresses and problems of puberty. 'He had no friends in London,' Ted Shine told me, 'and when he came home for the holidays there was nobody except myself, and by the time we were about 15 we had slowly grown apart. I went to a mixed day school and had a fairly good social life, but he was at a boys' boarding school and didn't have any girlfriends.' Stephen made the most of his holiday by shooting an 8mm cine film of the *Lock Up Your Daughters* tour, both onstage and off.

Freed at last from the treadmill of regular, humdrum television work and determined never again to run the risk of becoming typecast, Arthur now accepted as many unlikely parts as possible to distance himself from Leonard Swindley, among them roles in two way-out Russian productions at the increasingly progressive Royal Court Theatre. The first Russian play, which opened in October, was the British première of *Marya* by Isaac Babel, a Soviet writer who had been banned in Stalin's Russia and murdered in a Siberian concentration camp in 1941. It told of how all the hopes and idealism of the Russian Revolution had been betrayed by the tyranny of Lenin and the Bolsheviks, and by the civil war, state terror, hardship and misery that had followed. Arthur played two small parts in this unusual play: in the first scene as Yevstigneyich, a Red Army veteran with no legs ('Toulouse-Lautrec ... on a trolley,' said the *Daily Telegraph*); and later as Andrei, a building worker forced to scrub floors. Eric Shorter wrote approvingly in the *Telegraph*: 'Arthur Lowe in two minor roles distinguishes himself – as usual.'

Two months later Arthur was playing a corrupt mayor in another Russian play about Soviet tyranny, *The Dragon*, a fairy tale written in 1943 by Yevgeny Schwartz, though this time the parable's political message – a brave knight kills a monstrous dragon that has been oppressing and terrorising a town for 400 years – was dressed up as a jolly, magical children's Christmas pantomime, with fairy lights, acrobats, puppets, masks, a one-man band, a magic carpet and a talking cat. 'The acting of such Royal court regulars as Arthur Lowe ... is nearly always first-rate,' reported Shorter in the *Daily Telegraph*, and the *Sunday Telegraph* agreed: 'Arthur Lowe is a splendidly corrupt mayor, bursting with all the vices of petty officialdom.' It was a role that he now seemed to be playing almost every other time he stepped onto a stage. 'Arthur Lowe is superb as the rascally Mayor, half Kruschev, half West Riding tycoon.' said the *Tablet*. Having escaped Swindley at last, Arthur was now in danger of becoming typecast as the archetypal pompous northern businessman or bureaucrat. Yet his next part, as an ineffectual schoolmaster in Lindsay Anderson's film *If...*, was quite different.

If... was another Anderson allegory, this time about an English boarding school where three rebellious boys stage a violent revolt against the system and on Speech Day finally kill the headmaster, teachers, parents and dignitaries, including a general and a bishop, in a machine-gun massacre worthy of *The Godfather*. A powerful, visually beautiful film that alternated between realism and fantasy, with some scenes filmed in black-and-white and some in colour, it was another Andersonian plea for idealists to rebel against an unthinking, conformist society, and still makes excellent viewing today. Once again it seems an odd film for Arthur to appear in, given that it was such violently left-wing, anti-Establishment propaganda, but he liked appearing in unconventional films, admired Anderson and agreed to play a mild, weak housemaster, Mr Kemp, who allows his brutal prefects to rule his house without interference. Malcolm McDowell, then a wonderfully ugly 24-year-old making his third film, starred as the hero, Mick Travis, the tough but brainy rebel leader. Peter Jeffrey was the smug headmaster, Mona Washbourne a splendidly po-faced matron, and there was a gloriously wacky scene in which Arthur sat up in bed wearing striped pyjamas and singing while his wife tootled away on the recorder. And by nice coincidence, as smoke fills the hall on Speech Day at the end of the film, the General, who has been delivering the address, cries 'Don't panic! Don't panic!' in a manner worthy of Clive Dunn in *Dad's Army*.

Filming began in March 1968 amid the beautiful old buildings of three different schools, among them Anderson's old school, Cheltenham College, and Stephen's boarding school, Aldenham. Many years later David Wood, one of the young actors who had played one of the rebels, told Stephen that during a break from filming he and some of the other boy actors discussed loudly how awful Aldenham was with its peeling paint, unpleasant outdoor showers and general air of being utterly uncivilized, and agreed that any parent who sent his son there must be utterly inhumane. Later they discovered that Arthur had sent Stephen there and had heard every word they had said.

Although Arthur's part in the film was very small he was 'the best character actor you could ever possibly work with,' Malcolm McDowell told the BBC TV programme *The Unforgettables* in 2000. 'Although as a man he was very remote – he didn't muck in much, and he'd always keep himself rather separate from the rest of the film unit – he knew how to extract the humour out of any situation.'

Despite so many varied triumphs in 1967, the most significant of all the parts that Arthur played that year was at first sight hardly worth mentioning. He appeared in *Baked Beans and Caviar* at the Theatre Royal, Windsor – a 'terrible play', Bill Pertwee told me. In the audience one night were a young BBC producer, David Croft, and a young scriptwriter, Jimmy Perry, who were searching desperately for the right actor to play a leading role in their new TV comedy series about the wartime Home Guard, *The Fighting Tigers*. Dreadful play or not, they invited Arthur to lunch at the BBC. And then they changed the title of their new series. They decided to call it *Dad's Army*.

CHAPTER 8

Dad's Army

(1968)

Jimmy Perry was a 33-year-old actor who had never written a TV play, let alone a series, but was struck by inspiration one day in 1967 when he was travelling by train to Stratford East, in the East End of London, to appear on stage at Joan Littlewood's Theatre Royal. As a 16-year-old in Barnes and Watford during the Second World War, Perry had served in the Home Guard, that ramshackle, part-time army of men – at first known as the Local Defence Volunteers, or LDV – who were either too young or too old to join the proper army but pledged themselves to fight to the death if Hitler's Nazis ever invaded Britain. Films and plays about the war always seemed to do well, and Perry thought that if he wrote a TV series about the Home Guard he could include in it a part for himself that was based on his teenage experiences – a naïve mummy's boy called Private Pike. That weekend, on the Sunday afternoon, he saw the 1938 Will Hay film *Oh! Mr Porter* and realised with increasing excitement that one of the secrets of the film's success was that it had a superb balance of characters: a pompous idiot, an old man and a boy. In that moment were conceived the *Dad's Army* characters of Captain Mainwaring and Private Godfrey as well as Private Pike.

It was not a new idea. During the Second World War one of Arthur Lowe's idols, the Liverpudlian comedian Robb Wilton, regularly poked fun at the LDV in his comic monologues. People joked that LDV stood for 'Look, Duck and Vanish' and that it was going round putting tin helmets on sheep. In 1943, when Perry was 19, George Formby starred in a film about it, *Get Cracking*, which, like *Dad's Army*, began with Anthony Eden's radio broadcast announcing the formation of the Local Defence

Volunteers in May 1940. Like *Dad's Army*, too, *Get Cracking* depicted two shambolically amateurish, rival Home Guard platoons of bumbling volunteer soldiers who came from all walks of life and (again like *Dad's Army*) included an aristocrat, a butcher, a Scotsman, and a stupid boy.

Perry's own experiences in the Home Guard would have been hilarious had they not been so serious at a time when Britain was in real danger of invasion. At first the volunteers were armed only with sheath knives, coshes and bicycle chains, though Perry's commanding officer, a Major Todd, had worn a pistol strapped around his thigh, and had ended every parade by waving it in the air and bellowing 'Kill Germans!' Even when eventually they were issued with rifles only the older men were allowed to have ammunition. Perry was even instructed how to disable a German tank should it come rumbling down an English lane: he was supposed to light a petrol-soaked blanket under the tank's tracks, which were then supposed to seize up, upon which he was to creep up on the tank, prise its top open with a crowbar, and drop a Molotov cocktail into it.

Armed with such ludicrous memories, he wrote his first 30-minute script in six days, introducing a bunch of bumbling Home Guard volunteers in 1940 in a little English south-coast town called Brightsea-on-Sea, among them a pompous sergeant called Mainwaring. Perry showed the script to the BBC director David Croft, for whom he was playing a small part in a TV series, *Beggar My Neighbour*. Croft had himself been an air raid warden in 1939 before serving in the Royal Artillery and rising to the rank of major, and he was impressed by Perry's idea. He urged him to write a second episode and then showed both to Michael Mills, the BBC's head of situation comedy, who was equally keen on the idea but, in a moment of genius, suggested that the title should be changed to *Dad's Army*. Mills commissioned scripts for six 30-minute episodes even though Bill Cotton, the head of variety, told Croft he was out of his head to want to make a comedy about the Home Guard, and there were powerful figures at the BBC who asked 'Who will want to see a lot of old boys rushing about trying to play soldiers?' Mills was not one of them, but he insisted that Croft should collaborate with Perry in writing the scripts and suggested that the series needed a character who was not English – a Scotsman, perhaps – and so the dour Scots under-taker, Private Frazer, was born. Next to be created were the spiv, Private Walker, and the ancient butcher, Lance Corporal Jones, whose character was based on a real Home Guardsman Perry had known during the war: an old soldier who had fought in the Sudan at the Battle of Omdurman in 1898 and had kept reminiscing about fighting the 'fuzzy-wuzzies'. As for Jones's famous *Dad's Army* catchphrase, 'They don't like it up 'em!', it was a remark that had often been made by a sergeant who had taught Perry to use the bayonet when he was called up into the regular army in 1944. The pompous Mainwaring became a captain rather than a sergeant, and gradually Perry and Croft began to create some of the other main *Dad's Army* characters: the languid, aristocratic Sergeant Arthur Wilson; the belligerent air-raid warden, William Hodges; Private Pike's fussy mother, Mavis. And they changed the name of their fictional town to Walmington-on-Sea.

The first character to be cast was the lead: the pompous bank manager who commands the Home Guard platoon, Captain George Mainwaring. Jimmy Perry had long admired Arthur's acting and at first wanted him to play Mainwaring's subordinate, Sergeant Wilson. For Mainwaring himself the BBC approached Thorley Walters, a chubby, square-faced, moustachioed, 54-year-old character actor who had already appeared in 43 films, often playing buffoons or fussy, jumped-up, ineffectual officials, and who might well have been excellent as Captain Mainwaring. But he 'didn't fancy the part,' David Croft told me in 2001, and Jimmy Perry told me: 'Thorley Walters would probably have been very good but he said he didn't like to do shows in front of an audience.' The BBC then offered the part of Mainwaring to Bill Pertwee's cousin Jon Pertwee, who was later to be the third Dr Who in the long-running children's science-fiction series *Doctor Who* and to play the lead in *Worzel Gummidge*, the children's series about a walking, talking scarecrow. Pertwee also declined the part, because it clashed with a job he had agreed to do in America. Perry was still rooting for Arthur to be cast as Sergeant Wilson but Michael Mills was unconvinced, seeing Arthur as a mere commercial-TV soap-opera actor rather than a pukka BBC type despite his distinguished record in the theatre. 'Arthur Lowe?' said Mills loftily. 'We don't know him at the BBC. He doesn't work for us.' Perry, convinced that Arthur would be right for some part in the series, dragged Croft out to Windsor to see him in *Baked Beans and Caviar*. 'Arthur was *dreadful* in it,' said Perry. 'It wasn't his sort of thing at all.' But Croft still agreed that he could be right for the part of Mainwaring. Even then Arthur nearly blew it when, over lunch at the BBC restaurant in Broadcasting House, Croft asked him what sort of comedy programmes he liked and he replied: 'I'll tell you one I don't like: that thing *Hugh and I.*'

'I produce it,' said Croft.

Arthur barely blinked. 'This wine's not bad,' he said.

After lunch he gave Perry a lift to Sloane Square in his beloved old Daimler. 'You know, Jimmy,' he said, 'they don't make cars like this any more.' Perry tried to adjust the sunshield, which came apart in his hand, and he tucked it quickly under the seat, hoping that Arthur had not noticed. 'I realise then that a man who could be so naturally funny as this was a gift to any writer,' he said years later.

Michael Mills was keen for John le Mesurier to play Mainwaring, and there were long discussions at the BBC as to whether Arthur was classy enough to play an officer, but eventually he was offered the part of Captain Mainwaring, which he later described as 'a wonderful part … a sort of military extension of Mr Swindley'. At 52 he had finally found the role that was to make him immortal, and he knew already precisely how to play the part. 'Although Mainwaring thinks he is a little Montgomery, he is very brave,' he said. 'He is ridiculous, but if Hitler had landed, he would have been right there at the front.' Yet Croft still had his doubts about Arthur's suitability. 'We were taking a risk,' Croft told Richard Webber for his book *Dad's Army: A Celebration.* 'I needn't have worried though, because he slotted in to the role perfectly. The electricity between him and Wilson was wonderful.' It was in fact a spark of genius to cast tubby little lower-middle-class Arthur as the prickly, henpecked, chip-on-the-shoulder, grammar-school-educated officer, and lanky, laid-back John le Mesurier as his public-school-educated, aristocratic underling, the sergeant. First, though, the BBC asked le Mesurier if he could run. Yes, he said, but wrote in his autobiography 15 years later: 'The answer was no but so what? I could remember the real Home Guard and I never saw any of them run, save possibly to the pub.' At the age of 55 le Mesurier, whose name was prounounced to rhyme with 'treasurer', was even more famous than Arthur and had already appeared in 100 films. On television he had been in *The Avengers* and eight episodes of *Hancock's Half Hour,* and despite the languid, absent-minded, shambolic persona that he cultivated he was a consummate comedy actor. The BBC thought so highly of him that he was paid £262 (about £2,600 today) for each episode of the first *Dad's Army* series while Arthur was paid only £210 (about £2,100 today), the same as Clive Dunn.

Clive Dunn, who was cast as the geriatric butcher Lance Corporal Jack Jones after Jack Haig turned down the part, was convinced that he was offered the role only because his mother had once had an affair with David Croft's father. The distinguished 70-year-old Shakespearean actor John Laurie agreed to play the cynical, gloomy, wild-eyed Scot, Private James Frazer. Seventy-one-year-old Arnold Ridley was signed up to play the gentle, doddery, incontinent old bachelor, Private Charles Godfrey. A 21-year-old unknown, Ian Lavender, who was lucky enough to have Croft's wife as his agent, landed the part of the gormless, thumb-sucking teenager, Private Pike. Although Perry had hoped to play either Pike or the wise-cracking cockney spiv Private Joe Walker himself, Mills and Croft insisted that he should concentrate on writing the series rather than acting in it, and the part of the spiv was given to 38-year-old Jimmy Beck. Perry was given a little consolation prize by being allowed to make a brief appearance in the sixth episode as Charlie Cheeseman, the Cheerful Chump, a variety artiste who tops the bill at the Walmington Hippodrome Theatre. Finally the part of Hodges, the air-raid warden, went to 41-year-old Bill Pertwee, whose stage experience had been mainly in variety but who had worked with Croft on *Hugh and I* and had distinguished himself as the Indian Test cricket team's assistant baggage boy in 1946.

Lavender had only recently left the Bristol Old Vic drama school, had acted professionally for just one season at the Marlowe Theatre in Canterbury, and had appeared in just one television play, but the other four main actors had had distinguished careers in the theatre. During the 1930s John Laurie had earned himself a fine reputation as a classical actor and Shakespearean leading man at Stratford-on-Avon, where he had played Hamlet, Macbeth, Othello and Richard II, and he had appeared in Laurence Olivier's films *Henry V*, *Hamlet* and *Richard III*. When he was asked who had been the greatest Hamlet of all time, he replied: 'Me, laddie, me!' Arnold Ridley, who had as a young man played rugby for Bath, had written more than 30 plays, most notably the internationally successful *The Ghost Train* in 1923; had appeared several times in the West End and films; had for more than 20 years played Doughy Hood in the long-running radio serial *The Archers*; and had just appeared in *Coronation Street* as Minnie Caldwell's ageing admirer Herbert Whittle.

Clive Dunn had been acting professionally for 30 years and specialised in playing old men, most recently Old Johnson in the TV series *Bootsie and Snudge*, even though he was still only 47. Jimmy Beck, too, had appeared in *Coronation Street*, but much more importantly had won rave reviews as a leading man in rep playing Archie Rice in *The Entertainer* – which earned him a letter of congratulation from Laurence Olivier – and Shylock in *The Merchant of Venice* at the Theatre Royal, York. 'Everyone thought he was the finest Shylock they had seen,' Webber was told by Caroline Dowdeswell, who had been the assistant stage manager at York. 'I remember sobbing my heart out during rehearsals as he gave a truly poignant performance.' During the long run of *Dad's Army* Beck also played the lead in *Staircase* at the Palace Theatre, Watford, and when Dunn and le Mesurier saw him in it both said he was quite as superb as Paul Scofield had been in the part. So Arthur was far from being the only excellent actor in the cast.

Nor was he the only one to have served during the Second World War. Beck, Pertwee and Lavender had all been too young, but le Mesurier had been an air-raid warden in Chelsea and had then served in India and reached the rank of captain, though it has to be admitted that when he joined the army he disconcerted his commanding officer by arriving in a taxi with a set of golf clubs. Laurie and Ridley had both been in the real Home Guard in the Second World War after suffering horribly during the First, when Laurie had served as an artilleryman in the trenches and was invalided out of the army after fighting at the Battle of the Somme. Ridley had also fought at the Somme and had been so badly wounded there in 1917 that subsequently his left arm was almost completely useless and he suffered blackouts for the rest of his life. Nonetheless, he joined up again in 1939 as a major, only to be invalided out with severe shell shock during the retreat from France in 1940. Dunn's Second World War experiences had been equally unpleasant: he had joined the 4th Queen's Own Hussars and fought in Greece before being captured and spending four years in Nazi labour camps in Austria, at one of which he and his fellow POWs had been forced to march naked for 10 miles and right through a village.

None of the cast had particularly high hopes of *Dad's Army*. 'I assumed that we might just make the grade as a minor situation comedy,' le Mesurier confessed in his autobiography. 'My own feeling was that a comedy about the Home Guard would be riveting only to those who had been in the Home Guard or one of the other branches of civil defence.' He also thought that it would not last very long because it had few women in it and no romance. Dunn feared that it was being broadcast too soon after another military TV series, *The Army Game*, and Laurie told Perry: 'It's a ridiculous idea.' Only Pertwee was optimistic: when the cast and writers met for the first read-through in a back room of the Feather's pub at Chiswick in March 1968 he approached Perry during the coffee break and said 'I think this series is going to be a winner'. Later he explained:

By lunchtime I was convinced that we were witnessing the birth of something quite special. All seven platoon members had been wonderfully cast, but it was the slightly hesitant character of Arthur's Captain Mainwaring that was the magic ingredient and was to become the lynchpin of the show. Just as the great American comedian Jack Benny seemed to make you watch him even when he was doing less than anyone else, so it was with Arthur Lowe in that little back room in Chiswick.

Arthur was himself enthusiastic about playing Mainwaring even if he did not think it would last very long. 'At a party just after he'd started *Dad's Army*,' Christopher Bond told me, 'he said "I've got this marvellous script about all these old chaps in the Home Guard" and off he went, he was doing Mainwaring and they hadn't even started recording. He had him right from the start.' Arthur knew precisely how to play Mainwaring because 'our minor civil service, banks and post offices are full of Mainwarings,' he said. 'He's jumped up. He thinks he's made it.' And no, he said, Mainwaring was *not* based on his own bank manager: 'I have a good bank manager. I'm bloody glad he's not like Mainwaring.'

David Croft believed that Mainwaring was quite different from Swindley but others felt they were closely related. 'Mainwaring grew out of Swindley,' Tony Warren told me, and Derek Granger said:

They had much in common. Arthur virtually played one character on television, this archetype of the little middle-class Englishman, the bank manager. *Dad's Army* was his apotheosis, when suddenly he got the part that summed up almost every aspect of himself as an actor and as a man. Mainwaring became Arthur and Arthur became Mainwaring. It happens quite a lot in acting, particularly in soaps and long-running series, that the actor and the part fuse together so that you can't tell one from another. Mainwaring was everything he actually wanted. When you look at *Dad's Army* now it's superb, so delicate and clever, and it has enormous charm, and that's what he wanted to be doing when he was doing *Pardon the Expression*. He wanted to be in something really refined and *Dad's Army* was superb and quite a serious work of art.

Jimmy Perry agreed that Lowe and Mainwaring melted into each other. 'He revelled in the part and as the years went by David and I wrote so intimately for him, taking in every little quirk of his personality, that the man and the character became one,' he wrote in the *Guardian*.

The first episode, 'The Man and the Hour' – which describes Mainwaring's formation of Walmington-on-Sea's Home Guard in the town's church hall in May 1940 – establishes immediately the delicious contrast between the pompous, uptight bank manager, Mainwaring ('he who holds Walmington-on-Sea holds this island') and his casual subordinate, Wilson. 'Get the first man in,' says Mainwaring, looking in his bank manager's suit and prissy little moustache exactly like the future Labour Prime Minister Clem Attlee. 'Oh, very well,' says Wilson. He glances through the door at the first volunteer, the lugubrious Scots undertaker, Frazer. 'Would you mind stepping this way, please?' he says. Mainwaring cannot believe what he has heard. 'Wilson, Wilson,' he says. 'Come here, come here. I intend to mould those men out there into an aggressive fighting unit. I'm going to lead them, command them and inspire them to be ruthless killers, and I'm not going to get very far if you invite them to step this way, am I? Quick march is the order.' Wilson is contrite. 'I'm very sorry, sir. Quick march,' he says. Frazer fixes him with a beady eye. 'There's no point,' he says in his rich Scots brogue. 'I'm already here.'

When the first rehearsals were held at St Nicholas's church hall in Bennett Street in West London, Croft and Perry were appalled by the cast's sloppiness. 'I wasn't very happy with the first series,' said Perry. 'I wanted the performances sharper. In my view there was too much "underwater" acting [where no one makes much effort].' At first Croft agreed and was particularly worried about Arthur's performance: 'He was mumbling a lot, not really playing the part at all. The cast made terrible mistakes during that first get-together, which was very concerning, but we needn't have worried, because everything turned out fine for the actual recording.'

The first location filming began in the wilds of Norfolk on 2 April 1968. Although Walmington-on-Sea was meant to be on the south coast near Folkestone the series was also supposed to depict the summer of 1940 and Croft needed somewhere with plenty of evergreen trees and shrubs, so his production assistant Harold Snoad persuaded the Ministry of Defence to allow most of the outdoor scenes to be filmed on the army's military practical training area a few miles from Thetford, at Stanford, a vast practice battle area with 68 firing ranges littered with military debris and shells, some of them possibly still live. 'It was an active army range,' another BBC production assistant, Bob Spiers, told Richard Webber for his *The Complete A-Z of Dad's Army*,

and sometimes we'd be having breakfast when suddenly soldiers with guns would emerge from the bushes and have a free cup of tea before vanishing into the bushes again. There was also one occasion when we were given half an hour to move location because jets were coming in for an air strike. But the army were always cooperative, and the space gave us the chance to do some crazy things.

The cast and crew were warned not to wander off across such dangerous countryside. On one occasion filming was suddenly disrupted when a young, face-blackened officer in full camouflage uniform emerged from the bushes and told Snoad that he had orders to blow up the place in 10 minutes. 'That's ridiculous,' boomed Arthur, 'absolutely ridiculous. What do they think we're doing here? Playing games?' After a frantic telephone call – *Don't panic, Mr Mainwaring! Don't panic!* – the army agreed not to blow up the place until the next day. The advantages of filming at Stanford were that the area was remote and completely empty of modern houses, vehicles and people that would look out of place in a series set in the 1940s, and it offered a huge variety of countryside – roads, woods, open fields, a church, old farm buildings and cottages, even a river and a bridge – that could be used in all sorts of scenes. Within easy reach were a town hall, railway station, cinema, pier, mill and sandpits, all of which would in due course be used for filming.

On April Fool's Day most of the cast and crew checked into one of three hotels in Thetford – the Bell, the Anchor and the Central – which were to become homes from home for the *Dad's Army* team whenever they returned to film location shots for all the subsequent series over the next 10 years. Arthur went up a day later by train and checked into the Bell. The first full day of filming was not encouraging. As the cast was bussed out to the location at 9 a.m., dressed in their costumes, it started to snow, which was unfortunate since the episode was meant to be taking place on a summer's day. While the disgruntled actors waited for the weather to clear they huddled in David Croft's Rolls-Royce, which was parked in a field. At about 11 a.m. it stopped snowing and Croft asked Perry to assemble the cast. Because it was Perry's first TV series he was understandably excited and keen to start, but he told Richard Webber that

many of the cast didn't seem to share my enormous, mad, eccentric enthusiasm. The windows of the Rolls were steamed up as I pulled open one of the doors. Everyone was sitting there looking bellicose, and I was given the most terrible glares. I told them we were ready to film in ten minutes, and Arthur replied: 'We'll come when we're ready.' I went back to David and told him they were on the way before adding: 'We've got a miserable lot of old sods here.' But overall, we didn't have much trouble on the set. Some would mutter and get a bit sullen, but nothing to worry about.

The weather improved, too. That day was one of only three or four in 10 years of *Dad's Army* location shooting that the weather was not wonderfully good, and fine conditions became known as 'Croft's weather'. On one of the rare bad days the light became so poor that filming had to be abandoned, but the next day the sun was out again. 'This is better, isn't it?' Croft grinned.

'I suppose God sent you an apology as well,' said Arthur.

The first series required only five days of location shooting, and the rest of the first episode was recorded back in the studio at the BBC Television Centre in front of an audience of about 320 people on 15 April. After editing, the first broadcast went out in black and white three months later, at 8.20 p.m. on Wednesday, 31 July 1968, preceded by Jimmy Perry's new but wonderfully evocative, 1940s-style signature tune, 'Who Do You

Think You Are Kidding, Mr Hitler?', which the legendary wartime singer and Crazy Gang comedian Bud Flanagan had recorded (for £105) with the Band of the Coldstream Guards in February a few weeks before he died:

> *Who do you think you're kidding, Mr Hitler,*
> *If you think we're on the run?*
> *We are the boys who will stop your little game.*
> *We are the boys who will make you think again.*
> *'Cause who do you think you're kidding, Mr Hitler,*
> *If you think old England's done?*
>
> *Mr Brown goes off to town on the 8.21*
> *But he comes home each evening and he's ready with his gun.*
> *So watch out, Mr Hitler, you have met your match in us*
> *If you think you can crush us we're afraid you've missed the bus.*
> *'Cause who do you think you're kidding, Mr Hitler,*
> *If you think old England's done?*

Some of the first reviewers were unimpressed. The *Sunday Telegraph* said that the first script was 'pretty feeble, with an over-reliance on strained little jokes', and Peter Black reported in the *Daily Mail* that 'the trouble with this is that it isn't situation comedy or character comedy, it's only gag comedy, the easiest to write and the quickest wearing on the ear'. Jimmy Perry told me:

> It had a very lukewarm response. We had an audience survey when the first pilot was made and 90 per cent of the audience didn't like it. One woman said 'We've had enough of this wartime stuff. Can't they give it a rest?' Another one said 'And that bald-headed old man Arthur Lowe doesn't even know his lines!' I was very much downcast then.

But Stanley Reynolds of the *Guardian* thought that the first episode was amusing, Nancy Banks-Smith of the *Sun* said it was 'a nice little thing', and Sean Day-Lewis reckoned in the *Daily Telegraph* that Perry and Croft showed 'a real gift for satire'. Several other reviewers spotted the quality of *Dad's Army* immediately and were positively ecstatic. Ron

Boyle wrote in the *Daily Express*: 'I cannot say I cracked a rib, split my sides or even raised a good hearty belly-laugh – but some instinct is still telling me that the BBC is about to come up with a classic comedy series … the possibilities are tremendous.' Peter Tinniswood proclaimed it 'a real winner' in the *Western Mail*, and Fergus Wood wrote in the Glasgow *Evening Times*: 'I'm sure *Dad's Army* will go marching into the top charts.' As for Arthur, the *Daily Mirror*'s Mary Malone thought he was superb, and Michael Billington wrote in *The Times*: 'The one solid pleasure last night was watching the performance of Arthur Lowe.'

The second episode was transmitted a week later. In 'Museum Piece' the Home Guard platoon is still waiting for its uniforms and is armed only with one shotgun, 15 carving knives, an assegai that Jones had picked up in the Sudan 50 years previously, and one golf club, so it decides to raid a local museum of historic weapons and steals a Chinese rocket gun that then explodes. And so the series slowly began to establish itself. Pike turns up for parade wearing a muffler, with a note from his worried mother about his delicate chest. The weapons and uniforms still have not arrived so a plan is hatched to turn the platoon into a cavalry troop equipped with circus horses and ancient muskets. The men arrest a soldier with a suspicious accent only to learn that he is a Polish ally. They capture two downed German pilots. Jones is forced to undergo an assault course test to see if he is too old even for the Home Guard. And in episode five the uniforms arrive at last.

When the first series came to an end some viewers objected that the programme should not poke unpatriotic fun at a brave body of men like the Home Guard, but otherwise the initial audience reports were generally favourable. People said that they liked *Dad's Army* because it was clean, gentle, family entertainment as well as well written, funny, sometimes touching, always wonderfully observant of human nature, and vividly evocative of the nostalgic sights, sounds and songs of a braver, simpler, more decent golden age when Britons had been proud to be British – of Britian's finest hour. It was not, however, at all certain that the BBC would commission a second series, nor was the cast unanimous about wanting to carry on. John Laurie was particularly unenthusiastic and told Perry and Croft that they were illiterate. 'I have played every major Shakespearean role in the theatre,' he thundered, 'and I'm considered the finest speaker of verse in the country, and I end up becoming famous doing this crap!' But the first series had attracted an average weekly audience of more than 8 million viewers – pretty good considering it had been broadcast during the summer months, when people were away on holiday or enjoying outdoor activities at 8.20 p.m. on a Wednesday rather than watching television – and eventually, in August, the BBC agreed to commission another six episodes. A month later BBC TV's chief publicity officer, Keith Smith, sent Croft a note that said: 'There has been no comedy series in the last twelve months which has attracted anywhere near the number of reviews *Dad's Army* has. Nor has any series received this kind of universal praise.'

Early in October 1968 the whole *Dad's Army* circus moved up to Thetford again to film the location shots for the second series, and what was to become a regular trek to Norfolk once or twice a year began to establish a definite pattern. In the later series each batch of location shots would usually take a fortnight to film in and around Thetford, and wives joined the cast and crew for several days at a time at the Bell and the Anchor, where the atmosphere came to resemble a jolly party. 'It was like a summer school or a big family picnic,' said Ian Lavender. John le Mesurier 'likened it to going on holiday with the Boys' Club,' his widow Joan told Richard Webber. 'I went along quite often and the atmosphere was wonderful.' But 'normally the men preferred to be alone together,' she admitted in her autobiography *Lady Don't Fall Backwards*. 'It was like a rather exclusive club: everyone got on well together, genuinely admired each other's talent, and they all made each other laugh a lot.' The cast was 'in a high state of excitement like children going off to the seaside rather than work', she wrote in her book *Dear John*. 'It was rather like being in a gang, and we know how lads can be when they egg each other on.' Joan Lowe became a regular at these gatherings, and she and Arthur relished those weeks on location every year. They had always liked staying in hotels, although Arthur was renowned for this pernicketiness with waiters and receptionists and always carried in his jacket pocket a key with which he bled the air out of the radiators in their room as soon as they checked in. Stephen recalled him enquiring of one seaside hotel receptionist: 'Our room commands the most spectacular view of the service well. Do you have one which merely overlooks the sea?' He told another: 'I didn't sleep so well. I believe we are next to the rooms of ill repute.'

It was now that Arthur started to eat more than was good for him and to build the memorable paunch that was to round out his later years. 'He loved his grub,' Perry told Webber.

He'd have a full English breakfast, wade through bacon and sausage sandwiches at the 11 o'clock break, followed by a full lunch. For afternoon tea it would be Mr Kipling cakes and cucumber sandwiches. And back at the hotel he enjoyed browsing through the pile of menus to select his evening meal.

What was more, the cakes had to be Mr Kipling's; none other would do. He was in fact a creature of firm habits. He and Joan would smoke only Craven A cigarettes and he would complain loudly if the early morning tea-boy at the Bell put two tea-bags rather than just one in his pot: he insisted on weak tea and strong coffee. In the restaurant he was notoriously finicky and would quiz the waiter closely as to whether individual items of food were fresh or exactly how his meal would be cooked. Bill Pertwee, perfectly mimicking Arthur's deep, resonant, W. C. Fields tones (as did almost everyone to whom I spoke), remembered him asking a waiter: 'Is the kipper *whole*, or filleted? Is the ham off the *bo-o-o-ne* this morning? I don't want any of that plastic stuff out of a tin – and make sure the toast isn't burnt.' Stephen remembered his father enquiring suspiciously: 'I see you have kippers on the menu. Tell me, are they boil-in-the-bag or are they real' – waggling his hand – '*swim-about* kippers?' And at lunch he might ask in pretentious French for a *jambon* sandwich, which he pronounced 'jam bonne'. Not surprisingly he suffered terrible constipation and was often late for the daily 9 a.m. bus to the location. Perry told Webber:

He'd come out of the hotel doing up his belt, and breathing heavily, saying: 'These early mornings play havoc with my lavatorial arrangements.' I told him to eat bran for breakfast. He replied: 'Oh, I wouldn't take that muck, it's like mattress stuffing.' So I bought a packet and gave it to Arthur. About four days later he came out on time, and said: 'Eating bran has changed my life!'

'The drive out from the hotel early on those summer mornings is something I shall never forget,' said Pertwee in his autobiography.

The first picture of one of the most photographed actors ever: baby Arthur Lowe, just a few months old, at his parents' tiny terraced house at 112 Hemmons Road, Levenshulme, Manchester, in 1916.

Twenty-one-year-old Arthur in 1936 in the little feudal village where he was born: Hayfield in Derbyshire. Already he was wearing glasses, and five years previously his poor eyesight had cost him his boyhood dream of joining the merchant navy when he failed the Board of Trade eye test.

Arthur Lowe in the Duke of Lancaster's Own Yeomanry in 1939 with his army pony, Daisy. He had joined 'The Dukes' a year earlier, but as an old-fashioned cavalry regiment it was absurdly out of date, and Arthur's war was to be as farcical as anything that the scriptwriters would dream up for *Dad's Army*.

Arthur (second from the left in the back row), now a 24-year-old Bombardier and already going bald, with army comrades at Pembroke Dock in South Wales in 1940.

The poster advertising Arthur's first adult stage appearance, in a play performed by the amateur dramatics club that he formed with seven army comrades in the Palestine desert, at Rafah, when he was a corporal in January 1943.

Twenty-nine-year-old Sergeant-Major Lowe (centre, with spectacles) discusses a script with Captain Martin Benson in the wartime theatre that they set up together in Alexandria, Egypt, in 1944. On the left are two of the many young women, some of them in the forces, who helped with the theatre.

The love affair that lasted 36 years: Arthur and his fey, fragile young wife, the actress Joan Cooper, who saved him from being sacked after just a couple of weeks with his first professional theatrical company. On the front of her photograph she wrote 'All my love, darling Arthur' and on the back the inscription (below left): 'To my first and last love my own beloved Arthur. Joanie.'

To my first & last love my own beloved Arthur. Joanie

Arthur (cross-legged on the floor) and Joan (front row, fourth from the right) in 1947 with the rest of Derek Salberg's repertory company in Hereford. Several of the cast became the Lowes' lifelong friends: Christopher Bond (back row, third from left), Helen Uttley (back row, third from right), Richard Leech (back row, far right) and Peggy Bond (front row, second from right).

PRINCES

THEATRE · SHAFTESBURY AVENUE

JACK HYLTON

presents

the Bewitching Musical

"PAL JOEY" 6D.

Music by
RICHARD
RODGERS

Lyrics by
LORENZ
HART

Book by
JOHN
O'HARA

PROGRAMME

IN 1952 "PAL JOEY" WON THE NEW YORK CRITICS' CIRCLE AWARD FOR THE BEST MUSICAL OF THE YEAR

PAL JOEY

Cast in order of appearance :

Joey	RICHARD FRANCE
Mike	ARTHUR LOWE
Kid	MAUREEN CREIGH
Gladys	JEAN BRAMPTON
Adele	DIANA DAUBENEY
Sandra	BABS WARDEN
Gloria	ANN LYDEKKER
Dottie	JOANNA RIGBY
Dolores	LEANDER FEDDEN
Francine	SYLVIA RUSSELL
Linda	SALLY BAZELY
Vera Simpson	CAROL BRUCE
Valerie	VERA DAY
Escort	CALVIN VON REINHOLD
Amarilla	CAROL MONK
Agnes	JEAN ALLISON
Ernest	ERNST ULMAN
Victor	MALCOLM GODDARD
Delivery Boy	LIONEL BLAIR
Louis (the Tenor)	FREDERICK JAMES
Doorman	BILLY PETCH
Ludlow Lowell	LOU JACOBI
Melba	OLGA LOWE
O'Brien	SEAN O'FARRELL

DANCERS : Jean Allison, Maureen Creigh, Diana Daubeney, Patricia Ellis, Sheila Falconer, Leander Fedden, Gillian Low, Ann Lydekker, Sylvia Lynd, Carol Monk, Mary Reynolds, Joanna Rigby, Sylvia Russell, Babs Warden, Joan Wilshire, Bob Chandler, James Craigie, James Dark, Alexander Morrow, Billy Petch, Steven Shore.

Arthur's first big West End breaks came in three lavish American musicals in which he sang and hoofed it with the best of them: *Call Me Madam* in 1952, *Pal Joey* in 1954 and *The Pajama Game* in 1955. *Pal Joey* ran in London for seven months.

Arthur and Joan taking tea on the roof terrace of the converted granary in Pavilion Road, Chelsea, London, where they lived from 1958 to 1970.

Arthur and Joan's five-year-old, sailor-suited son Stephen with Honor Blackman in the 1959 film *A Night to Remember*, which was based on Walter Lord's book about the sinking of the *Titanic* and starred Kenneth More as the First Officer.

Arthur (far left) finally made the breakthrough to TV stardom in 1961, at the late age of 46, when he played a pompous northern haberdasher and lay preacher, Leonard Swindley, in the new twice-weekly soap opera *Coronation Street*.

In the best of all Arthur's *Coronation Street* episodes his nervy, strait-laced business partner, the spinster Emily Nugent, played by Eileen Derbyshire, invited him to dinner and nervously proposed to him in a scene of memorable poignancy.

Opposite:
The third great love of Arthur's life, after Joan and the theatre, was this 83-year-old wooden Victorian steam yacht that he bought in 1968, the *Amazon*.

Arthur, Joan and Stephen with their beloved 1948 Daimler, Henry, in the early 1960s. Arthur knew nothing about cars and spent almost as much time under the bonnet as in the driving seat.

Although Arthur was best known for his parts on television, he was also acclaimed for his numerous appearances on stage even at the height of his TV fame. In 1967 he won rave reviews for his parts in two bawdy, rollicking Restoration comedies: *The Soldier's Fortune* and *Lock Up Your Daughters* (right).

Right: Consummate actor that he was, Arthur always insisted on dressing for the part and would strut proudly around the deck wearing this ginger suede cap and playing to perfection the part of the gnarled old sea salt dreaming of distant horizons.

Below decks the *Amazon* had a stateroom, saloon, galley, captain's suite, dressing room and bathroom, and she was gradually fitted out with teak panelling, a Victorian fireplace, central heating, a Rayburn solid fuel stove, mahogany lavatory seats and even a harmonium, which Joan would play in the evenings while Arthur sang.

The magnificent seven in full flight: the much-loved stars of the phenomenally successful TV series *Dad's Army*. From the left: Clive Dunn (Corporal Jones), Jimmy Beck (Private Walker), John le Mesurier (Sergeant Wilson), Arthur Lowe (Captain Mainwaring), John Laurie (Private Frazer), Ian Lavender (Private Pike) and Arnold Ridley (Private Godfrey).

'Don't panic, Mr Mainwaring!' Arthur as Captain Mainwaring and Clive Dunn as Corporal Jones on the roof of a runaway railway carriage in an episode of *Dad's Army* that was first screened in 1973: 'The Royal Train', in which the Walmington-on-Sea platoon is ordered to form a guard of honour as King George VI's train rattles by.

Above: Arthur (left) as bank manager Mainwaring with his deputy Arthur Wilson (John le Mesurier) and the spiv Joe Walker (Jimmy Beck) in a very early episode of *Dad's Army*, 'Command Decision', broadcast in 1968. Their Home Guard uniforms and weapons have not yet arrived, so they are wearing armbands marked LDV: Local Defence Volunteers, though jokers claimed that the letters stood for 'Look, Duck and Vanish'.

The indomitable *Dad's Army* British bulldog spirit of 1940: bank manager George Mainwaring defiant and armed to the teeth. As Bud Flanagan sang in the series' theme song: 'Mr Brown goes off to town on the 8.21, but he comes home each evening and he's ready with his gun. So watch out, Mr Hitler, you have met your match in us...'

Arthur and the other *Dad's Army* stars are introduced to Queen Elizabeth II by the impresario Bernard Delfont after a Royal Variety Performance at the London Palladium in 1975 when the Queen and Prince Philip had been entertained by more than 300 performers.

Arthur with his and Joan's son Stephen in the 1970s. Theirs was always a difficult relationship, mainly because Arthur was so obsessed by his work, the theatre and Joan that he seemed to have little time to spare for Stephen.

Arthur with 83-year-old J. B. Priestley, the author of the stage play *Laburnum Grove*, an old-fashioned 1930s comedy in which Arthur and Joan appeared together in 1977 and which they took on tour.

Arthur loved playing Shakespeare on stage and scored a memorable triumph as Stephano in Peter Hall's production of *The Tempest* with Sir John Gielgud in 1974. But not everything that Arthur touched turned to gold. When he played Dogberry (above) in a BBC TV recording of *Much Ado About Nothing* with Penelope Keith in 1978 the programme was eventually 'considered unsuitable' by the powers-that-were and was never transmitted.

Arthur appeared in many cinema films but never made the big Hollywood breakthrough of which he dreamed. But one film that he enjoyed especially was *The Lady Vanishes*, in which he and Ian Carmichael (above) played two cricket-mad old English buffers aboard a train in Nazi Germany as Europe teetered on the brink of the Second World War.

Cambridge Arts Theatre

Founded by Lord Keynes in 1936   Manager and Licensee: Andrew R. Blackwood
Box Office (Telephone 352000)   Open Mondays to Friday 11am to 8pm   Saturdays 10.00am to 8pm
MON. 13 APRIL to SAT. 18 APRIL   Monday to Friday 8.0   Saturday 4.30 & 8.15
Prices: Monday to Friday Eves. & Saturday Mat. £4, £3.30, £2.50   Saturday Eves. £4.25, £3.65, £3
all prices include VAT   All Seats bookable in advance

NEWPALM PRODUCTIONS present

ARTHUR LOWE

IN

Beyond A Joke

DEREK BENFIELD'S LATEST
SMASH HIT COMEDY

with

JOAN COOPER   ISABEL METLISS   VYVIAN HALL
RODNEY COTTAM   MICHAEL BEVIS   PEGGY ASHBY

and DEBORAH WATLING

DIRECTED BY
VYVIAN HALL

Arthur Lowe of televisions 'Potter', 'Bless Me Father' and 'Dads Army' stars in this very funny new comedy
"Ideal holiday entertainment for all the family"

Right: To bolster Joan's career Arthur formed their own little repertory company in 1979 so that they could control every aspect of the plays they took on tour, and they persuaded their old friend Christopher Bond to direct their first play for them, *Beyond a Joke*.

In September 1981, at Box Hill School in Surrey, Arthur recorded six episodes of his final television series, *A. J. Wentworth, B.A.*, in which he played a bumbling old 1940s prep-school master whose pupils run rings around him. Sadly the series was not nearly as funny as the hilarious book by H. F. Ellis on which it was based.

In love right to the very end: Arthur's fond glance at Joan says it all. They had been devoted to each other for 32 years, and when he collapsed in his dressing room at the Alexandra Theatre in Birmingham and died in April 1982 she struggled on but was eventually inconsolable.

The roads were almost empty, and … the coach had to avoid pheasants running out of the woods and dashing hither and thither across its path … The journey would probably only take half an hour or less, but in that time it seemed reminiscent of naughty schoolboys going on an outing. It was the start of a day out for the *Dad's Army* Club.

In the evenings Arthur followed a rigid routine if the cast was back at the hotel in time. At six he and Joan would bathe and at 7.30 he would order drinks to be sent up to the room: two *large* gins in *big* glasses, a slice of *cucumber* in each, two bottles of *unpoured* tonic water, and a *separate* dish of ice. Hapless waiters invariably got one or more of these careful instructions wrong and a great deal of sighing, rumbling, muttering and reordering would ensue. Later the Lowes would have a second double gin each in the bar before going in to dinner, where Joan would eat almost nothing but would knock back a glass of white wine with the starter, and they would share a bottle of red with the main course. As she became increasingly drunk through dinner she would chatter away while Arthur nodded and grunted. After dinner they would have a couple of liqueurs: perhaps an Armagnac for him, maybe an Amoretti for Joan, who was by now so drunk that she had to be helped to bed. 'Unconsummated love would slip into self-pity,' wrote Stephen in his book,

and she would crash perhaps on the bed, perhaps on the floor. Arthur would undress her and get her into bed. Then he would get room service to bring up a cold beer, and he would sit on the side of the bed in his vest unable himself to find sleep. They followed this routine for many years.

In Thetford the routine at night was sometimes different: after dinner, at about 10.30 p.m., the cast would repair to the town's little cinema after the end of the public performance to watch the latest rough-cut rushes that had been filmed two to three days previously and printed in London. Arthur would generally fall asleep but back at the hotel, even if it was nearly midnight, he was always thirsty enough for a nightcap.

At first he was as standoffish as ever and in London 'he used to disappear straight after rehearsals,' Caroline Dowdeswell told Webber. 'I can't remember him ever going to the bar with the rest of us.' Perry told me that because he and Arthur had appeared in hundreds of plays in rep they would often discuss the parts they had played and they became 'very good friends even though he was seven years older than me. But I knew very little about him. Arthur was a very warm, kind man, but I knew nothing about his private life.' Pertwee found it very difficult to get to know Arthur at first – 'he had that thing "until I get to know you I don't want to know you" ' – and Joan le Mesurier told me: 'He was very witty, very dry, and always made me laugh, and he was endearing, but I was in awe of him. He was very much the star, the leader of the pack.' Lavender had trouble getting to know him too, but in his case that was understandable since he was 30 years younger than Arthur:

He did assume leadership, a role of authority, and he *was* the leading man, and he frightened a lot of people because he was a star. He could sit and read his script and ignore you, and it took two or three years for him to decide that he liked me and wanted to be a friend, but we didn't live in each other's pockets. None of us did. We worked together for 10 weeks a year and saw each other two or three times a year, and that was it. But I liked him enormously, I really did. Yes, he and Joan sometimes ate separately in the evenings, and it did upset some people, but then we'd been in each other's pockets all day filming.

In due course, as the cast and crew lived and worked together, Arthur was more sociable and even invited a few back to Pavilion Road for drinks or dinner when they were in London. Working on *Dad's Army*, Joan Lowe told Pertwee years later, 'gave us the happiest years of our life together. To be a part of that wonderful family of actors was a great delight.' Eventually Arthur became not only the acknowledged leader of the squad, both on screen and off, but also its jovial musical director: if there was a delay in filming the platoon would start a sing-song and he would conduct. He was also notably kind and considerate towards younger actors like Rose Hill and Don Estelle (later Lofty in the TV series *It Ain't Half Hot, Mum*), and when he noticed that Ian Lavender had very little to do during the first series he advised him to stand close to him so that he was on screen as much as possible.

The other actors, however, became increasingly irritated that Arthur never read his script until the last moment and continually failed to learn his lines properly. He refused to take his script home. 'Certainly not,' he told Croft. 'I'm not having any rubbish like that in my house.' The result was that Arthur would often suddenly paraphrase his lines. 'This kept everyone on their toes in case they had to rephrase their lines in order for them to make sense,' said Croft. 'I suppose that this accounted for some of the wonderful spontaneity of their playing.' Harold Snoad, who was Croft's right-hand production man for six years and directed six of the episodes, told me he had finally had enough:

> When Arthur came in not knowing his lines other people decided they wouldn't bother either, so we had a lot of fluffs during recordings. There were so many retakes that one day I announced to the cast: 'Listen, folks, I've just had a nightmare experience editing this and I have to say you don't know this stuff. You've really got to get down and learn it.' There was a stunned silence and David and Jimmy both said to me later that I was the only person brave enough to tell them they ought to get their finger out. Arthur came up to me afterwards and said 'A very brave thing to say, Harold', and I said 'Well, it's true', and he said 'Well, I suppose there is a degree of truth in that, yes, mmm', and it did get a lot better.

Some found Arthur's behaviour especially irritating because he was notoriously intolerant of anyone else's unprofessionalism. 'Bobby and Chuck, two wonderfully funny props men who had worked with everybody in the business, nicknamed Arthur "Kitty" because he was always a bit fussy,' Joan le Mesurier told me. 'Chuck was short, fat and very Cockney, effing and blinding all over the place, and one day he said to John: "D'you know, in one day I've had more fucking trouble with Kitty than I had with Charlton Heston in the whole of *El Cid*."' Arthur's fussiness became legendary. 'His clothes were always spot on,' said Stephen. 'His desk was organised to the nearest millimetre. Dinner always had to be at 8 p.m., never 7.59 p.m. or 8.01 p.m., or he'd get very cross.' And he always carried a pair of nail clippers in his pocket.

Not surprisingly Arthur could not abide John le Mesurier's air of utter disorganisation and dishevelled helplessness, and was annoyed by the amount of attention it attracted from the girls in the wardrobe department, who fought a constant skirmish to keep le Mez looking soldierly. 'I could never find a make-up girl to powder me down, as they were all fussing over John,' Caroline Dowdeswell, who played Mainwaring's bank cashier, told Webber.

> He always seemed to have about three of them around him: one doing his hair, one giving him a manicure and another running errands or getting him a sandwich. He was always so languid and would call everyone 'dear lady' in a world-wearied drawl while they fell over themselves fetching and carrying for him.

Harold Snoad once told le Mesurier that his watch had stopped 'and he said "Oh yes, could you wind it up for me?" He was *totally* impractical.' The make-up girls did not make a fuss over Arthur, perhaps because he was rarely at ease with women and refused even to let them wash his hair, insisting that Joan should do it. He was also puritanical about anything that might be considered vulgar or sexually suggestive. The oldest and gentlest member of the cast, Arnold Ridley, sometimes startled the girls in the crew by telling unexpectedly risqué jokes, but Arthur, 20 years younger, 'was quite prim sexually,' said Snoad. 'He never made any risqué comments or flirted with the girls, or said of anyone "She's rather pretty." He never had the normal male wandering eye. Eventually the same applied to his relationship with Joan, which seemed to lose some of its sparkle.' Snoad's wife, Jean, agreed. 'Arthur wasn't at all sexy,' she said. 'There was no chemistry at all. But Joan was quite sexy and she loved a dirty joke.' Joan le Mesurier told me: 'It wouldn't surprise me if Joan was very highly sexed and Arthur wasn't. He wasn't sexy at all, and not just because he was fat. Hancock was rotund and I fancied Hancock, but he was very sexy, whereas Arthur didn't have any sex appeal and never flirted with women.' Even Pam Cundell, who came as close to Arthur as any woman except Joan – 'because', she said, 'I was jolly and made him laugh' – admitted to me that he had no sex appeal at all:

> They really adored each other but it wasn't a sexy marriage. She looked after him but I can't say they ever kissed and cuddled. Arthur wouldn't have wanted to do that. I used to put my arms around him and cuddle him, but he never cuddled back. He would never have had another girlfriend. Never. But Joan loved dirty jokes and naughty stories and shrieked with laughter, and when she laughed it was a really deep-throated laugh.

Pertwee believed that Arthur derived more pleasure from acting than from sex. 'That might have explained Joan's drinking,' he told me.

Arthur could be quite prim, but Joan liked a saucy story and she had a dirty smoker's/drinker's laugh. I think that Arthur had not had much of a spark in his private life and he got his spark from turning in a good performance and getting a good notice. But Joan would always put her arm in his if they were walking up the street, and in the hotel at night he would touch her hand and say 'All right, sweetheart?'

Lavender, on the other hand, suspected that

it was a sexy marriage and they had great fun. When Arthur wasn't working, for instance, he'd spend Thursdays in bed. Joanie said he should have one day a week in bed, so he did, and she brought him breakfast and lunch and then joined him in bed in the afternoon. It sounds very sexy. And one night we were all sitting around in the lounge in the hotel in Thetford and eventually Arthur and Joan went off to bed. First they went one way and then they returned two minutes later – '*goodnight, good-night*' – this tiny 60-year-old couple going off to bed, Arthur about 5'7" tall, Joanie even smaller, and they were carrying a rose bush, two open bottles of Guinness and a length of hosepipe! '*Goodnight, goodnight.*' Gawd knows what the hosepipe was for! But I can't believe they had anything but fun together, whatever they were doing.

On screen, though, Arthur shunned the merest hint of sexual impropriety and refused even to be filmed marching in longjohn under-wear, as the rest of the platoon did when they filmed the *Dad's Army* movie in 1970, let alone having a bomb down his trousers while John Laurie groped around for it, as one script demanded in the sixth TV series. 'He'd had that script for several weeks but didn't actually mention his objection until the day of filming,' said Snoad. 'That was a bit unprofessional.' Arthur felt so strongly about it that he insisted on having it written into his contract that he would never again be asked to remove his trousers or to have bombs thrust down them.

But his acting was always so superb that they forgave him everything. 'He was one of the greatest comedy actors of our time,' said Perry, and

Croft explained it by saying that he was so good because he never made a conscious effort to be funny, 'which is death to comedy'. 'He was a brilliant comic actor,' said Ian Lavender. 'What he left unsaid made you laugh.' And Jean Snoad told me:

> Arthur instilled respect, not fear. With some actors the whole production team is in a state of trepidation in case they upset them or the make-up or wardrobe isn't right, because he or she will go ballistic, but there was never that with Arthur. The team respected him and wanted to do the right thing. He would never have a whipping boy, like some actors. One member of the BBC crew, Des Stewart, once took his nine-year-old son to watch the filming of an episode at Thetford, and the boy made the mistake of suddenly saying 'It's raining' just as Arthur was speaking to camera. Arthur was understandably annoyed by the interruption, but when the boy started crying Arthur walked over to him, ruffled his hair and said 'Don't cry, lad. It's only a film. We would have had to do it again anyway as there are spots of rain on the camera lens.' Said the boy's father: 'I always thought of him as a rather grumpy fellow. How wrong I was.'

Arthur's acting was particularly outstanding in his scenes with le Mesurier, but they never became close friends. Although they both loved drinking, jazz and cricket – le Mez was an excellent jazz pianist and had played cricket for Suffolk – 'John was very witty and sophisticated, and used to laugh at Arthur behind his back,' Clive Dunn told me. In turn Arthur disapproved of le Mesurier's apparently lazy style of acting and resented the fact that le Mez was at first paid more than he was. 'He used to think that John was not acting but purely behaving like John le Mesurier, which of course he was,' Pertwee told me. 'John was a personality actor, like some of the Americans. Gary Grant always played Cary Grant and John always played John, whereas Arthur liked to get under the skin of a character.' He also disapproved of le Mesurier's untidy, disorganised bohemian private life. 'John used to go to Ronnie Scott's jazz club until five o'clock in the morning but was always on set at 9 a.m., word perfect,' Pertwee told me. 'This irritated Arthur immensely and he would growl "What's the game?"' Well, the game was that when it came to learning a script le Mez had a photographic memory despite his heavy drinking. On one rare occasion he forgot one of his lines but said to the stage manager, 'Don't tell me. It's at the top of the next page, after the bit in capital letters.' Le Mesurier had also been married three times and his third wife, Joan, who came from a circus and fairground family, had just had a wild, adulterous affair with Tony Hancock. Le Mesurier and Arthur 'were not soul mates and would not naturally spend time together', Lavender told me. Yet together on screen they were magic. Even Croft and Perry 'could be surprised by Arthur's extra lift of the eyebrow or movement of the hand that had not been there at a previous run-through,' wrote Pertwee in his book *Dad's Army: The Making of a Television Legend*. 'He was, you see, a natural humorist, not a manufactured actor.' And it was during rehearsals for this series that Arthur suddenly called Lavender 'you stupid boy' even though it was not in the script. Croft pounced on it. 'We'll keep that in,' he said.

'As I got to know Arthur more it became obvious that Mainwaring had been waiting for him and he for Mainwaring,' said Pertwee. 'The two fitted like a split screen merging into one.' Arthur constantly denied that he and Mainwaring were similar characters, but David Croft told Graham McCann for his book *Dad's Army*: 'Arthur was *enormously* like Mainwaring. No doubt about it at all. And Jimmy and I took all kinds of things from his own personality and wrote them into the part. Somehow he never seemed to notice.' And Pam Cundell, who played Mrs Fox, Jones's girlfriend and ultimately his wife, and became a close friend of the Lowes, told me: 'He was a pompous little man and he got more pompous as *Dad's Army* went on, because he got to believe that he *was* Captain Mainwaring, but he was kind and sweet and I loved him to death.' Mainwaring 'probably *was* closest to his own nature and he found it very easy,' said Christopher Bond, and Harold Snoad told me: 'There *were* shades of Mainwaring's pomposity in Arthur. On the first day's location filming he was boarding the coach and one or two of the extras said "Morning, Arthur" and he sat down alongside me and said "Arthur? That'll have to change." But he might have been semi-joking.' Ian Lavender was convinced that Arthur was joking and that his pomposity was put on for effect.

Yes, he *was* Mainwaring, essentially, but whereas Mainwaring's pompous balloon was burst by the characters around him in the show,

Arthur tended to burst his own bubble, but you wouldn't know that until he had decided to let you in as a friend. If he and Joanie were coming round to us in Wandsworth for supper, for instance, he'd say 'Ah, we'll bring the wine' just to make sure that they got good wine, knowing that we couldn't afford it. Are you going to call that pompous? I'm not. He only wanted to drink good wine and we couldn't afford it, so fine. He enjoyed playing at being a pompous little man: it got him a long way, just as John le Mesurier got a long way socially and sexually by being vague and helpless. John played at being fey, Arthur at being pompous. He was partly sending himself up.

Bond agreed. 'He played the pompous idiot quite a lot of the time in real life,' he said, 'but I think he was sending himself up. A lot of people were taken in by this and thought that's what he was really like.' In 1998 Lavender explained to the *Daily Mail*:

In a way we weren't actors. I think one of the reasons why *Dad's Army* made such an impression was that in a way we all played ourselves. If you look at the very earliest scripts, you'll see they are very different to the ones that followed. The reason was that the scriptwriters had got to know all of the actors and they started to write the scripts around our personalities.

There were certainly times when it was difficult to tell Arthur and Mainwaring apart. Arthur's beloved Daimler, Henry, for instance, had a strange gearbox that allowed it to drive off without anyone at the wheel, and Arthur could not resist showing it off. In a car park one day he started Henry's engine, put the lever into first gear, closed the car door, and watched proudly as it started to move slowly away. But then he could not open the car door to stop it, and as Henry picked up speed across the car park he chased after it – *Don't panic, Mr Mainwaring! Don't panic!* – in vain. It crashed into a brick wall. Other incidents could have come straight from a *Dad's Army* script. Pertwee said that Arthur stopped the car one day at the side of the road to relieve himself into a ditch by a telegraph pole but slipped and ended up hanging from the pole by his braces: 'It was hysterical.' Dunn claimed in one of his books that Arthur was driving out in the country when he ran over a cockerel and killed it.

Gentlemanly as ever, he took the dead fowl to a nearby farmhouse and told the farmer that he would like to replace the cockerel. 'Please yourself,' shrugged the farmer. 'The hens are round the back.'

Arthur had few close friends but got on well with most of the cast and crew, especially Pertwee and Lavender, though Laurie thought he was ridiculously pompous. One problem was that like a typical Derbyshire countryman he was notoriously tight-fisted. 'He could be slightly frugal,' said Snoad. 'Well, yes, mean.' Jimmy Beck's widow, Kay, was very fond of Arthur and Joan but admitted to me:

> He was always very careful with money. During one cocktail party at their flat in London they gave us avocados and he let us all know he'd got them at a special price. And he hated waste. Jimmy loved light and used to leave all the lights on in our house, but even there Arthur would go round turning them all off. If he invited us out for dinner he'd always carefully divide the bill exactly into two afterwards, even though *he'd* invited *us*!

Richard Leech disagreed: 'He wasn't mean. He was very generous and gave wonderful parties, but they said he was mean because sometimes he used to take a packed lunch when he went on location and people said "Look, the old bugger's even too mean to go and buy some lunch." '

The closest friendships in the cast were those between le Mesurier, Dunn and Beck – their wives also became good friends and the six would regularly meet for dinner – and the three men and Pertwee would often drive off for dinner on their own to the Bull at Barton Mills or the Angel Hotel in Bury St Edmunds. Le Mesurier and Beck were heavy boozers and would often sit up drinking together for half the night and sometimes misbehave. One night le Mesurier met an old colonel friend from his army days in the hotel bar and when it closed invited him, Beck and a couple of make-up girls up to his room for a few more snifters. Pertwee decided to surprise them well after midnight by bursting into le Mesurier's room naked except for his air-raid warden's boots and white helmet. Beck slipped out of the room and slammed Pertwee's door, locking him out naked in the corridor. 'We all became rather hysterical,' Pertwee recalled.

> The one worry now was that Arthur Lowe, whose room was just down the corridor, would come out and see what was going on at one o'clock

in the morning, so I hid in a broom cupboard for several minutes until John and Jimmy had telephoned reception to get a pass key from the night porter. When the porter came up Jimmy said to him, 'The warden has just been visiting the vicar.'

Not surprisingly Jimmy Beck sometimes arrived on the set the next morning late and with a crashing hangover, though le Mesurier was less affected. Dunn was with him one New Year's Eve in Trafalgar Square when le Mez asked a policeman where he might find Alcoholics Anonymous. 'Why?' asked the bobby. 'Do you want to join?' 'No,' said le Mesurier, 'I want to resign.'

Another warm friendship was forged between Laurie and Lavender, despite the 49-year difference in their ages. In *Dad's Army* Arthur was always calling Lavender 'you stupid boy!' but in fact Lavender was highly intelligent and he and Laurie would compete with each other and Joan Lowe to finish *The Times* crossword first every morning. The notoriously caustic and eccentric Laurie was often condescending about Arnold Ridley and would say of him 'Poor old boy, look at him, he's falling apart', even though Ridley was only a year older than he. One day when Croft was leaning into a car and shaking Ridley's hand Laurie cried excitedly: 'Look, they're pumping him up! They're pumping him up!' Ridley himself was often irritated by the inevitable delays of filming and would walk up and down muttering: 'Come on, come on, get on with it!' But Pertwee was friendly with everyone and would often defuse any threat of friction between the others by cracking a joke. 'The bottom line is that they were a marvellous bunch of pros that you don't get today,' Jimmy Perry told me. 'There was no sort of volatile animosity between anybody.'

That was not in fact strictly true. 'People said that John Laurie hated Arthur,' Lavender told me, 'but John hated *everybody* at one moment or another.' And Arthur himself was not exactly fond of Dunn and disapproved strongly of Dunn's socialist views, his fund-raising work for the Labour Party and his friendship with the Prime Minister, Harold Wilson. Dunn in turn was offended by some of what he called Arthur's 'totally outrageous' right-wing opinions. 'As an actor I'd give him 10 out of 10 in his field,' Dunn told me,

but he was a bit pompous and a bit of a prude – he wouldn't even take his tie off – and I was never on intimate terms with him. When the dustmen's strike was on Arthur said 'They should run over a few of them, that would teach them a lesson.' But you couldn't tell whether he meant it or whether it was a comedy line.

It would obviously be wrong to take everything that Arthur said at face value since his dry, throwaway remarks were often meant to be witty rather than serious. On one occasion, for instance, Pertwee remarked that London was becoming a bit rough and violent and Arthur replied: 'Yes, I'd round them all up and put them on a raft and float them out to sea.'

'What would they eat?' asked Pertwee.

'They can eat each other,' said Arthur.

'Those sort of things were said to make us laugh,' Pertwee told me.

Bill Harman, a young, idealistic assistant floor manager, reckoned that Arthur was 'somewhat right of Genghis Khan [and] a big fan of Enoch Powell, and claimed to be a prominent contributor to the fund set up to promote Powell into the PM's job'. Harman was appalled during the dustmen's strike to hear Arthur remark: 'I want to open my morning paper and see "Forty dustmen shot this morning". Then we'll get this country moving!' Arthur saw that Harman was shocked. 'Do you know what the eighth deadly sin is?' he asked. 'Tolerance.' But 'I could see a twinkle in his eye as he said it', reported Harman. Arthur was 'obviously tickled at the reaction his statements provoked'. Perhaps, like the Lewis Carroll little boy, he did it only to annoy.

On another occasion, when there was not enough rehearsal rooms at the BBC Television Centre and the *Dad's Army* cast had to use a building across the road where London Transport trained their budding bus conductors, Arthur had to find a lavatory by pushing his way through a canteen crammed with 70 or 80 jolly West Indians. Of course they recognised him, called out 'You stupid boy!' and 'Don't panic, Mr Mainwaring!', patted him on the back, jostled him, and asked for autographs. Hot and flustered, he finally struggled back through the crowd and slammed the door behind him. 'Fucking cannibals!' he rumbled. As a joke, surely. 'Arthur was not exactly a racist,' Dunn told me, 'but he was quite aware of them being not quite as grand as him. Underneath he was possibly quite a rough little character.'

There was also professional jealousy in Arthur's dislike of Dunn.

'Arthur did think that Clive was getting too many laughs,' I was told by Snoad. 'He was aware of him as competition. He was a threat.' Pam Cundell saw it differently. 'Clive used to get up Arthur's nose,' she told me.

He didn't like Clive much because he was an untidy performer, for a start: he never did or said the same thing twice, so he was very difficult to work with. And Clive was very bossy and was always making denigratory remarks about *Dad's Army* and saying it was a load of rubbish, and that got up Arthur's nose too because he really thought they were a proper platoon and really believed in that blasted Home Guard in the end. It became a real thing.

When Dunn was awarded the OBE in 1975 Arthur was 'incensed,' said Ms Cundell.

Arthur said 'He's let the platoon down by accepting the OBE because he's a Labour man', and he never forgave him. Maybe he thought *he* should have got it, and he *should* have done. I don't know why Arthur was never offered anything and he would have been bitter. He would have liked an honour.

Snoad agreed: 'He was certainly jealous of Clive's OBE,' he said, but Arthur himself told Pertwee that he would never accept any honour as humble as an OBE. 'When it comes to me,' he said, 'I'd never agree to that bargain basement stuff.' Nothing less than a knighthood would have done for him. David Croft, who was himself to be given the OBE in 1978 along with Jimmy Perry, admitted that 'we were all a little surprised because Clive's award came allegedly direct from Harold Wilson and a little prematurely.' Croft was in fact so surprised by the award that when he heard the announcement he dropped his boiled egg. Most caustic of all was John Laurie's reaction. 'Clive's been up Wilson's arse for years,' he sneered. Arthur might also have resented the fact that Dunn and Ridley were both the subjects of *This Is Your Life* television tribute programmes while he never was, but Croft told me: 'Arthur never wanted to appear on *This is Your Life* and gave express instructions to his wife to reject any approach,' and he added: 'I think Arthur would in due course have been offered a knighthood.'

As for any animosity between the wives, Joan Lowe was not the most popular, although Pam Cundell became very fond of her and Kay Beck told me: 'She was a wonderful woman and Arthur adored her. They were a lovely couple, very loving, and never went anywhere without each other. Even when he had to help her gently up the stairs because she had drunk too much he did it in the most loving way.' Just before that happened, as it did almost every evening, said Lavender, 'Joanie would be talking vivaciously to you and then suddenly she'd just slump. She'd be gone, and he'd say: "I think it's time we went to bed."' Joan le Mesurier actively disliked her. She told me:

The other wives were a really close bunch, but when Joan had had a few she got very haughty and remote. I think she thought that she was better than everyone else and she had delusions of grandeur about being a great actress. One of the group called her and Arthur the Lunts!' [a reference to the celebrated theatrical couple Alfred Lunt and Lynn Fontanne]. Arthur and Joan were both rather grand and both often had one over the eight, but Arthur always kept his dignity and got more pompous when he was pissed: rigid and upright, wonderfully funny.

The second series of *Dad's Army*, which was still in black and white, was transmitted in March and April 1969. Unbelievably the BBC kept only one of the six episodes in its archives. The tapes of the other five disappeared. The first, 'Operation Kilt', was a particularly funny episode, Perry told Richard Webber:

The platoon was involved in an exercise and were spying on their opponents. Jones was supposed to be in a field dressed up as a panto-mime cow, although it was really a couple of stuntmen. In the same field were forty real cows. Suddenly they went crazy, following the panto cow everywhere. We filmed it all, it was wonderfully funny.

It was unforgivable that these episodes were treated so carelessly, since the *Dad's Army* audience for the second series leapt from an average of 8 million viewers a week to 12 million, and it must have been obvious even to the BBC that it had a hit on its hands. Then in 2001, miraculously, after Croft and Perry had searched in vain for more than 30 years for copies of the missing episodes, the first two, 'Operation Kilt' and 'The Battle of Godfrey's Cottage', were rediscovered when an anonymous man came forward to say that a friend had found them among a pile of rusting cans of film in a skip at Elstree film studios in the 1970s and had kept them for years in his garden shed without realising what they were. The cans were so rusty that they had to be opened with a chisel. The films themselves, however, looked as good as new when they were screened again on TV just after Christmas that year, attracting a huge audience.

The weekly *Dad's Army* audience was to grow to more than 14 million for the third series in 1969 and over 16 million for the fourth in 1970. 'The series had everything right,' Jimmy Perry told Byron Rogers of the *Sunday Telegraph* in 1995.

It was one of those shows in which the cast was right, the time was right and the subject was right. People come up to me, they say high-falutin' things like 'I see a terrific resemblance between that episode and the scene before Agincourt.' Sometimes I say 'Excuse me, all we did was write a funny show.' But sometimes I say 'yes'.

The *Daily Telegraph*'s TV reviewer Sylvia Clayton came up with a theory worthy of the medieval alchemists when she suggested in 1972 that the three main stars of *Dad's Army* had turned Croft and Perry's raw material into gold because they embodied three of the classic medieval humours: choler (Arthur), melancholy (le Mesurier), and sanguineness (Dunn). More convincingly Professor Jeffrey Richards suggested in his book *Films and British National Identity* that *Dad's Army* became so hugely popular in Britain because its characters and humour are as immortally English as those of Dickens and Shakespeare – the 'rude mechanicals' in *A Midsummer Night's Dream*, for instance, or Dogberry and the Messina watch in *Much Ado About Nothing*. 'Shakespeare had his pompous and officious functionaries (Malvolio), his "stupid boys" (Sir Andrew Aguecheek), his spivs (Autolycus),' wrote Professor Richards. 'He even mustered a Tudor Dad's Army as Sir John Falstaff and Justice Shallow recruited their volunteer force in *King Henry IV Part Two*: Mouldy, Shadow, Wart, Feeble and Bullcalf are the ancestors of Jones, Pike, Frazer, Godfrey and Walker.' In 1978 Arthur was actually to play the part of Dogberry in a TV version of *Much Ado*, and as for the comparison with Dickens, Professor Richards observed that 'Captain Mainwaring is almost a Dickensian character.' So too of course was Arthur himself, which may explain why he had been so good at playing Mr Pickwick on television and was to be excellent again in 1974 as Mr Micawber in a TV adaptation of *David Copperfield*. To clinch his theory, Professor Richards pointed out that *Dad's Army* has in it every one of the six essential characteristics of Englishness as cited by Sir Ernest Barker in his book *The Character of England*: a social cohesion cemented by snobbery; a love of amateurism; a gentlemanly code of conduct; a propensity to volunteer; eccentricity; and an eternal boyishness. Mainwaring and Arthur himself exemplified perfectly all six characteristics, which may explain why both achieved such a firm grip on the affections of British viewers. Fat, pompous, red-faced and irritable though they were, they came to personify all the old-fashioned British virtues of decency, fair play, indomitable courage and patriotism. They reminded us of John Bull and Winston Churchill. They became the personification of the British bulldog.

Arthur never could explain the success of *Dad's Army*. 'If we knew that, we'd all be millionaires,' he said, but he reckoned that you could spot if a comedy programme might become a classic if you turned the colour off and the sound down and found that you were still laughing at it. In any case he was far too busy to waste his time theorising about it. As soon as the first series of *Dad's Army* was in the can he bought himself at last the boat that he and Joan had always dreamed of owning: his huge, beloved, Victorian steam yacht, the *Amazon*, the third and last great love of his life.

CHAPTER 9

Stinker, Sailor, Soldier, Singer
(1968–1971)

On a beautiful Sunday in August 1968 Arthur and Joan were relaxing in deckchairs on their roof terrace garden in Pavilion Road when he spotted among the classified ads in *The Sunday Times* an advertisement for the *Amazon*: an 83-year-old, 53-ton, wooden steam yacht, 104 feet long and 15 feet wide, which was lying only four miles away on the Thames at Cubitts Yacht Basin in Chiswick. It had been built in Southampton in 1885, apparently of 'Burma teak sheathed in copper', and could sleep as many as 10 people. The asking price was £2,000 (about £20,000 today). 'I love the atmosphere of a ship,' he explained, 'the hum of ventilators and generators, the smell of diesel.' The next day they took Stephen, now 15, and Henry the Daimler and tootled out to Chiswick to have a look at the *Amazon*. She was moored in a backwater among an untidy gaggle of houseboats and had been lying there for 30 years. She was a real stinker: she looked and smelled dingy, dirty and derelict. There were hen coops and chicken runs on the linoleum-covered deck, a rickety gangway, wood-worm in the timbers, mildew in the furnishings, and her side had been splintered by a V-bomb during the war, yet all three Lowes were enchanted by her. She had wonderfully slender, elegant lines, the hull was sound, and under all the rot, rust, decay and disrepair – and beneath the wheel and deckhouse – she had a stateroom, saloon, galley, captain's suite, dressing room and bathroom. Who cared if she needed a few repairs? This would be the start of a new adventure as well as giving them somewhere stylish to retire. Within two days Arthur had bought her for £1,850. 'It was the gingerbread on the prow that won us,' he said.

The ship had been designed by a famous Victorian yacht designer,

Dixon Kemp, and built for a Southampton shipyard owner and Member of Parliament, Tankerville Chamberlayne. 'I expect Edward VII himself goosed the Jersey Lily in her panelled staterooms,' chuckled Richard Leech. The *Amazon* had made her last voyage in 1937 and had then been bought by Sir Randle Holme, whom Arthur called Randle the Vandal because he had torn out her engines, moored her in Battersea Reach, installed cocktail cabinets and art deco fretwork, covered her in cheap plywood and chocolate paint, and turned her into a gin palace. Arthur claimed that in those days the ship had been 'a floating brothel'. If so, along with his ex-whorehouse flat in Pavilion Road, he had achieved an extraordinary double for a man of such rigid sexual principles.

A few days later the three Lowes and three Shines descended on the *Amazon* for days on end and stripped it clean, burning the rubbish on a bonfire while Arthur and Stephen took turns with the ciné camera filming it all in black and white. Arthur found the original plans for the boat and old photographs of her in the National Martime Museum at Greenwich and the craftsmen were called in – carpenters, plumbers, electricians, metal workers, engineers – to restore her to her original condition, right down to the brass fittings, with a new deck, twin masts, diesel engine, generator, portholes, galley and aluminium funnel. As the ship became increasingly beautiful the ciné film blossomed into full colour, Lindsay Anderson style, to heighten the contrast.

Arthur was determined not only to renovate her but to make her sea-worthy and take her out again on the open ocean. Below decks the *Amazon* was gradually fitted out with teak panelling, a Victorian fireplace, central heating, a Rayburn solid-fuel stove, luxurious furnishings, Hunting Stewart tartan drapes, and mahogany lavatory seats. The work was carried out at the Tough Brothers shipyard four miles away at Teddington, where the 'Burma teak' turned out to be pine and oak below the waterline. In the lavatory the brass and porcelain heads – all levers and pumps – had to be sent to the original manufacturers in Gosport to be completely refurbished. The new deck, which on its own cost £1,000 (£10,000 in modern terms), started to leak and had to be relaid again in teak. Within two years Arthur's bank overdraft was running at £10,000 (£90,000 today) and in all he spent about £40,000 on the *Amazon*, nearly £400,000 in current terms. 'All his money went on *Amazon*, every penny,' Christopher Bond told me, but Arthur never regretted it. He did not own a house so why not spend his money on a boat instead? He was convinced that it would be a good investment and eventually worth twice what it had cost. 'It's unique,' he said. 'When I have finished, it will be the oldest private yacht in commission, so it's quite impossible to put a price on it.' A fairground painter called Mr Pocket put the final touches to the bow and stern – in elegant gold leaf, ivory and azure – and on 20 June 1971 Arthur's dream was finally realised: the *Amazon* moved again at last under her own steam and he wrote jubilantly in his diary, 'Twelve knots against the tide. First voyage for 35 years!'

He moored the ship on the Thames near the television studios at Teddington, and during the 1970s he and Joan would sometimes live on board for as much as six months of the year. Consummate actor that he was, he always insisted on dressing for the part and even in hot weather would strut proudly around the deck wearing a thick, padded, kapok Arctic suit that Joan had bought for him and a ginger suede cap, playing to perfection the part of gnarled old sea salt dreaming of distant horizons. But whenever he wanted to sail the *Amazon* away from the safety of her mooring he hired a professional skipper or in later years asked Stephen to do it. When friends came aboard he affected a nautical manner – 'Ahoy, there' – and David Croft reported that 'there was a lot of looking over the side'. Bill Pertwee, whose wife, Marion, often sat on deck painting with Joan, told me:

One day Arthur said, 'Right, weigh anchor, slip the bollards', and all this sort of thing, shouting down to a non-existent crew. He moved the boat about 200 yards and said 'Right, drop anchor', and I said 'We've only moved a couple of hundred yards, Arthur', and he said 'Yes, we're not going to have lunch watching that snotty-nosed little boy on the other bank picking his nose.'

'He loved playing the part of the skipper,' Christopher Bond told me, 'and he believed it. Stephen was the crew and he was the Master.' Even so there were numerous moments of Arthur's nautical life that could have come straight out of *Dad's Army*. When Harold Snoad was on board one day the ship's port side was being painted at Teddington and the *Amazon* had to be sailed out into the Thames, turned around, and brought back to her mooring with the starboard side facing the bank so that the painters could get at it. He told me:

> They reversed the boat into the main river and suddenly the engine
> conked out. It was quite a long boat and there we were across the
> Thames, starting to drift and blocking the other boats that were coming
> up and down. We jammed the river for about 35 minutes before they
> could get another boat to haul us in with a rope. Arthur was very put out.

'He behaved on board as if it were the Orient Express,' Joan told
Romany Bain of *TV Times Magazine* in 1982.

> Each evening he washed and changed, and as the sun went over the
> yardarm, he donned his yachting cap and blazer and went up on deck.
> The boat was his sea mistress, and he treated her with all the old-world
> courtesy and good manners to which he felt she should be accustomed.

Sometimes they would have a party on board for as many as 50 people,
some of them from *Dad's Army*, and Arthur would squeeze behind the
wooden bar – out of which a semi-circle had been cut to accommodate his
burgeoning paunch – and pour the drinks, especially one that he had
concocted himself: the Amazon, which was a large slug of gin and ginger
ale and two slices of cucumber. John and Joan le Mesurier were invited a
couple of times 'and when he served drinks,' she said, 'they were always
very small ones in small glasses – he was always a bit mean – and it was
done very formally on a silver salver.' Even when guests came on board
for dinner he nagged them to switch off lights and not to waste water,
claiming that 'the vessel's safety' depended on it even though the vessel
rarely left its mooring.

Joan bought an old harmonium and installed it on board, and because
they had no close neighbours she would play it at night while Arthur
sang. Sometimes they danced together on deck, just the two of them, to
scratchy melodies from their wind-up gramophone. Beneath that gruff,
conventional exterior there beat the heart of an incurable romantic.
'Probably our best times as a family were the times we spent on board the
boat,' said Stephen. 'He had a terribly romantic view of life generally. He
would buy flowers all the time and he would choose romantic places to
spend weekends.' Pam Cundell agreed. 'He *adored* Joan,' she said. 'It was

always "What does Joan want?" Always.' And Peter Campbell recalled that 'on Valentine's Day and birthdays he used to choose very carefully little tokens of love and affection.'

There was also a modest side to Arthur, for at times he could not believe his good fortune. 'I remember him standing here in Barnes at our window overlooking the Thames,' said Christopher Bond, 'and saying "who would have thought all those years ago in Hereford that you would end up here with all this and me with *Amazon*."' The producer John Newman told me that 'the only time I've seen Arthur totally at home and at peace with himself was when he was on board that boat with his captain's cap on.' The Lowes started to give little candlelit dinner parties, graced by the expensive bottles of wine they had started to drink. 'Those people are drinking Mateus Rosé, James,' Arthur once remarked to Jimmy Perry in a restaurant. 'Are they insane?' He took to wearing flamboyant headgear: a tweed cap, an Australian outback hat, a strange blue-and-white titfer, and a black trilby, which he called his Mafia hat. Sadly, however, he was putting on so much weight that he could not indulge his extrovert taste for bright clothes.

When they moored the *Amazon* in places that were accessible to the public the sight of 'Captain Mainwaring' polishing brass or swabbing decks inevitably attracted unwelcome attention and cries of 'Now gather round, men!' and 'You stupid boy!' In Ramsgate Arthur was irritated by a couple who kept appearing on the dock and calling out to him. '' Allo, Arthur, 'allo!' they would cry, waving. 'Oi, Arthur, 'ow yer doin'? Don't panic, Mr Mainwaring! They don't like it up 'em, you stupid boy!' Doggedly Arthur ignored them and continued to polish his brasses until eventually the woman said to her husband: 'Well, we know what we can do with 'im, don't we? We'll switch 'im off!'

Arthur loved the *Amazon* so much that he told Pam Cundell he would be quite happy to retire and live on board and never work again,

to sit on the deck and just look, maybe go to Amsterdam and just watch all the people go by. But Joan pushed him all the time and made him work because she realised his potential. And it was a full-time job looking after Arthur. It was like having a baby. 'I've got to get the old boy off, get him to work,' Joan would say.

Whenever Arthur was offered a new part Joan always read the script first and he would never take anything on unless she recommended it. 'She encouraged him enormously,' said Peter Campbell. 'She was his Svengali.' Pertwee told me:

Arthur wasn't henpecked but he relied on her for advice almost more than she relied on him. He needed her to hold him together. He had to open a fête in Eastbourne once and he should have had a written speech but he didn't and he wasn't in command of himself at all, and afterwards she said 'You're a naughty boy, aren't you? You should have made some notes, shouldn't you?' And he said 'Yes, you're quite right, quite right, Joan's quite right', and he said he would never open another fête again. But sometimes the amount of work he'd take on was ridiculous. He liked to get booked up several months in advance and he'd be doing a voice-over at nine o'clock and would then come for *Dad's Army* rehearsals at ten. I think he still had the mentality of the rep performer where you had to watch your money because you weren't earning much.

That year of 1968 Arthur made two more films, one of which was Dick Lester's bizarre, *Monty Python*-esque film of Spike Milligan's long-running stage hit, *The Bed Sitting Room*, which was filmed in a disused quarry at Chobham Common in Surrey. The film, a surrealist, pacifist fantasy, depicted the weird lives of a group of bewildered survivors in a devastated wasteland Britain three years after civilization has been destroyed in a nuclear war. Among them is a girl who has been pregnant for 18 months (played by Rita Tushingham), her mother (Mona Washbourne) and father (Arthur), who live on a London underground train and survive by breaking into the Tube's chocolate-vending machines. Other barmy parts were played by Milligan, Michael Hordern, Roy Kinnear, Harry Secombe, Marty Feldman, Ronald Fraser, Dandy Nichols, Jimmy Edwards, Peter Cook and Dudley Moore. Because of nuclear radiation the characters eventually mutate into other things. Ralph Richardson turns into an actual bedsitting room of bricks and mortar, Dudley Moore into a dog, Mona Washbourne into a cupboard, and Arthur becomes a green parrot that is roasted and eaten. Nobody had much of a clue as to what it was all about and the film is so embarrassingly corny and unfunny that it was a commercial flop, but Arthur is hilarious when he starts to turn into a parrot, scratches the back of his head, makes clicking noises, whistles piercingly, and squawks 'pretty Poll, pretty Poll'.

And still he never eased up. On the night that BBC-1 broadcast the last episode of the first series of *Dad's Army*, 11 September 1968, he was back on the same channel a few minutes later – promoted to the rank of colonel – in a *Wednesday Play* by William Trevor entitled *A Night With Mrs Da Tanka*.

A fortnight later Joan at last returned to the stage on her own when she went without him up to Dundee Rep in Scotland to appear as the mother in *The Reluctant Debutante* by William Douglas Home. Since it was her big chance to rebuild her career she tried desperately to control her drinking. 'In a week I've had two single gins, $^1\!/_2$ of $^1\!/_2$ a bottle of white wine, three light ales and one glass of red wine!' she wrote to Diana Shine before the first night. 'Just wait till I get home! ... Oh well, it's an interesting experiment for me!' She added nervously: 'Everyone is very kind – let's just hope I shall be good enough to justify it.' She signed her letter 'Giovanetta'. A few days later, after the play had opened, she wrote again:

Well, I've done it twice now and found the 2nd time quite enjoyable really! They laugh like drains anyway and both the houses have been big enough to hold the first curtain-up! So, with luck, it will grow to be quite fun – at least I can't complain of being bored – I don't even have time for a <u>cigarette</u> except in the interval.

But she was vulnerable without them and Arthur. In the first letter she wrote 'I really must go to my sickeningly lonely bed now,' and in the second,

I must have been crazy to think I wouldn't pine for you all in a month – I feel like an exile in Siberia ... I'm just longing to be back with you all and my lovely Pavilion and my darling Amazon. Ten days – & most of all 'Himself'.
Tons of love, Gio.

By the end of the play's run she was desperate to return home to Arthur and wrote to him:

Oh my darling,

I am certainly 'feeling the pull of the old place' as Mich Murrell would say – I can't really be bothered to do the last two performances (particularly as I've already been <u>paid</u>) – oh how seriously these children take their work! I just want to come HOME to <u>YOU</u>!! Golly, I never realised just how hopeless it would be without you. Of course I've been spoiled, mostly by 30 commercial travellers … and of course I've been happy in the dressing room with the girls – but it's just not <u>important</u> enough – it is if they laugh like drains – like on Wednesday then it's marvellous – but audiences are such <u>wets</u> – they really only deserve television – I'm glad I've done it – if only to find out that it isn't enough!

Soon be Sunday now!

Longing to hold you close.

Must try to sleep, but I'm so excited –

Goodnight, my Tim,

So glad you like your lamps,

Oodles and oodles,

Pony.

They are playing 'Pennsylvania 65000' which of course makes it even worse!

As soon as Arthur finished the second series of *Dad's Army* – which won for Perry and Croft the Writers' Guild award for the best comedy script of the year – he was thrilled when Sir Laurence Olivier asked him to join his classy National Theatre Company at the Old Vic in London to appear in Somerset Maugham's cynical comedy *Home and Beauty*. Geraldine McEwan played the First World War widow who marries her hero husband's best friend only to discover that her first husband is still alive and has returned home. Robert Stephens and Robert Lang played the two husbands and Arthur was the dubious divorce solicitor, A. B. Raham, who steals the third act when he lectures the widow and her husbands as to how one can prove desertion, cruelty and adultery to get a divorce and provides them with a professional lady co-respondent. The reviewers were lukewarm about the play itself, finding it old-fashioned and unpleasantly misogynist, but unanimous in praise of Arthur's performance: 'a gem', 'a superb little vignette', 'a delightful cameo', 'wonderfully funny', 'excellently played'. 'Arthur Lowe gives a performance of Dickensian dimension' – Dickens again – wrote Frank Marcus in the *Sunday Telegraph*, and Hugh Leonard reported in *Plays and Players* that Arthur's performance was 'marvellous … as fruity as an orchard in autumn'. Arthur was proud to work at the National but could not resist amusing Joan at home by regaling her with cruel impersonations of Olivier, who nevertheless paid him the ultimate compliment, when Arthur left *Home and Beauty* at the end of January to rehearse a new musical, by stepping into his shoes at the National and playing Raham. Not many actors have had Olivier as their understudy.

Suddenly everybody seemed to be after Arthur, not just for plays, films or TV series but to star on chat shows as a 'Personality', to make after-dinner speeches – he enjoyed speaking at elegant guild-hall functions in London – and to help raise money for charities, especially for the sea-going charity that was closest to his heart, the Royal National Lifeboat Institution, to which he sent the money that he received when he started charging for his autograph and of which he was to become Vice-President in 1970 and President in 1977.

In February 1969 he opened in Coventry with Dorothy Tutin, Hy Hazell and Ian Lavender in a new musical, *Ann Veronica*, a version of H. G. Wells's 1909 novel about suffragettes and women's emancipation, which was directed by David Croft. Arthur played the lecherous old business-man, Mr Ramage, who tries to seduce young Ann Veronica while they are having dinner in the private upstairs room of an expensive restaurant. Croft, to keep his *Dad's Army* star as sweet as possible, let Joan play the small part of Molly Stanley. Arthur revelled in his role and sang several songs, notably the jolly, rollicking duet 'Too Much Meat' with Hy Hazell, who played the militant, bowler-hatted suffragette Mrs Miniver. 'Too Much Meat' was a roistering echo of all those boisterous songs that he had belted out in the Fifties in *Call Me Madam* and *The Pajama Game*. In it Hy Hazell jeered at him for daring to have such disgustingly lustful thoughts when he was so fat and ugly and advised him to curb his passion by eating less meat:

> All that meat! It makes your system overheat.
> I hope you don't mind my saying, bit by bit you're decaying …
> Your flabby flesh sags and sprawls

And both those roving eyes are sticking out like ping-pong balls ...
All that flesh! It makes you anything but virile and fresh.
Look at that paunch! Look at that neck!
You're not a man, you're more a wreck!
A disgrace, from your bald-headed face to your two fat cheeks.
Too much meat! Too much meat! Too much meat!

Undeterred by this uncomfortably accurate assessment of his looks in real life as well as on stage, Arthur responded with vigour:

All that veg must give your temper quite an edge.
Although the face may be placid, both lips drip prussic acid.
All your chums: they must have rubbish-bins for tums,
And do they think, silly clods, the nectar of the gods
Is made from stewing senna pods?
Your bust may be ample to the eye, but will it do for nuzzling too?
I'd have to be drunk to try. All those nuts
Must get a constipating grip on the guts.
Think of that wheat! Think of that bran!
You need some meat, then you need a man! ...
I do believe if you were Eve the choice I'd make would be the snake!

Arthur's understudy was the young John Inman, who was later to illuminate David Croft's department-store comedy *Are You Being Served?* as the gloriously camp – 'I'm free!' – Mr Humphreys. 'Arthur could sing extremely well in a deep baritone voice,' Inman told me, 'but his dancing in *Ann Veronica* was soft-shoe shuffle, not high kicking.' Inman played the waiter in the restaurant seduction scene:

The upstairs room was all Victorian drapes and the chaise longue and 'Come on, my dear, tight lacing has never been good for a girl. Have some Madeira, m'dear', and Arthur was wonderful in the part. I used to try to open a bottle of champagne and he'd say 'Oh, give it to me, *give it to me!*' and he'd get the bottle between his legs and start tugging and one night he put in a sudden ad-lib – 'Damned Froggies! They bung things in with never a thought of how they're going to come out!' – and it got a huge laugh.

On 1 March the BBC started to screen the second series of *Dad's Army*. The episode where Jimmy Beck and John Laurie are dressed as a panto-mime cow and attract the attention of a real bull and a herd of cows sent Peter Black of the *Daily Mail* 'into one of those long, happy, tearful paroxysms of laughter that only a visual gag brings'. Black added: 'Arthur Lowe's gift for projecting doubtful but obstinate self-confidence is so spendidly and perfectly set off by his part as the bank manager/Home Guard Officer that you get the impression the part was laid out for him by some benevolent predestination.'

Arthur and Joan went to Brighton with *Ann Veronica* and back to London when the musical opened at the Cambridge Theatre in Covent Garden with Mary Miller replacing Dorothy Tutin, who had found that her voice was not strong enough to conquer the orchestra. The critics judged the musical to be a disaster. In the *Daily Telegraph* Sean Day-Lewis denounced Arthur's seduction scene as 'appallingly vulgar … full of simple-minded *double entendre*, typified by the forward waiter who enters carrying a goose and asks: "Will you be fancying the bird now, sir?"' Day-Lewis did not blame Arthur personally, writing: 'Arthur Lowe as Ramage only succeeds in demonstrating how unfair it is that such an accomplished actor should be saddled with such a part.' In the *Sunday Telegraph* Rosemary Say was rude even about Arthur and what she called his 'strident vaudeville performance'. Arthur was furious with the critics and complained that they had been unfair and even unpatriotic in savaging a musical that could have attracted thousands of American and Japanese tourists to London and provided employment not only to the actors and theatre staff but also to local hotels, restaurants and taxis, but it was naïve of him to expect the reviewers simply for 'patriotic' reasons to be nice about a production that they all disliked. The play ran for only eight weeks in the West End and was rumoured to have lost £60,000 (the equivalent of nearly £600,000 today), yet Inman had happy memories of it.

Arthur and I got on extremely well and we used to talk about a north-country comic, Frank Randle, whom we both admired. Randle was a rebel: he'd smash up dressing rooms and take the scenery out to the car park, and not turn up because he was totally drunk, but his timing was brilliant and for us he could do no wrong. Arthur was funny and he relished telling one joke about this waitress to whom he had said 'We'll have a nice bottle of wine. Have you got a white Macon?' and she said 'No, this is me overall.' He loved that joke. He would tell it time and again.

In May Arthur went to Thetford again to record the third series of *Dad's Army*, in the first episode of which 38-year-old Frank Williams, a lay preacher in real life, appeared for the first time as the vicar, the Reverend Timothy Farthing, and in the eighth episode of which, 'The Day the Balloon Went Up', Mainwaring is carried off by a runaway barrage balloon, though the figure dangling from the balloon was not Arthur but 42-year-old Johnny Scripps, one of three professional stuntmen who stood in for him at dangerous moments. David Croft, always keen to keep Arthur happy, let Joan appear in the penultimate episode as an undertaker's receptionist. In 1969 Arthur made five more films, among them David Frost's satirical comedy *The Rise and Rise of Michael Rimmer*. This film, in which Arthur plays the bumbling managing director of a seedy advertising agency, shows how an efficiency expert could take over an ad agency and quickly make himself an MP, Cabinet minister, and finally President of the United Kingdom, and was packed with such comic actors as John Cleese, Peter Cook, Denholm Elliott, Roland Culver, Julian Glover, Dennis Price and Ronnie Corbett. Arthur was also in four radio programmes, most notably with Jimmy Beck in the Gogol play *The Government Inspector*, which had been adapted by his old friend Henry Livings. He made five commercials that year, for which he was paid on average £1,000 a time (£10,000 today). To prove that he didn't care whose products he endorsed so long as they paid him well, one of the ads was for Cambridge cigarettes even though Arthur smoked nothing but Craven A, and another was for Lyons cakes even though his favourites were Mr Kipling's. 'The man's got no dignity,' sniffed John Laurie. 'Pay him a thousand poons and he'd dress up as a monkey.' That year Arthur even made a solo LP record, *Bless 'em All*, on which he sang nostalgic songs of the Second World War – including 'Kiss Me Goodnight, Sergeant-Major', 'Lili Marlene', and 'We're Gonna Hang Out the Washing on the Siegfried Line' – as well as five singles, among them 'Who Do You Think You Are Kidding, Mr Hitler?' and 'Making Whoopee'.

In the spring of 1970 the Lowes' lease on the flat in Pavilion Road expired and the building was scheduled for demolition. Arthur and Joan bought a short-term lease on another two-bedroom flat: Flat C at 2 Maida Avenue, the ground floor of a two-storey Victorian villa in London's Little Venice, in Maida Vale, in a leafy avenue beside a quiet canal that housed numerous narrowboats. They made it their own by putting their piano in a corner of the living room and Joan's small paintings on the walls. Stephen had his own room and Arthur a study where he housed an impressive collection of miniature Dinky Toy cars that eventually filled a six-foot-long shelf. They kept themselves to themselves to such an extent that although their next-door neighbour was the novelist Doris Lessing, she told me that in all the years that he was there she had no idea that he lived next door. Nice though the new flat was, Joan pined for Pavilion Road. 'She didn't give a toffee after that went,' said Stephen. 'I've met people who are dearly attached to houses since, but none like her; she was like a cat. She properly existed only in that time and place.'

Now 17, Stephen left school that summer and became a merchant seaman, joining the Ellerman City Line and sailing to India. Arthur was delighted that his son had fulfilled his own boyhood dream of going to sea and he was equally proud of David, now 28 and a music master at Manchester Grammar School. Arthur and Joan kept in touch with his parents, too, and she wrote to Diana Shine: 'We had a pleasant evening with A's parents who ate and drank us under the table – these 80-year-olds are fabulous.' Big Arthur was now 81 and Nan 85, but both were still regulars in the village pubs and drank deep day and night. 'Big Arthur was very proud of Little Arthur,' Ann Middleton told me, 'but Little Arthur was so pompous and snobbish. He thought he was one cut above the rest of us and he'd ignore you. He was also dreadfully tight-fisted. I didn't like him.' Her taxi driver husband Trevor agreed, but Eric Smith, who was then the landlord of the George Hotel, where the Lowes stayed whenever they came to the village, told me:

He wasn't big-headed at all. They'd come in the bar after closing time, about 10.30 or 11 at night – they both liked their drink, they liked Guinness – and they were great. We'd get out the portable gramophone and records and we used to dance round the pub until about 12. He was quite light on his feet and very much like Captain Mainwaring.

Smith's wife, Dorothy, agreed:

Arthur was never arrogant. He was a gentleman. He just didn't suffer fools and he couldn't stand silly people. And he could be mischievous. He once phoned Pete Murray [the radio disc jockey] pretending to be an irate listener whose son had sent in a request and it hadn't been played. He was a great practical joker.

Arthur and Joan also drank often in the dark, snug Pack Horse pub and often drank too much. But 'Joan was a lovely lady even when she was drunk,' I was told by the pub's part-owner Richard Rowbottom.

Everything they ate had alcohol in it – port and melon, steak Diane, sherry trifle – and they loved good wines. We'd put her at a table in the corner next to the wall so that if she fell to one side the wall would keep her up. Once she stumbled and fell and we had to pretend that she'd caught her foot in a hole in the carpet. But they were both lovely.

That spring Arthur and Richard Briers recorded for television seven of Ben Travers' old 1920s and 1930s Aldwych farces – among them *Rookery Nook*, in which Joan also had a small part, *A Cuckoo in the Nest* and *Turkey Time*. Briers and Arthur both argued that they should have top billing. 'I was just a bit more famous than he was then,' Briers told me,

and since I was playing the leading parts, while Arthur was playing the supporting parts, we had an awful duel about the billing. I said 'Well, naturally I have star billing' and he said 'No you bloody well won't!' In the end we had to have a gentlemen's agreement in which the billing alternated every week.

In later years Arthur loved to recall how Briers tried at the end of the series to find a ticket to keep as a souvenir and the only one he could find was one that gave Arthur top billing. They worked on the series for three months but even Travers, who was now 83, admitted afterwards that it was not a success although he thought that Arthur and Briers were ideal for their parts. 'Those farces didn't really come off,' Briers told me, 'because they were stage plays, and when you do stage plays on the telly they're always a bit old-fashioned and stagey.' Arthur, he said, was 'marvellous' even though he was lazy and never really learned his lines.

'He was wonderful at showing outrage, at *bridling*. Outraged respectability was his great thing.'

As work on the *Amazon* progressed Arthur started fantasising about retiring and sailing off into the sunset. 'He always said to me "I'm going to get out early",' said Briers. 'He wanted to sail away in this wonderful boat, and said to me, "I'm off. I'm not buggering about with this for much longer."' Yet he kept taking on more work and popping up all over the place on radio and television. In February he was a guest on *The Val Doonican Show* and *The Tommy Cooper Show* and in June he played Charles Dickens' father, John, in the dramatised TV documentary *The Great Inimitable Mr Dickens*; to fit the job in he rehearsed the Travers farces in the mornings and the documentary in the afternoons. In September he joined Judi Dench and Frank Muir on the TV game show *Call My Bluff* and in December he was the subject of the *Desert Islands Discs* radio programme, on which he chose his eight favourite records. He picked his old Glenn Miller favourite, 'At Last', the song that he and Joan had adopted as their own; Bud Flanagan singing 'Who Do You Think You Are Kidding, Mr Hitler?'; Shani Wallis and Jeff Warren singing the Irving Berlin song 'It's a Lovely Day Today' from *Call Me Madam* and, his teenage favourite, Al Bowlly crooning 'Love is the Sweetest Thing'. He also chose Peter Dawson singing 'Parted' because it reminded him of his father singing the song during their happy musical evenings in Manchester during his childhood; Litolff's *Concerto Symphonique No 4 in D minor*; Bach's *Concerto in C minor*; and *La Mer* by Debussy. As his desert island luxuries he chose a dozen cases of his best claret and a book about tropical plants so that he would know which of the island's berries he could eat.

That year he also made 13 episodes and two special short sketches of *Dad's Army* and a full-length *Dad's Army* feature film. The series was the Queen's favourite TV programme, so in May the platoon took part in a Royal Television Gala Performance with a sketch in which they were guarding Buckingham Palace during the Second World War, the highlight of which was the moment when two girls, obviously the young princesses Elizabeth and Margaret, emerged from the palace with cups of cocoa for the shivering platoon. From June to August they recorded the first six episodes of the fourth series, from August to October they filmed the *Dad's Army* movie, and from October to December they recorded seven more episodes of the fourth series.

The full-length film was generally considered to be a disappointment, especially by the writers and cast themselves, who did not enjoy making it, partly because the American movie moguls at Columbia Pictures insisted that filming should be rushed through in eight weeks and that changes should be made to the Perry-Croft script, which thus lost much of the close-knit spirit of the TV series. And they were stunned when they met the film's 54-year-old director, Norman Cohen, and he told them that he had never seen even one episode of the TV series. The film was shot at the inland Buckinghamshire town of Chalfont St Giles, which, with the help of a few sandbags, gas masks, rationing notices, small boats and fishing nets, was made to impersonate the fictional wartime seaside town of Walmington-on-Sea. One of the funniest moments happened off-camera when Arthur decided that his pistol was too heavy to carry around and that a plastic replica would do and terrified the staff of a nearby Woolworth's store by marching in dressed as Captain Mainwaring to demand a pistol, accompanied by Paul Dawkins dressed as a Nazi general. Arthur's trip was in vain and he left the store muttering: 'You could always buy a sixpenny pistol in Woolworth's when I was a lad.'

The second half of the fourth TV series was much more successful and included three of the best remembered episodes: 'Mum's Army', a parody of the romantic film *Brief Encounter* in which Mainwaring falls in love with Mrs Gray, played by Carmen Silvera; 'The Test', in which Hodges challenges Mainwaring to a cricket match and the England cricketer Freddie Trueman plays a fictional fast bowler; and 'Fallen Idol', in which Mainwaring gets drunk during an officers' party, lurches back to his tent, grabs his tent pole for support, and spins around it muttering 'Damned revolving doors' – an unscripted line that he suddenly came up with himself. 'Mum's Army' and 'Fallen Idol' demonstrated just how powerful and varied Arthur's acting could be even when he was playing Mainwaring: in 'Mum's Army' he is an unhappily married, middle-aged man who is suddenly desperately in love, tender and touchingly vulnerable; in 'Fallen Idol' he is superb, as he always was when he played a drunk, perhaps because he lived with one. The fact that at first Arthur hated the script for 'Mum's Army' suggests that neither he nor Joan was always a reliable judge of a script. At the first read-through he grumbled, 'If I'd read this script before I came to rehearsal, I would have refused to do it', but a few days later he was saying: 'This script is sheer genius.' As for 'The Test', he was a lifelong lover of cricket and much enjoyed filming with Freddie Trueman, even though he was hit on the temple and bruised by a ball while batting, and on the way back at the end of the day Arthur, Trueman and Don Estelle led a sing-song on board the coach.

When the last episode of the fourth series was broadcast on 18 December 1970 the BBC did not plan to make any more and it was widely assumed that that was the end of *Dad's Army* except for one short TV sketch on Christmas Day, 'The Cornish Floral Dance'. In a farewell tribute Sylvia Clayton in the *Daily Telegraph* called it 'the most resilient and expert comedy team on television'. In the *Sunday Telegraph* Philip Purser wrote that Captain Mainwaring had become 'one of the great comic characterisations of the past decade', and the Variety Club of Great Britain elected Arthur as its BBC-TV Personality of the Year. Little did anyone realise that after two years and 39 episodes of *Dad's Army* – now top of the comedy ratings with an average weekly audience of 14½ million, and about to win yet again the Writers' Guild award for the year's best comedy script – still had seven years of life ahead and 41 more episodes to go. Despite the programme's popularity it was to be 10 months before the cast came together again to make the next episode – a one-off, 55-minute special for Christmas 1971 – and 18 months before they recorded another series.

In the meantime Clive Dunn had a huge No. 1 hit record when his sentimental little song 'Grandad' was released in November 1970 and he appeared on the TV teenage music programme *Top of the Pops*. Arthur, once again determined not to be upstaged by Dunn, decided to make a sentimental record of his own, 'My Little Girl, My Little Boy', with a B-side called 'How I Won the War'. Backed by the Mike Sammes singers and released in 1972, 'My Little Girl, My Little Boy' was a sentimental little number, lush with the sounds of strings and piano, and warm with Arthur's strong, deep voice:

> *Little boys and little girls, freckled faces, shining curls,*
> *They hurry through each day playing games I used to play.*
> *If you'll be a sparrow than I'll be your tree*
> *Then every night you'll fly home to me.*

Arthur spoke the next verse, murmuring fondly:

If you'll be a mountain, then I'll be your stream,
Sing you my song, tell you my dream,
And if you should ask me if dreams do *come true,*
When I'm with you [chuckle] oh yes – they do.

And then, singing again:

For who fills my world with sunshine and joy?
My little girl, my little boy.
Oh yes: my little girl and my little boy.

The song was not a hit: sentimentality about small children might just be credible from Jonesy but not from the childless Captain Mainwaring. But Arthur hardly needed to be seen on *Top of the Pops* and certainly did not need the money. By now he was earning £600 for each episode of *Dad's Army*, about £5,300 in today's terms, so that in 1970 he earned more than £200,000 in modern terms, though it has to be remembered that at that time, under a Labour government, he had to pay 83 per cent in income tax. Even so he told Jenny Campbell of the *Radio Times* in May 1971: 'The money's an embarrassment. No, really. It needs so much looking after.' He bought a lot of Rolls-Royce shares only to see their value collapse. Arthur was 'very careful with his pennies', said the ex-*Coronation Street* producer Bill Podmore in his book *Coronation Street: The Inside Story*, and 'appeared to have lost a small fortune. His only crumb of comfort was that his pal Ernie Wise had lost even more.' Podmore tried to lighten the gloom by telling Arthur that he had heard that a Swiss consortium was about to bail Rolls-Royce out. 'They're going to make Swiss Rolls,' he joked: 'Arthur was not amused. He stomped off muttering darkly, "Oh, very droll, very droll indeed." '

Free of *Dad's Army* for a year and a half except for the one Christmas special, Arthur popped up almost immediately in two other TV series: *Doctor At Large* in March and April and *The Last of the Baskets* in May and June. *Doctor At Large* was already a popular series and Arthur appeared in five episodes as Dr Maxwell, 'The Major', a pompous ex-Indian Army medical officer now running an antiquated general practice in Britain. By contrast *The Last of the Baskets*, for which he had been lured back to Manchester by Granada to play the starring role, had been written especially for him, was produced and directed by Bill Podmore, and was to run for six episodes in 1971 and for seven more in 1972. Arthur played an owlish, snooty, old-fashioned butler, Redvers Bodkin, who is appalled when his bankrupt employer, the Earl of Clogborough, dies and his title, derelict stately home and huge debts are inherited by a mysterious missing relative, the last of his family line, Clifford Basket, an uncouth, dim-witted, northern yob who lives in a council house and has just been sacked from his job as a sweeper in the boiler room of a factory making chiming doorbells. Bodkin takes the vulgar new earl under his wing and tries to teach him how to be a gentleman. Arthur and Peter Campbell both tried to persuade Granada to let Joan play the new earl's boozy mother, but they refused and the mother was played in the first episode by Hermione Baddeley. As the star of the show Arthur was once again up to his old trick of trying to cut everyone else's funny lines and Baddeley walked out and was replaced by Patricia Hayes. Campbell was Baddeley's agent as well as the Lowes' and believed that Arthur behaved so badly towards Baddeley because Joan was jealous of her getting the part. The reviews were decidedly mixed. The *Daily Telegraph* lamented that an actor as 'excellently accomplished' as Arthur should be involved in such a humdrum sitcom, and Barry Norman wrote in *The Times*: 'Bodkin owes rather too much to the characters Mr Lowe played in *Dad's Army* and *Coronation Street*. He could be Captain Mainwaring come down in the world or Mr Swindley risen.'

Arthur was beginning to corner the market in butlers as well as drunks, and his next major role combined the two when he was cast as a drunken butler in the Peter O'Toole film *The Ruling Class*. 'Arthur loved talking about butlers swigging the port and watering the gin and taking backhanders from tradesmen,' said Jimmy Perry, 'because one of his ancestors had been in service. He played a superb butler and we often discussed the idea of writing a series for him as an old retainer.' *The Ruling Class*, a bizarre musical black comedy about the British class system, started shooting at Twickenham Studios in May 1971, and although O'Toole was the star and gave a memorable and surprisingly touching performance it was generally agreed that the film was stolen by Arthur as the boozy, bolshy butler and Alastair Sim as the batty, bewildered bishop. When Arthur and Joan arrived to begin filming – she had a small part as a nurse – they were greeted by a note from O'Toole that read 'Blessed are they that steal the best parts', and O'Toole told others: 'I've gathered these lunatics just to ruin me. I stand no chance. First Arthur Lowe steals the scene, then Sim. I'm just the feed. They're all pissing on my grave.'

Like *The Last of the Baskets*, the film starts with the death of an earl, this time the mad, fetishistic Earl of Gurney, played by Harry Andrews, who dies kinkily when trying to half-hang himself while wearing a ballet tutu, a red military jacket, a white-plumed cocked hat and a sword. He leaves his title and stately home to his even madder son, Jack – a Christlike O'Toole with flowing blond locks, brown monk's habit and sandals – who has been living in a lunatic asylum, is convinced he is God, and likes to meditate on a large cross. Asked why he is so sure that he is God, he replies languidly: 'Simple. When I pray to Him, I find I'm talking to myself.' The dead earl has also left £30,000 to his Communist butler, Daniel Tucker, and when the will is read out Arthur greets his good fortune with a glorious moment of hesitation, a blink, and a whoop of joy. 'Thirty thousand smackers!' he yells, 'Yippee!', and dances merrily across the room in tailcoat and squeaky shoes, tossing his bowler hat into the air and singing 'Gilbert, the filbert, the kernel of the nuts'. Until now Tucker has hidden his deep bolshevik hatred of the Gurneys, whom he has served for 40 years, by spitting in their soup and peeing on their Wedgwood plates, but freed by his inheritance he comes into his own, remarking, 'Rich snobs and privileged arseholes can afford to be bonkers.' As the family squabbles over the will he smokes a cigar and hurls a priceless heirloom to the floor, and as the film progresses he becomes increasingly drunk, uppitty and funny and dances from one hangover to the next with the help of a flask of whisky and astonishingly light feet. His performance is unforgettable: when he sits carefully drinking on a sofa, wonderfully red-faced, exhausted, and hungover; when he attends O'Toole's wedding to a stripper, staggeringly drunk in tasselled red fez and carnation, gives a superbly alcoholic raspberry, and does yet another beautifully executed drunken dance; when he finds one of the noble family (played by Coral Browne) stabbed to death and yells ecstatically, glass in hand, 'One less! Praise the Lord! Hallelujah!'; and when he is finally dragged away by the police on a charge of murder, singing and wearing a straw boater, a red bow tie, red-striped blazer, white trousers, and black-and-white co-respondent's shoes, and honours the hated Gurneys with a final V-sign. It was 'the performance of his life', wrote

Richard Leech at the time, and Joan told Bill Pertwee that Arthur had loved making the film because for once he had been able to forget his puritanical attitude towards television and family entertainment. In later years Arthur felt that this was his finest film performance.

The Ruling Class was shot at Cliveden, Shere, and an old country mansion in Lincolnshire as well as at Twickenham, and it turned out to be so long – more than two and a half hours – that United Artists demanded cuts, but O'Toole, who had paid £55,000 for the film rights (£450,000 today), refused, which may have ruined its chances at the box office. A financial disaster, it was nevertheless chosen to be the main British entry at the Cannes Film Festival in May 1972, was castigated as blasphemous in *The Times*, and earned excellent reviews. Arthur's performance was 'a ravishing character sketch', said the *Sunday Telegraph*, and it earned him the friendship of the ebullient O'Toole, who would join him and some of the crew for an informal game of cricket during the lunch breaks. 'They used to talk cricket a lot,' Bill Pertwee told me. 'He loved Peter O'Toole, and O'Toole said he loved working with Arthur.' O'Toole threw numerous exuberant parties at the house that he and James Villiers shared during the shooting of the film, and the Lowes invited O'Toole and others to join them for boozy parties on the *Amazon*. 'There we were driving up and down the bloody Thames in this dirty great boat with people playing the organ,' said O'Toole later. 'A boat with an organ! We used to call him Admiral Bligh.'

Arthur actually played Captain Bligh of the *Bounty* in April when he appeared on the hugely popular *Morecambe and Wise Show* in a comic sketch deliberately misspelt *Monty on the Bonty*; Arthur was given one of the best lines in the show when le Mesurier asked him 'Is that wise, sir?' and Arthur replied, 'No, *this* is Wise; the one with the short, fat, hairy legs.' Successful though he was, he was not the only member of the *Dad's Army* team for whom 1971 was a vintage year. Clive Dunn was the subject of a *This is Your Life* TV tribute, and John le Mesurier played the charming but sinister British Soviet spy Kim Philby in Dennis Potter's TV play *Traitor* so well that he won the British Association of Film and Television Arts (BAFTA) award as the best actor of the year. Jimmy Perry won the Ivor Novello Award for the best theme tune for 'Who Do You Think You Are Kidding, Mr Hitler?' and *Dad's Army* won the BAFTA award for the best TV situation comedy of the year and (for the third year in a row) the Writers' Guild award for the best comedy script. And the Variety Club chose to give all seven of the *Dad's Army* stars one of its heart-shaped awards. 'At the awards lunch the stage was tiny,' Ian Lavender told me, 'and Arthur said "I think it would be better if I go up and receive them on behalf of us all", to which John le Mez said "No you fucking won't, we're all going", so we all trooped up.'

But 1971 brought sadness too. On 12 August Arthur's father died in his cottage in Hayfield. He was 82 and after a lifetime working for the railways was probably saddened that the 102-year-old Hayfield railway branch line and station had been closed the previous year under the swingeing nationwide railway cuts that had been inspired by the government's adviser Dr Beeching. Nan was with him when he died, of a heart attack and chronic bronchitis, and Arthur and Joan went up to Derbyshire for the funeral at Stockport crematorium. Big Arthur left everything to Nan, but it was not much: just £4,336.38 (£35,000 in today's terms), little more than the value of their cottage alone. Luckily Little Arthur was rich enough to be able if necessary to help his mother, who was 86 and had 10 more years to live, and he hired a local woman, Alice MacDonald, to clean the cottage and keep an eye on her. But according to Arthur's boyhood friend Victor Turner Nan found herself relying increasingly on her next-door neighbours, Nellie and Albert Jepson, because

although Arthur did come to see his mother now and then, the Jepsons looked after his mother and if they asked him to do something for her, he wasn't very interested. Albert Jepson became very disenchanted with him because he was so arrogant. He wasn't very popular in Hayfield in later years. Joan was very nice, but he got too big for his boots and a lot of people agree with me.

Some villagers did not agree at all, and maybe Arthur's apparent arrogance was actually something else, for at about this time, said Stephen, Arthur was taking 'happy pills and vitamin B_2 injections and had long bouts of bad temper. It was as if, for all the pushing and shoving and striving, he couldn't move his career along fast enough.'

He was 56 and time was running out.

CHAPTER 10

Prime Time

(1971–1977)

Arthur may have believed that his career was not moving fast enough, but the 1970s were to be the prime of his acting life. Only one new episode of *Dad's Army* was made in 1971 – a 55-minute Christmas special, 'Battle of the Giants' – but 15 earlier episodes were repeated and he took on a huge variety of other work. In November he and Ian Lavender joined Kenneth Connor for a radio comedy series about a small railway station in the years before Dr Beeching's massacre of the railways, *Parsley Sidings*, in which Arthur was the station manager, Lavender his idiot son, and Connor the porter as well as Clara the chicken. 'Arthur was in hysterics watching and listening to Kenny Connor,' Lavender told me. 'He loved comics. I've a sneaking suspicion he'd rather like to have been a stand-up comic himself.'

In January 1972 Arthur plunged into a six-part comedy murder serial, *It's Murder. But is it Art?*, in which he played another of the pompous, irascible, comic busybodies that were becoming one of his trademarks, this time Phineas Drake, a retired amateur sleuth who tries to solve the murder of a pretty blonde. Drake is a poseur who wears a grey beard, moustache, belted tweed jacket and dog-tooth-checked deerstalker hat, drives a pony and trap, does yoga on top of a chest of drawers, rings church bells as a hobby, and remarks when told that the main suspect is a brigadier: 'Soldiers don't go around killing people.' The critics were not amused. They found it contrived, unfunny and 50 years out of date, although Peter Knight wrote in the *Daily Telegraph*: 'The only credit entry of an otherwise barren sheet was Arthur Lowe, who played the eccentric detective with splendid dash and style.' If Joan really did choose

Arthur's parts for him – and he claimed that every week she read four or five scripts – it was another indication that she was losing her touch, and he began to appear on television in some decidedly humdrum programmes.

His next film, too, was pedestrian – Spike Milligan's story of his service as a conscript during the Second World War, *Adolf Hitler, My Part in His Downfall,* in which Arthur played yet another army officer, Major Drysdale – but much worse was Lindsay Anderson's unbearably long, boring, jerky and embarrassingly pretentious film *O Lucky Man!* A sequel to *If...,* it attempted to attack almost every British institution as being hopelessly corrupt and uncaring but succeeded only in making Anderson look like a pseud and a poseur. Malcolm McDowell again played Mick Travis, now an ambitious young innocent-abroad coffee salesman who undergoes a pilgrim's progress through a maze of corruption. Anderson's favourite actors were on parade: Ralph Richardson, Rachel Roberts, Mona Washbourne, Graham Crowden, Dandy Nichols, Peter Jeffrey, all playing several parts. Arthur had three roles – as a coffee company's very Mainwaringesque sales manager, a shifty porn-loving mayor, and an African dictator – and they were to win him a BAFTA award as the best supporting actor of the year. His portrayal of the gleamingly black African president, Dr Munda, with his wet, red, grin, light blue three-piece suit, close-cropped grey hair, dark glasses and Robert Mugabe voice, was superb, but the film itself was an affected, contrived disaster, peppered with hectoring silent-movie propaganda messages, in which at the end a smug, lizard-like Anderson unwisely appeared as himself auditioning McDowell for his part in the film. It is astonishing that Arthur was prepared to appear in such a dreadful film, not least because in one scene McDowell approaches a woman in church and suckles her breast, and in another a naked judge is flagellated by his female court usher.

Much more fun was a jokey Vincent Price horror movie, *Theatre of Blood,* in which Price is an old Shakespearean ham actor who takes his revenge on the critics by killing them off in a variety of horribly appropriate Shakespearean ways. Michael Hordern is hacked to death while Price declaims 'Pardon me, thou bleeding piece of earth.' Robert Morley is force-fed with a pie made out of his pet poodles. Robert Coote drowns in a barrel of wine. And Arthur has his head sawn off – like Cloten in *Cymbeline* – as he lies in bed with his wife. The severed head is discovered by another critic (Ian Hendry) when he opens his door in the morning and finds Arthur's head perched on a pint of milk. The film is most enjoyable, but after seeing it Joan had nightmares about Arthur's decapitation and would wake sweating and feeling in panic for his head. Arthur loved making films like this and dreamed of appearing in a really successful one, but he feared that now it would never happen. 'I would like to have had that telegram from Hollywood saying "Come immediately", he confessed to the *Evening Standard*. And maybe *Theatre of Blood* reminded him only too vividly of his mortality, for in April 1972 he made a will.

In May the *Dad's Army* team gathered again at Thetford to shoot the location scenes for the 13 episodes of the fifth series, which was to prove the most popular of them all, with an average weekly audience of more than 16 million. It included some of the best of all the episodes, among them 'Keep Young and Beautiful', in which Mainwaring buys a toupée in an attempt to look younger but succeeds only in looking ludicrous. In 'A Soldier's Farewell' he dreams he is Napoleon, and in 'Time On My Hands' a German pilot bales out and becomes tangled with a clock tower, and once again Arthur managed to wangle a small part for Joan.

Despite Arthur's wealth and popularity with producers, film directors, advertisers and the public, his fear of unemployment was still acute. It was more than three years since he had appeared in the West End theatre and 'there's still the worry of being out of work' he told Weston Taylor of the *News of the World* in September.

What have you seen, for example, of Raymond Francis on the screen lately? Nothing, have you? Yet for years he had it made as the detective in *No Hiding Place* ... This is a terrifying situation that has happened to all kinds of well-known actors because they have been famous in one particular role on television. I don't want that kind of thing to happen to me.

He need not have worried. For the rest of his life he always had more offers of work than he could handle. Chat-show hosts fell over each other to book him and on Christmas Day the *Dad's Army* platoon was back on TV with a 15-minute sketch called 'Broadcast to the Empire'. In 1972 and 1973 he made 11 commercials at more than £1,000 a time, equal to

£90,000 today. In the first quarter of 1972 he appeared in two television plays as well as a film with Ronnie Corbett and Beryl Reid, the lively, lunatic farce *No Sex, Please, We're British*, in which Ian Ogilvy and Susan Penhaligon were a young couple who worked in a bank and kept being sent unsolicited porn.

Arthur still avoided making personal appearances at fêtes and charity fund-raising occasions except for the RNLI. He made an exception in July when he and Clive Dunn spent a weekend helping young people to clear debris from the foreshore of the Thames between Kew and Greenwich to raise money for a charity for the homeless. After much cajoling from David Croft and Jimmy Perry he also made another disgruntled exception when the stars of *Dad's Army* were invited to switch on the illuminations along Blackpool's Golden Mile, though when their train stopped at Crewe and a crowd of fans, delighted to see them eating lunch in the buffet car, pressed against the window and called out ' 'Ello, Arthur! 'ello, Arthur!' he rapped firmly on the window and barked: 'Go away! Clear off!'

'What a miserable old sod!' yelled one of the fans.

Arthur sipped his wine. 'Take no notice,' he muttered as the train fortunately began to pull away from the angry crowd on the station.

'Then he winked at me,' said Perry. 'He had to keep up his image. Arthur had a great sense of humour and loved to send himself up.' Perry remembered another occasion when Arthur was less than welcoming to a stranger who came too close. They were eating in a restaurant in Great Yarmouth when a guitarist approached to serenade them. 'Not here,' muttered Arthur, waving his hand. 'Go away.'

Arthur quickly regretted his agreement to go to Blackpool. His disgruntlement began even before the lighting ceremony, when the cast was served a meagre dinner without any wine 'due, apparently, to a previous celebrity having over-indulged and made a mess of things during the switch-on', wrote Joan le Mesurier in her book *Dear John*. Afterwards Arthur switched on the lights and the cast was driven through the streets in a freezing coach and marched in pairs onto the stage of the Winter Gardens ballroom amid a sort of fairy grotto. 'Hello,' grunted Arthur, 'it's the Ideal Gnome Exhibition.' They were seated at a long table loaded with pieces of Kunzel cake and pork pie, but once again there was no alcohol. Glumly they munched their cake and pie while the audience gawped at them. In desperation Arthur summoned a waiter and ordered two large scotches. 'We're not allowed to serve doubles,' the waiter said. 'In that case,' said Arthur grimly, 'bring us two singles, then go away and bring us two more.' They were forced to listen to a string of civic speeches, after which one of the dignitaries invited the cast to meet some of the local people. 'Not bloody likely,' growled Arthur. 'We've sung for our supper and now we're off to the Lemon Tree' – a Blackpool nightclub where there was a jazz band and the drink did not flow like glue.

In June they recorded the first 20 of 67 episodes of the radio version of *Dad's Army*, which was being adapted by Harold Snoad and Michael Knowles, who was later to play the silly-ass Captain Ashwood in the Croft–Perry TV series *It Ain't Half Hot, Mum*. They also began to shoot on location at Thetford the seven episodes of the sixth TV series, and again Arthur was harassed by the fans. Frank Williams told me:

A lot of villagers were asking for autographs, and Arthur said 'No, no, no, I don't do that.' In the afternoon more villagers came out and one said 'There's Arthur Lowe, I'll go and ask him', and one who'd been there in the morning said 'It's no good askin' *'im*, he'm a *miserable* old toad, 'e is.' That kind of recognition is very irritating. I did a commercial for Tunes lozenges once, and people came up to me and said *tyooonz* at me, and there's no reply to that, really. The one that always got me was 'What've you done with Captain Mainwaring?' How do you reply to that?

Bill Pertwee remembered having dinner with Arthur in a restaurant when a drunken fan approached them, planted his hand in the middle of Arthur's *boeuf bourguignon*, and tried to hold an incoherent conversation. On another evening, when the cast was eating in a restaurant in Manchester, about 50 people collected outside and gaped at them through the window. Arthur sighed. 'Now I know how the monkeys must feel at the zoo,' he said. 'He often used to take us out for a meal,' Phyllis Bateman told me,

and Joan would go in first and find a table in the corner and Arthur would sit with his back to the rest of the restaurant because he didn't like people interrupting his meal. He was very shy, but he wasn't rude to people. We were in Bath once and he was buying some underwear in

Debenhams and two ladies said 'Ooh, Mr Mainwaring, what are you doing?' and he said 'I'm buying some underwear, madam.' He was very kind and generous with us, but very mean with himself. Joan had told him he must buy himself some new underwear because his usual ones were full of holes.

The first episode of the new series was to become Perry's favourite of them all, 'The Deadly Attachment', in which the platoon captures the crew of a German U-boat. In 1999 the scene in which Mainwaring is threatened by the smooth but sinister U-boat captain, played by Philip Madoc, was voted Britain's favourite moment of TV comedy ever:

CAPT MAINWARING: I'm going to have a word with these prisoners of war.

SGT WILSON: You can't speak any German, can you, sir?

MAINWARING: They'll know by the tone of my voice that I'm in charge. They'll recognise authority when they see it. You'd better come with me.

WILSON: Yes, of course.

MAINWARING: Now pay attention.

[*The Germans snap to attention.*]

WILSON: I say, they're awfully well disciplined, aren't they, sir?

MAINWARING: Nothing of the sort. It's slavish, blind obedience. I tell you, Wilson, they're a nation of automatons led by a lunatic who looks like Charlie Chaplin.

U-BOAT CAPTAIN: How dare you compare our glorious leader with that non-Aryan clown?

MAINWARING: Now look here…

U-BOAT CAPTAIN: I am making notes, captain, and your name will go on the list, and when we win the war you will be brought to account.

MAINWARING: You can write what you like. You're not going to win this war.

U-BOAT CAPTAIN: Oh yes we are.

MAINWARING: Oh no you're not.

U-BOAT CAPTAIN: Oh yes we are.

PRIVATE PIKE [*singing*]: Whistle while you work. Hitler is a twerp. He's half barmy, so's his army. Whistle while you work.

U-BOAT CAPTAIN: Your name will also go on the list. What is it?
MAINWARING: Don't tell him, Pike!

Another classic episode was 'The Royal Train', in which King George VI's carriage is about to rattle through Walmington-on-Sea and the platoon has to provide a guard of honour on the station platform, and Arthur was hilarious in the fifth episode, 'The Honourable Man', in which he is incensed to learn that Sergeant Wilson has not only become the Honourable Arthur Wilson because his uncle has died but has also been invited to join the golf club because of his new title.

Tragically 'The Honourable Man' was the last complete episode in which Jimmy Beck appeared: a month after it was recorded he was dead. Beck and Arthur had begun to work together on a TV series based on Tony Hancock's 13-year-old comedy series *Hancock's Half Hour*. Hancock had died five years previously and Arthur took on his role – though now he was a retired bank manager rather than a down-at-heel suburban loser from Railway Cuttings, East Cheam. Beck took the part that had been played originally by Hancock's sidekick, Sid James. The title was changed to *Bunclerke-with-an-E*, although the scripts were almost the same as the originals, and a pilot programme was made. 'Lowe was marvellous,' said Alan Simpson, who wrote the series with Ray Galton. 'He had exactly that same pompous quality as Hancock, though of course he was more middle class.' But in July, while opening a charity fête, Beck suddenly suffered a dreadful pain and was rushed to hospital with chronic pancreatitis, which is usually caused by drinking too much alcohol. 'Arthur was wonderful,' Beck's widow, Kay, told Richard Webber. 'He said "Leave it to me" and he arranged for a specialist to see Jimmy. For that I'll always be grateful.' Beck survived in Queen Mary's Hospital, Roehampton, for three weeks and underwent an operation for a suspected ulcer. During the operation his pancreas burst, his kidneys failed, and he died of a heart attack, aged 44, on 6 August 1973. The *Dad's Army* cast and crew were devastated. Not only had he been a highly talented actor, painter, sculptor, linguist, and opera buff, he had also been great fun to have around, the sort of life-enchancer who would arrive on the set and start the day with a funny impersonation of Humphrey Bogart or W. C. Fields. 'Arthur was very helpful when Jimmy died,' Kay Beck told me. 'He was always there for me.' But he felt superstitiously that two deaths

– Hancock's and now Beck's – meant that *Bunclerke-with-an-E* was cursed. He refused to go on with it and the series was shelved.

Despite this setback Arthur's career blossomed over the next 18 months. In November he and Joan went off for several weeks to Paris and Chamonix in the French Alps to record scenes for a four-part dramatised TV documentary, *Microbes and Men*, in which he played the nineteenth-century French scientist Louis Pasteur. It was one of his favourite parts because it was serious and factual rather than comic, he had to age from 32 to 73, and he felt that he had really got inside Pasteur's skin. When filming at Pasteur's house at Arbois local people constantly told Arthur how closely he resembled Pasteur. And in the Alps he and Joan had 'a very romantic time,' said Stephen. 'The altitude suited them both and just for a while I thought I glimpsed young lovers again.'

Early in 1974 Arthur rejoined Laurence Olivier's National Theatre Company and returned to the West End stage, after an absence of nearly five years, to play yet another drunken butler, Stephano, in Peter Hall's production of *The Tempest*, which starred Sir John Gielgud as Prospero, Denis Quilley as Caliban, and Julian Orchard as Trinculo. The National had been nagging Arthur for some time to become a regular member of the company and to sign a year's contract, but he was as loth to tie himself down for so long with the National as he had been with Granada TV. 'The part isn't only comedy, that's why I wanted to do it,' he explained. 'There is a scene where Caliban tries to enlist Stephano's help to kill Prospero and then the jolly drunk becomes someone who is very dangerous indeed.'

He was outstanding as Stephano, but the production itself was widely considered to be a failure. Michael Billington described it in the *Guardian* as one of the four worst Shakespeare productions he had ever seen. It was Peter Hall's first play as the new director of the National and he admitted that the production did not come off. Arthur, however, was brilliant right from the first depressing day of rehearsals, 2 January, of which Hall wrote in his diary: 'Arthur Lowe was just naturally funny as soon as he opened his mouth. It is a joy to have a clown as a clown.' After the first night, on 4 March, Hall wrote in his diary that Gielgud was 'a little woolly' but that Arthur was 'wonderful'.

'Arthur was very proud of his more prestigious theatre work,' said Peter Campbell. 'He was genuinely honoured to play alongside Gielgud and

Olivier.' He also relished the fact that he could excel onstage in Shakespeare as well as in avant-garde films and popular television series. David Gatehouse, now 32 and director of music at Stowe School in Buckinghamshire, was immensely impressed by his performance in *The Tempest*. 'He was an exceptionally good actor and I think it's terribly sad that he's only remembered for *Dad's Army*,' Gatehouse told me. 'He was hugely proud of his work for the National Theatre and *The Tempest* was the big thing for him, immensely satisfying.' The critics were equally impressed, 'Inspired casting!' said Arthur Thirkell in the *Daily Mirror*, and Irving Wardle reported in *The Times*: 'Mr Orchard, a fleshy ladylike stooge in cap and bells, and Mr Lowe, a dangerous buffoon with a powerful sense of his own dignity, make something very real of the sub-plot; and their enslavement of Caliban is genuinely disturbing.'

Even more pleasing for Arthur were the congratulations of fellow actors. Gielgud sent him a note that read: 'Dear Arthur, A great privilege to work with you and I wish you all success. Sincerely, John G.' Ralph Richardson wrote: 'Dear Arthur, I have not had better pleasure than when you took the peak of your wonderful part with "we will inherit here" and I cannot resist telling you so. EVER affectionately, Ralph. FAN LETTER NOT TO BE ANSWERED.' Dame Flora Robson sent him a signed photograph with the message: 'To my favourite comedian, Arthur Lowe, my homage, Flora Robson'. And Peter Hall told him that he was now good enough to play the great Shakespearean character parts and suggested that he might soon play Falstaff for the National – another inspired piece of casting which sadly never came to pass.

Legend has it that Prospero's farewell at the end of *The Tempest* was Shakespeare's own farewell to the stage and London, and that he then retired to Stratford to live as a rich landowner, so it seems strangely appropriate that Arthur's next stage role – in *Bingo* by Edward Bond at the Royal Court – showed Shakespeare in retirement and was to be Arthur's last straight West End play. *Bingo* depicted Shakespeare, played by Gielgud, being visited by several people from his past, including his rival playwright, the envious, Rabelaisian Ben Jonson, played by Arthur. This Bard was a gloomy, corrupt, materialistic old grouch, not at all the humane idealist you would expect after seeing his great plays but a man who hated his bullying, harridan wife and daughter and cared nothing for injustice or the dreadful sufferings of his poor tenants. He commits suicide by swallowing poison pills given to him by Jonson after a long, witty, drunken meeting in Stratford during which the red-wigged, red-bearded Jonson tells him that the Globe Theatre in London has burned down and tries to cadge a loan.

'Gielgud was delighted when Arthur was given the part,' Edward Bond told me.

> He admired him immensely, as I did too. Arthur had great subtlety – he provoked 'audience work', which is one of the abilities of great actors. They suggest something rather than dramatically overstating it. The suggestion isn't, though, a mere gesture, it is complete in itself, a total artistry, often having great finesse. It is a window into the human soul. One of the pleasures of watching actors such as Arthur is that they remind us of the subtlety and basic goodness of human nature. And for a writer there is a great comfort in knowing that what you've written is in the hands of someone as perfect as Arthur. You know that every word will be thoroughly 'used' and that what you've written is made better by the performance.

Bond did notice, however, that Arthur suffered from 'a sort of restricted professionalism':

> His performance in *Bingo* was wonderful but it was 'isolated'. He didn't attend the rehearsals of scenes in which he did not take part and I'm told he did not show any interest in integrating his scene with the rest of the play. But he was a great actor, probably wasted by our stupid theatre. He was also a wonderful man.

When *Bingo* opened at the Royal Court in August 1974 Arthur received good luck telegrams from Peter Hall and Lindsay Anderson, one that read 'Keep it manly. O'Toole', and a note from Gielgud that said: 'Dear Arthur, Very proud to be with you again.' Five days later Hall saw the play and wrote in his diary that Arthur's boozy argument with Gielgud 'is one of the high spots of my theatregoing for years'. Later Joan said that his performance in *Bingo* was the best of his entire career, and when Arthur died Francis King wrote in the *Sunday Telegraph* that he 'must be one of the few actors ever to have succeeded in acting John Gielgud off the stage'. The reviewers were caustic about Gielgud and the play though they were full of praise for Arthur, yet he never played the star or the luvvie. On the first night Edward Bond went backstage after the final curtain. 'You could hardly get into Gielgud's dressing room,' he told me.

The corridor outside was crowded, the room seemed to be full of several layers of people. There was champagne and cards, and Gielgud, whom I greatly admired, was blessing the multitude and, I imagine, turning five fishes into food for the mob. There was a lot of noise. I then sought out Arthur's dressing room. One person was leaving it as I arrived. I went in. He was utterly alone. He was sitting in front of his dressing mirror working at some forms. Afterwards I was told he was doing his tax return.

Arthur was by now so successful that he had a great deal of income to declare for tax, including that from the first of numerous lucrative jobs as the narrator of the *Mister Men* series of children's cartoon films. In 1974 he appeared in nine television programmes apart from *Dad's Army*, most notably in September as Pasteur. In the *Daily Telegraph* Richard Last was awed by Arthur's 'beautifully concise, authoritative performance as the testy, crippled Pasteur', and the headline over Shaun Usher's rave in the *Daily Mail* read: 'Forget the comedy, … what an actor!' In October it was back to Thetford to start recording the location scenes for the seventh series of *Dad's Army*. The cast was so saddened by Jimmy Beck's death that some wondered whether the series could survive without him. 'It was very odd without Jimmy,' Ian Lavender told Richard Webber.

We stopped doing lots of silly little things. Often when we were standing around waiting to shoot a scene on location we'd have a bit of a sing-song while Arthur Lowe conducted. Somebody started doing it while we were waiting to shoot the first episode of that series and no one joined in. It just didn't seem right.

In December Arthur was back on TV in yet another Dickens role, as Mr Micawber in the six-part BBC serial *David Copperfield*. To do it he had to work a hectic seven-day week from 9 a.m. to 10 p.m., rehearsing for both *Dad's Army* and *Copperfield* every day, and it earned him more ecstatic reviews. Sylvia Clayton in the *Daily Telegraph* and Alan Coren in *The Times* both said that Arthur's Micawber was superb. Coren wrote:

> When that empurpled conk first burst into the bottle shop last night, the felt hat at the perfect angle, the belly flourished like a huge fifth limb, and when that booming whine rattled out the first grand circumlocution, could I have been alone in feeling the prick of gooseflesh? For was this not W. C. Fields back from the grave?

For Arthur that was the ultimate compliment.

At the end of that year he took a rare break to enjoy a family Christmas on board the *Amazon* with David, his wife Sylvia, their sons Peter and Timothy, aged 10 and nine, and Stephen, who was now 22 and had left the merchant navy to become a highly paid deep-sea diver working on a North Sea oil rig off Aberdeen. It was a lonely, monastic life on the rigs, where young men were confined for weeks at a time, and a month after Christmas, during one of his shore leaves, Stephen had an affair with a 20-year-old Aberdeen shop assistant, Susan Turner, and she became pregnant. Nobly he stood by her, went to live with her on a caravan site and married her in Aberdeen in September, seven weeks before their son Jack was born. Sadly the marriage was to last only six years. 'It was a grave mistake and was virtually over before it even started,' Ted Shine told me. 'Arthur and Joan didn't think much of her at all and were slagging her off right from the start. They even suggested that she was on the game. There was a lot of money in Aberdeen at the time and there were a lot of girls up there.' For a couple of years Stephen, Susan and Jack lived aboard the *Amazon* in Ramsgate yacht marina and he continued to work as a deep-sea diver, but the marriage eventually ended in divorce in 1981. In later years Stephen was to drift into a variety of other jobs as a dock worker, skipper of the *Amazon* and long-distance lorry driver, and at one stage he was banned from driving because of drunkenness. Bill Pertwee and Phyllis Bateman both thought that Arthur was disappointed in Stephen, and Harold Snoad told me: 'There was a distance between Stephen and his dad. Perhaps Arthur thought he was a bit of a layabout.' For several years Jean Snoad had the impression that Arthur and Joan had only one son, by her previous marriage: 'I didn't think of Arthur as being a father.' Other friends of the Lowes never heard them mention Stephen, and met him only once or twice in 30 years.

In addition to his other work in 1974 Arthur made nine commercials, 28 national radio programmes and played the part of a property developer in an embarrassingly thin TV-comedy-series spin-off film, *Man About the House*. This suggests that he would now do anything for money even though he was making so much that he told Sheridan Morley: 'The pressure's off at last and I can turn down the rougher jobs. Also it means I can have holidays without worrying about losing work, but the trouble is that I went so long without holidays, now I don't know how to spend them.' So 1975 was as busy as ever, with nine TV appearances apart from *Dad's Army* (most notably as Sir Oliver Surface in *The School for Scandal*), a *Dad's Army* stage show, 32 radio programmes, 10 commercials, and three films, including a disastrously bad musical romp, *The Bawdy Adventures of Tom Jones*, in which Joan also had a small part. That year, too, he made a rare foray into politics by joining the Britain In Europe group, which supported Britain's entry into the European Economic Community and included Graham Greene, Benjamin Britten and Alec Guinness.

After writing 66 TV episodes of *Dad's Army* Croft and Perry had had enough of it, but it was still drawing a weekly audience of nearly 15 million and David Attenborough, the controller of BBC1, persuaded them to write two more series. Among those 14 episodes was one of the most memorable of them all. Entitled 'My Brother and I', this special for Boxing Day showed Arthur not only as the uptight Mainwaring but also as his drunken, ne'er-do-well, travelling salesman brother, Barry. As always Arthur showed an uncanny aptitude for playing a drunk, and as a heavy drinker himself he identified more with the red-faced, cynical, boozy brother than he ever had with Mainwaring. 'He's a much more lovable character,' he said. 'In fact I think he deserves a series of his own.'

By now there were *Dad's Army* videos, records, books, board games, mugs, T-shirts and fan clubs in Britain and New Zealand, and for millions of viewers Arthur *was* Captain Mainwaring. In May he made a delightful guest appearance on *The Black and White Minstrel Show* dressed as Mainwaring and sang a rousing medley of wartime songs in his warm baritone voice: 'Roll Out the Barrel', 'We're Going to Hang Out the Washing on the Siegfried Line' and 'Run Rabbit, Run Rabbit, Run, Run,

Run'. He also did a nifty soft-shoe shuffle routine with the four girl dancers and pretended to be shocked when they surrounded him and sang 'Kiss Me Goodnight, Capt Mainwaring'. He ended tenderly with two poignant solos, 'Lili Marlene' and 'The White Cliffs of Dover'. It was an endearing demonstration of his remarkable versatility: he could hold his own onstage in Shakespeare with Gielgud and Olivier, and he could also sing and dance with the Black and White Minstrels without looking foolish.

Four months later – after recording six more episodes of *Dad's Army*, in one of which Joan appeared again as Godfrey's sister Dolly – Arthur and the platoon were singing and dancing every night in a musical stage show version of *Dad's Army*. A series of sketches and songs, it offered such delights as the entire platoon prancing around as Morris Men with bells on their knees; Ian Lavender zipped into a huge plastic banana and singing the wartime hit song 'When Can I Have a Banana Again?'; Bill Pertwee dressed as a Nazi general with a monocle; John le Mesurier hauntingly half-singing, half-speaking the nostalgic wartime melody 'A Nightingale Sang in Berkeley Square'; and le Mez and Arthur (dressed like Bud Flanagan in a straw hat and long, tatty fur coat) crooning the Flanagan and Allen Crazy Gang wartime classic 'Hometown' and gathering on stage the entire cast all dressed as Flanagan or Allen. That scene brought the London audience to its feet on the first night at the Shaftesbury Theatre, applauding and cheering for ages, when Arthur came on to sing the song with 81-year-old Chesney Allen himself. Joan landed not just one part in the show, but three: as a voluntary worker; as Godfrey's sister Dolly; and as Gert of the wartime duo Gert and Daisy, which allowed her to sing a duet with Pam Cundell. Arthur played no fewer than four parts: Captain Mainwaring; the wartime radio character Mr Lovejoy; his old radio and music hall idol Robb Wilton; and Bud Flanagan. Audiences were deeply moved by the final scene, set as the war came to an end in 1945, when Arthur as Captain Mainwaring stood on a deserted beach, pompous no more, and spoke with simple dignity the spine-tingling epilogue.

The Home Guard never went into battle, but the two million men – shop assistants, factory workers, doctors, lawyers, men from every walk of life – gave of their spare time and, in some cases, their lives, to defend their homeland. And if ever this island were in danger again, men like those would be there once more, standing ready.

And then he sang 'Who Do You Think You Are Kidding, Mr Hitler?' as the orchestra and the rest of the cast gradually joined in:

> *Who do you think you're kidding, Mr Hitler,*
> *If you think we're on the run?*
> *We are the boys who will stop your little game.*
> *We are the boys who will make you think again,*
> *'Cause who do you think you're kidding, Mr Hitler,*
> *If you think old England's done?*

Not all of the cast were keen on the idea of a stage show. John Laurie, now 78 and increasingly breathless, felt that he was too old to cavort about a stage every night for months and was replaced as Frazer by Hamish Roughead; and Clive Dunn, who did not want to be away from his family for too long, agreed to appear in the show only for the first nine months and was replaced for the last three by Jack Haig. Even so the show was a huge success, opening in September in Billingham, County Durham – a week before Stephen's wedding in Aberdeen – and a month later at the Shaftesbury Theatre in London, where it ran for five months before taking off on a nationwide tour from March to September 1976. During the London run the cast performed one of the most successful scenes at the Royal Variety Performance at the London Palladium in the presence of the Queen and Prince Philip: 'The Choir Practice', in which jazz-loving John le Mesurier played the piano while Arthur attempted to conduct the entire cast for 'The Floral Dance'. Also at the Palladium that night were more than 300 other performers, among them Vera Lynn, Charles Aznavour, Harry Secombe, Bruce Forsyth, Telly Savalas and Count Basie, who congratulated le Mesurier on his piano playing. Two weeks previously, with the birth of Stephen's son Jack, Arthur had become a grandfather, and as the cast waited for the final line-up they found themselves next to the African Kwa Zulu dancers, one of whom was breastfeeding her baby. 'The baby and his mother's breast were level with Arthur's eye line,' recalled Bill Pertwee. 'Arthur did one of his double takes and then said to the lady, "Enjoys a drink, does he? I could do with one right now!"'

Yet Arthur could still be surprisingly prim. During the Morris Dance scene Mainwaring explained to Pike that it was a sort of fertility dance, and when Frazer started beating Jones with a stick Dunn ad-libbed one night: 'Frazer was trying to fertilise me, sir!' 'It got a roar of laughter,' Dunn told me, 'the belly laugh that comics dream of', but Arthur was not amused. 'On the way up to the dressing room afterwards he came up and said "You won't say that again, will you?" So was he a prude, or didn't he like me getting that belly laugh?' On another occasion, when one of the lesser-known actors introduced a piece of 'business' that Arthur considered vulgar, the fellow said defensively, 'Well, it gets a good laugh.' Arthur peered at him over his spectacles and snapped: 'If I walked down to the front and peed in the pit it would get a good laugh but it wouldn't be the right one.'

'He didn't like any kind of lavatory humour,' Frank Williams told me.

In one of the radio scripts they'd written something for me like 'Can you pass water through the window?' and he suddenly cottoned on to the double meaning and said 'No, no, we can't have that line.' He felt that slightly lavatorial humour didn't fit with the programme, and he was absolutely right.

The rest of the cast and sometimes even the writers and directors tended to defer to him. 'He clearly was the leader, not only in the character,' said Williams. 'When we were on tour with the stage show it was Arthur who actually sorted problems out.' As for Joan,

she was the sort of mother of the company. She was a clever woman and I liked her very much, but I can remember once in a restaurant two knives being crossed and she said superstitiously 'For goodness' sake uncross those knives', which struck me as odd for an intelligent woman.

Arthur's reputation was now so great that he was asked to play God – a bearded, one-legged eccentric called Javitt – in a TV adaptation of Graham Greene's story *Under the Garden*, for which he had to hop about on some slippery rocks in Chislehurst Caves in Kent with his leg strapped up. He also had his portrait painted by John Bratby but disliked the result and refused to buy it when Bratby offered to sell it to him for £200 (about £900 today). Busy though he was, he found time to write a kind letter and send a tie to John Laurie, who was unwell with emphysema and resting at his home in Chalfont St Peter in Buckinghamshire. 'My dear Arthur,' replied Laurie,

I feel very lonely without you all sometimes, and am sad not to be busy, as you are. But the slightest physical exertion puffs me out, and I've long accepted that my defection was inevitable. Mind you, if we were called on location to Thetford tomorrow, I'd be there! Thank you for sending on the tie – a kindly thought, from both Cheshire and you. My love to dear Joan, and all the best to you and the gang.
John L.

Once or twice a year the Lowes drove up to Hayfield to see Arthur's mother. He was amused to discover in the summer of 1975 that Nan, who was 90, had no idea how famous he had become. One day the village's new doctor introduced himself and when Arthur told Nan that he had just met her doctor she was astonished. 'But how on earth did he know your name?' she exclaimed.

One of his visits to Hayfield is still remembered gratefully. He had given the cricket club an Arthur Lowe Cup in memory of Big Arthur, and the club had made him its Vice-President. Now the committee asked if he could help them to raise about £5,000 (£20,000 today) to buy and improve the cricket ground where they and their forebears had been playing for 150 years. Arthur promised to bring a *Dad's Army* team to play against the village and with great generosity started the fund off by donating £400, the equivalent of £1,600 today. The *Dad's Army* team arrived by coach on Sunday, 9 May 1976 when the cast was appearing in the stage show 30 miles away in Bradford. It was a lovely sunny day and 3,000 people turned out to watch, among them Nan and her minder, Alice MacDonald. Proceedings started with a boozy lunch: 'Ba goom,' growled Arthur proudly, 'we've stopped a few barrels going sour today.' Although he and le Mesurier had signed contracts that forebade them to play any sports, Arthur donned a flat cap and strode on to the field before the game to inspect the *Dad's Army* team with their bats sloped in military fashion on their shoulders. Hayfield won the toss, batted first, and made 172 while

Arthur and le Mez sat in a marquee and sold their autographs. The villagers finally won by 25 runs when the *Dad's Army* team was all out for 147. At the end of the day the stars had raised the £5,000 and celebrated by staying overnight in Hayfield. 'We stopped a few more barrels going sour in the evening,' Pertwee remembered. The next morning they returned by coach to Bradford. 'Arthur was in one of his skittish moods,' said Pertwee,

> and when the coach was stopped to allow the gentlemen in the party to relieve themselves on the side of the road, hidden by the coach, Arthur quietly told the coach driver to move on. The sight of a dozen males standing in a straight line hastily adjusting their dress was like something out of a French farce.

When the show reached Richmond in Surrey in July one of the actors, 31-year-old Jeffrey Holland – who was later to play Spike Dixon in another Croft–Perry TV comedy series, *Hi-De-Hi!* – heard that his wife had gone into labour in hospital and dashed off to be with her without telling anyone except his two understudies. Arthur was furious. When Holland returned the next day he bellowed that people had had babies before and the show must go on, and accused Holland of being unprofessional. But the first bouquet of flowers to arrive at Mrs Holland's bedside was labelled 'From Arthur and Joan Lowe, with love'. To be fair to Arthur he was probably thoroughly fed up with babies because when the show reached Eastbourne and Brighton they were living aboard the *Amazon*, which was moored at Shoreham, with Stephen, Susan and nine-month-old Jack on board as well. 'It wasn't without its tensions,' said Stephen.

By the end of 1976 Arthur had reached the pinnacle of his career. He appeared for the first time in *Who's Who*, was asked to make a long radio programme about his favourite prose and poetry ('I don't think anything will be any funnier than P. G. Wodehouse'), and was earning so much money – he made 13 commercials and training films – that he took on an accountant, Lawrence Newman. 'Arthur was a very quiet, self-effacing person, quite shy, and as nervous as I was when we met, but we got on well and I was his accountant until he died,' Newman told me.

When I first met him he said 'Comedy is when you laugh at other people, and farce is when you laugh at yourself.' Arthur always laughed at himself, never at other people, and I was very impressed by this: it was really a very nice way to behave.

As for his tax affairs,

they were quite straightforward and he simply wanted his accounts prepared so that he didn't have any trouble with the Revenue. He was very careful about keeping bills and receipts, and he did his own VAT returns and always kept the money for the VAT in a separate account because if he didn't do it, he wouldn't have the money to pay them at the end of the quarter, but he found it difficult to do a tax return. His only asset of any note was *Amazon*, and he didn't earn as much as you might think. Even a leading actor's fees weren't *that* great, and he never earned more than £100,000 a year, though of course that would be worth much more now [in fact, £400,000 now].

Much of Arthur's income was taxed at the ferocious top rate of 83 per cent. '*Amazon* took up a lot of money,' said Newman.

It was always breaking down and needing expensive repairs, and he made some expensive trips in it. But apart from that he spent his earnings. I think he supported Stephen a lot and he certainly supported Joan, who earned very little indeed. The Revenue would allow him to claim his hotel expenses against tax, and if there was a hotel bill we'd charge the bill even if it included Joan, but they once asked me what meals he charged in his accounts and said they'd allow breakfast and dinner, because that was 'travelling and subsistence', but lunch was not allowed because that was not wholly and exclusively for the purpose of business but apparently for the domestic purpose of keeping yourself alive! So I recommended him to have a big breakfast and a big dinner but a very light lunch!

Now that Arthur was 61 Newman advised him to put at least 20 per cent of his income into a pension fund – a dangerously small percentage considering his age and the fact that he had no real savings, but 'that seemed to him a very high amount to give to a pension company' and he did not do it. By spending up to the hilt and not saving for his old age Arthur was flirting with disaster, for by 1976 his health was fast deteriorating; maybe he knew he had only a few years left and so decided that there was little point in contributing to a pension. 'He had put on more weight, he was more often irritable, and an air of general dissatisfaction pervaded,' said Stephen. He had also started to suffer from narcolepsy, which made him fall asleep in taxis, restaurants, during a play or recording, even in the middle of a sentence. In a restaurant once he slumped forward into a bowl of soup. A moment later he lifted his dripping face out of the bowl. 'The mulligatawny's not as good as it was,' he muttered. Sometimes people assumed he was drunk, and maybe sometimes he was. Certainly his heavy drinking cannot have helped his affliction. When he invited the Pertwees to dinner, Bill Pertwee told me,

he had the wine in a plastic bucket under the sink. 'It helps it to breathe, you know,' he said. 'There are two bottles in there' – and he poured directly from the bucket into the glasses. Then he fell asleep at dinner. When he woke up Joan said 'The soup's cold', and Arthur said 'Mmmm. Wine's very good.'

He had to give up driving and from now on relied on taxis and chauffeurs. 'The fact that he fell asleep did embarrass Joan,' Frank Williams told me. 'She was very apologetic.' She told Phyllis Bateman that she was enduring long hours of loneliness as she sat in hotel bedrooms while Arthur was asleep. To pass the time she would sit and paint the view from the window. Along with Arthur's drowsiness came a new hesitancy so that Croft and Perry found that increasingly they had to edit out of the *Dad's Army* recordings dozens of Arthur's *um*s, *er*s and *ah*s, and he found it more difficult than ever to learn his lines because he could barely keep awake long enough to read a page. During the stage show at the Shaftesbury Theatre Jimmy Perry once heard Joan telling Arthur in the dressing room: 'You'll have to learn it, Arthur, you know. You can't just wing it.'

Joan, too, had health problems. She was painfully thin, frail and undernourished, drank and smoked far too much, and suffered badly from the skin disease psoriasis. 'She used to put polythene bags on her thin legs to stop the itching,' Pam Cundell told me. 'I think it worried her – scratch, scratch, scratch, scratch – and she was a bit nervy.'

In January 1977 Arthur kept dozing off during the filming of a zany one-hour comedy film for television about the grandsons of Sherlock Holmes and Dr Watson. In *The Strange Case of the End of Civilisation As We Know It*, set in London in the 1970s, John Cleese played Holmes, Arthur was Watson, and they found themselves up against a plot to destroy civilisation by the evil grandson of the original Professor Moriarty. Cleese's inefficient Holmes is completely unless as a sleuth, his 'brilliant' deductions utterly obvious, and Arthur's stunningly dim Watson is an appalling doctor who kills the Commissioner of Police by mistake and tries to return the body to Scotland Yard in a brown paper parcel. 'The point about playing comedy successfully is that you must be totally serious about it,' Arthur told David Lewin of the *Daily Mail* during a break in filming.

> No matter how ridiculous what you say or do or wear is, you must never let it appear to be the slightest bit odd or out of place. When you start something new in comedy there are three panic points. The first is when you say 'Will I ever learn it?' The second is when you say 'How did I ever get into this one?' And the third is when you break up laughing in rehearsal because suddenly it is so funny. That is the period of release. When you're through that you're fine.

A few months later he made the same point to Reginald Brace of the *Yorkshire Post*:

> I treat every comic part as a straight part. The more seriously you play the part, the funnier it is. You see, people are only funny to other people, never to themselves. They are going about their business quite seriously, not realising other people find them funny. I mean, the man who slips on a banana skin doesn't do it on purpose.

He put this technique to such good use during the filming of his next half-hour TV play that Shaun Usher wrote in his *Daily Mail* review: 'Arthur Lowe is never happier than when apparently in deadly earnest – the indignant, baked-potato expression or the narrow, sniffing stare of somebody regarding life across a bad egg.' The play was *Car Along the Pass* by Ray Galton and Alan Simpson, in which Arthur played

Captain Mainwaring's double, Henry Duckworth, a loud, rude, bossy, chauvinistic, xenophobic Englishman on a two-week camping holiday in the Swiss Alps and hating every moment of it. He finds himself stranded in a broken-down cable car near St Anton with a German aristocrat who was educated at the English public school Haileybury, flew in the Luftwaffe during the war, dropped leaflets on Britain, and speaks excellent English – a combination of factors that is guaranteed to enrage Mainwaring/Duckworth, who even says at one point: 'Pay attention, everybody!'

THE GERMAN: 'Excuse me, old chap. I could not help overhearing. You have not enjoyed your holiday?'
DUCKWORTH (*suspiciously*): 'Have we met?'
'Excuse me. Permit me to introduce myself. Heinz Steiner.'
'German?'
'*Ja.*'
'I see.'
'From Baden-Baden. And you?'
'Henry Duckworth from Twickenham-Twickenham.'

To be frank the play was laboured and not that funny, but Arthur's performance delighted the authors. 'As soon as we were three or four pages into the script we knew the part was just right for Arthur,' said Simpson, and Galton added: 'There isn't a line we ever wrote for Hancock that Arthur couldn't do, and vice versa. They represent very similar English types.'

Three months later Arthur again demonstrated his remarkable versatility by playing something completely different: a serious part in a serious television play by Ian Curteis, *Philby, Burgess and Maclean*. His role was that of the one-eyed Labour Foreign Secretary Herbert Morrison, who had to deal with the 1951 spy scandal when the British traitors Guy Burgess and Donald Maclean defected to the Soviet Union and their fellow traitor, Kim Philby, was wrongly cleared of treachery before defecting in 1963. Arthur confessed that he would never have cast himself in the part, but by adopting a cockney accent and wearing a grey wig and heavy, round, black-rimmed spectacles with one frosted lens he even looked exactly like Morrison. His performance was once again hailed by the critics. It was 'a beautifully observed and controlled little cameo,' reported Peter Knight in the *Daily Telegraph*. By 1977 it seemed that he could do no wrong. In play after play, year after year, he hit exactly the right note. Despite his fame in *Dad's Army* and his reputation as a comedy actor he was so credible even in a spy thriller like *Philby, Burgess and Maclean* that he was chosen that summer as the first actor to play the part of John le Carré's English spymaster, George Smiley, in a documentary sketch. In 2000 le Carré told *The Times* that he would have been quite happy for Arthur to have gone on to play Smiley in the subsequent TV series *Tinker, Tailor, Soldier, Spy* in 1979 and *Smiley's People* in 1981 had not Alec Guinness come along and played the part superbly.

In June the Lowes went up to Thetford for the last time to record the location scenes for the six episodes of the ninth and final series of *Dad's Army*. Sadly all was not well with the cast. John le Mesurier had recently collapsed in Australia with liver failure caused by drinking too much alcohol and had been rushed to hospital. He turned up in Thetford looking so dreadfully thin and strained that during the shooting of one episode Croft ordered all the lights to be brought together and switched on so as to warm him up. Teddy Sinclair, the Verger, did not look at all well either, and Arthur had such trouble learning his lines that when they shot the indoor scenes he kept them in the top drawer of Mainwaring's desk so that when he forgot them he could stall for time by rumbling 'Wilson, Wilson, Wilson' while he pulled the drawer out in a desperate search for his next line.

In this last series the platoon pretended to be fifth columnists; dressed up in medieval costumes to stage the battle between St George and the Dragon; and in episode 80, 'Never Too Old', the last of them all, attended the wedding of Lance-Corporal Jones and Mrs Fox, who was played by Pam Cundell, an episode in which Joan appeared yet again as Godfrey's sister Dolly. At the wedding Mrs Fox was given away by Captain Mainwaring, and right to the end Arthur's nose for comic 'business' was infallible. During rehearsal he and Pam Cundell walked through a door together and became jammed in the doorway. 'Don't do it again until the actual take,' muttered Arthur, 'and we'll do it then and everybody will be in stitches.' He was right. In the marriage scene Croft and Perry invited all the wives with Equity cards to play the wedding guests, and Croft told Richard Webber:

The last recording was a very emotional experience for us all. The production gallery was unusually quiet during the recording and a truck-load of lumps were in a lot of throats … We had all enjoyed a glorious run of success and to stop, albeit at the top, was a wrench.

'Never Too Old' ended with the platoon drinking a toast to the Home Guard as Mainwaring delivered his final patriotic speech:

Anybody tries to take our homes or our freedom away from us, they'll find out what we can do. We'll fight. And we're not alone, there are thousands of us all over England … Scotland … Great Britain, in fact. Men who'll stand together when their country needs them.

Said Croft: 'As they assembled for the last shot and raised their tea mugs to join Arthur's toast, "To Britain's Home Guard", there wasn't a dry eye in the studio.' And that was it. No sensational ending, no fanfare. The series ended quietly, with a whimper.

Soon after recording the final episode Teddy Sinclair died of a heart attack at the age of 63. With Beck and Sinclair dead, le Mesurier looking as if he were on his last legs, Laurie and Ridley now 80 and 81, and Arthur dozing off and forgetting his lines, Croft turned to the cast after Sinclair's funeral and said 'I think that's about it', and they all nodded.

The cast and crew were appalled that the BBC neglected to throw a farewell party to mark the passing of one of the greatest comedy series ever, a series that had attracted more than 10 million viewers a week right to the end and was sold all around the world. It was left to Croft and Perry to organise a supper in a Notting Hill restaurant and the *Daily Mirror* to arrange a dinner at the Café Royal in London for the cast, their wives and friends, and to present the stars with medals inscribed 'For Services to Television Entertainment'. Almost everyone made a speech, including Joan Lowe, 'who was inclined to get rather merry,' David Croft told Graham McCann. 'She'd been going about three or four minutes when, all of a sudden, she slipped under the table – just like that – and Arthur, of course, took no notice and just carried on as if nothing had happened.'

'Bill Pertwee got up and said a lot of lovely things, as he always does, bless his heart, saying now lovely everybody was,' Clive Dunn told me.

Then Arthur got up in his usual diplomatic manner and said 'Personally, I never read the *Daily Mirror*. I wouldn't have it in my house.' Then somebody else got up, and then John Laurie got up and said 'We've heard a lot of things this evening but what nobody has mentioned is that actors are A LOAD OF CUNTS! He shouted it! I laughed so much I fell off my chair: I actually fell on to the floor. It was wonderful. Dear old John didn't give a sod for anybody.

Eventually the BBC Board of Governors was shamed into inviting the cast to a belated lunch. 'The BBC seemed strangely reluctant to show any appreciation,' wrote le Mesurier in his autobiography. 'Eventually, and I'm sure after much soul-searching and cost calculating, we were summoned to an official leaving party. A rather formal occasion which none of us enjoyed much, but it signalled the end.'

The greatest days of Arthur's life were over.

Together to the End
(1977–1982)

At 62 Arthur still felt unfulfilled as an actor even though he was now so famous that he made 18 commercials in 1977, more than ever, from Coleman's Mustard to the Australian airline Qantas. One was decidedly risqué for an actor so renowned for being straitlaced: in an ad for Cadbury's Hanky-Panky popcorn he sat on a park bench beside a woman and asked her 'Would you care for a bit of Hanky-Panky?' She slapped his face. 'I was only offering you a little nibble!' he protested, and she slapped his face again. But he feared he would never achieve all that he wanted, especially the big breakthrough into films. 'I think he saw time running out,' said Stephen, 'and he got depressed. Funny men do. My mum would buy my dad yellow waistcoats to cheer him up.'

Unfortunately she was drunker than ever every night and their rows became worse. 'There wasn't one dinner when she wasn't smashed by the end of it,' Peter Campbell told me, and Richard Gatehouse said: 'David told me she was very unhappy, God only knows why. She was ill a lot with arthritis and angina, and she always had a bottle of sal volatile around and when she felt her heart was ticking she would take a swig of it.' Sal volatile, of course, contains alcohol. Joan was now insisting that Arthur should never take on any stage play unless there was a part in it for her as well, and from now on he never appeared in a play without her and never again in the West End except in one pantomime. His last years were spent touring the provinces with her and many believe that Joan's insistence on acting with him destroyed his career. 'The Joan problem became worse and worse,' said Campbell.

At one stage Arthur verbally agreed to do a play for Michael Codron, who kept saying that there was nothing in it for Joan, but Arthur insisted. There was a policeman at the end of the play, so Codron said 'If we change the policeman to a policewoman would that appease the situation?' Joan said nothing, but later Arthur rang me and said 'I have to see you. I'm coming now.' When he arrived in my office he broke down. He walked in through the door and burst into tears. 'I've just had the worst weekend of my life,' he said. 'If there are any theatre offers don't even tell me if there's not a part for Joan.' It was a nightmare. She wasn't violent but she was quite a devious person. The main problem was drink, but frankly the talent just wasn't there, either. He was too bloody good not to be aware of it, but he loved her too much.

Harold Snoad told me that Arthur 'knew she wasn't as good as him but I think she was giving him a hard time about it. It may be that the marriage was getting a bit rocky and he thought this was a way of pulling it together.'

Other friends saw it differently. 'It was an act of devotion and in no way to "save" his marriage,' David Croft told me. Stephen wrote in his book that although it was 'a dreadfully disappointing sacrifice ... his motive in making such bitter sacrifices was the love he had for Joanie.' But Ian Lavender told me:

I never felt it was any hardship to him to turn down work later because of her. Yes, she was a pretty bad actress and she played as you imagine they did in rep in 1938, very dramatic and stagey, but he didn't want to leave her alone and he wanted to be with her. He loved her.

Arthur himself told Bill Pertwee: 'I don't like leaving her for too long and I don't like travelling on my own now, and she's not terribly well.' Christopher Bond told me: 'Up to a point he did sacrifice his career for her towards the end', but he also believed that Arthur deliberately narrowed his horizons and took on provincial tours because he could no longer keep learning new lines. 'Frankly, I think he'd *gone*,' said Bond, 'and this was one of the reasons why he turned to the theatre.' Jimmy Perry agreed: 'Arthur was getting on a bit and he hated studying new lines, so it was comfortable touring with Joan.' Richard Leech told me: 'I don't believe that Joanie was a witch. I know he enjoyed touring and I think he was a happy man going round the smalls of England, even though he was already very ill.' Frank Williams concurred.

I think Arthur deliberately chose to do those tours with her simply in order to be with her. If it did hold him back it was only because he chose to be held back. My guess is that he adored her so much he didn't like to see her unhappy. To me, it was a great love story. But yes, the booze may well have been a substitute for sex.

Pam Cundell felt that since Joan had 'devoted her life to Arthur', it was perfectly understandable that 'when he became famous she felt she'd like to have a little bit of fame herself and she insisted that she went out in plays with him. If it hadn't been for Joan I don't suppose he would have done anything because she was the one behind him.' But she agreed that Joan was not much of an actress. 'She had to say the lines and then walk, or walk and then say the lines, but she couldn't walk and say the lines together, so it was a bit of a stilted, old-fashioned performance.' However much Arthur loved Joan, it was surely a major sacrifice when Warren Beatty asked him to appear in his highly successful 1978 film *Heaven Can Wait* and he turned down the offer because of Joan. Richard Leech was still unimpressed. 'I can well believe that he would have said "I'd prefer to stay with my wife, thank you. I've got a good living over here and fuck Hollywood."' Stephen disagreed. 'Arthur would have had to go to America for the filming, something he would have loved,' he said, 'but he turned it down because there was no part for Joanie.' Arthur even considered buying the theatre on Brighton pier so that she could have one of her own to run, but in the end he backed off because the theatre needed a lot of refurbishment.

On the surface he seemed happy to downsize his career. 'What a perfect life it is, going on tour, with the wife in the same show,' he told Pearson Philips of the *London Evening News* in October 1977. 'You have all day to potter about doing things, and there is always something to do in the evening. Not only that, you are getting paid for it as well.' A year later he was telling Romany Bain of *TV Times*: 'We just like being together more than anything else. We visit nice places like Eastbourne and Bournemouth, and stay in nice hotels.' He also argued that it was good therapy for an actor to return regularly to the provincial theatre. He and Joan loved exploring new towns and poking around in antique shops, and he added that he thought of touring as 'a paid holiday when we can be together. God forbid, the idea of lying on a beach bores me stupid.' As for the possibility of retiring, he told Ivan Waterman of the *News of the World*:

Never. I never take a rest either. Who needs a rest? Joan and I are never going to retire ... Instead of us having to worry about our children settling down, it's Joan and I who never sit still. We're like rebellious kids roaming around playing parts we enjoy.

The first tour that they did together, at the end of 1977, was J. B. Priestley's *Laburnum Grove*, an old-fashioned 1930s comedy about the Depression, suburban hypocrisy, and a dull, middle-class, English family, where the pipe-smoking, slipper-shod, knitted-cardigan father, George Radfern, played by Arthur, tells his greedy, sponging, po-faced relatives that he is in fact a forger and counterfeiter, and that they owe everything they have to crime. Arthur and the producer, Duncan Weldon, went to see Priestley, who was 83, had just been awarded the Order of Merit, and told Arthur that he would have had him in mind to play Radfern had he known about him when the play was first produced in 1933.

Joan, as Radfern's wife, played a surprisingly large part – far too large in Weldon's opinion. When the play opened in Harrogate he telephoned Peter Campbell in desperation and told him that Joan's acting was so bad that they would never get the play into the West End unless they replaced her, but Arthur refused to continue unless she stayed. Although *Laburnum Grove* did eventually make it into London after playing in Birmingham and Leeds, not one critic mentioned Joan, despite her big part. She retaliated by producing a handwritten, spoof programme of a play called *Laburnum Grave* that sneered at everyone except Arthur and called Duncan Weldon 'Duncan Welldone'. Attached were quotes from spoof newspaper reviews: 'Sue Storr's production makes sure it drags from beginning to end'; 'Mr Bates proves himself once again to be the master of the inaudible line, treading the tightrope between tedium and total boredom'; 'breathtakingly meagre'.

The real reviews were kinder. 'The central glory of the production is, of course, Arthur Lowe,' wrote Frank Marcus in the *Sunday Telegraph*. 'He is perfectly cast: outwardly the epitome of boring conformity, but containing within him an impish anarchism.' 'His timing is perfect,' said Eric Shorter in the *Daily Telegraph*, and John Braine, author of *Room at the Top*, who later wrote a biography of Priestley, described Arthur as 'a comic actor of genius' and reckoned that he was one of a very few actors who could have played Radfern properly. Christopher Bond was less impressed. 'When we saw it at the Duke of York's Theatre in London, it wasn't a very comfortable evening,' he told me. 'The theatre was very empty and it's a creaky old play, not very up to date, and it didn't run long.'

The first episode of the last series of *Dad's Army* was broadcast on 2 October and Arthur delivered his own final salute to Captain Mainwaring when he told Reginald Brace a few days previously that Mainwaring was

a military Swindley, if you like. He was pompous, but courageous and sincere, too. Although he was always having his pomposity pricked, he always emerged with some sort of dignity, and he had a deep-rooted belief in all his potty schemes. He was a chauvinist to the death who actually believed that the Warmington-on-Sea platoon could save the South Coast. Maybe there was a bit of overspill of me in him, but not too much I hope. An actor is an actor is an actor.

As for the series itself, 'I don't think anyone believes it has ended yet,' he said. 'We were such a closely knit, happy team.'

The final episode of *Dad's Army* was broadcast on Sunday, 13 November 1977 and in the *Sunday Telegraph* Philip Purser hailed Arthur's performance over nine years as 'one of the comic creations of the age'. The platoon fell in one final time on TV when they appeared on the *Morecambe and Wise Christmas Show* on Christmas Day 1977 with a regiment of showbiz stars, among them Elton John, Richard Briers, Paul Eddington, Penelope Keith, Angela Rippon, and the racing driver James Hunt. It was the last time that Arthur played Mainwaring.

Not everything that Arthur touched turned to gold, and that year he suffered two rare setbacks. He played Dogberry in a BBC TV recording of *Much Ado About Nothing* with Penelope Keith, but the programme was eventually 'considered unsuitable' by the powers-that-were and never transmitted. The second disappointment was over a projected one-man stage show. Ever since he had so enjoyed playing Louis Pasteur four years earlier, and then Herbert Morrison in 1977, he had dreamed of portraying the conductor Sir Thomas Beecham on stage because he relished researching and playing the part of a real person. In the end the writers, Ned Sherrin and Caryl Brahms, chose Roy Dotrice instead of Arthur, and Ms Brahms told *The Times* why. 'I'm afraid we had a difference of opinion with Arthur as to how he should portray Sir Thomas,' she said. 'He wanted to play him as something of a ladies' man. Ned and I thought otherwise.' After years of being so prim about sex, Arthur seemed to be experiencing a quickening libido in his sixties. Perhaps it was just as well that he was about to play the part of a celibate priest: in a new TV comedy series, *Bless Me, Father*, he starred as a wily, mischievous old Irish Roman Catholic, Father Duddleswell, complete with cassock, collar, biretta, Irish accent, a penchant for saying 'Jaysus', and a feuding housekeeper, Mrs Pring. Arthur relished the part, which allowed him to deliver elegant Gaelicisms such as 'What are me chances? Slighter than the thin white vest clinging to the inside of an eggshell'; and 'Jaysus, 'tis as useless as hammering cold iron with a hair of me head.' When his newly ordained, naïve young curate, Father Boyd, asks if Catholics and Protestants have separate areas in the local cemetery, old Duddleswell replies:

Indeed. We do not believe in mixed funerals, you follow? At the Last Day, St Michael will blow loud the Trumpet Blast, and winds wild as angels on horseback will blow from the four corners of heaven, and God will start His resurrecting, like, in this sacred little plot of Catholic earth. 'Stand up, Seamus Flynn,' He will cry. 'Stand up, Mary Ryan. Stand up, Micky O'Brien, if you are yet sober.'

Duddleswell was quite different from Mainwaring and Swindley, softer and more tolerant. Arthur was not himself at all religious. 'Sunday is my day of rest,' he said, and 'it would be a bit odd for me to see the light at my age. If the fee's right, that's the only light I can see. My eyes light up every Friday.' Unhappily the seven-part series barely lit up at all. It is embarrassingly thin and not nearly as enjoyable as the delightful Peter De Rosa novel on which it was based. Even Arthur's admirer Sylvia Clayton of the *Daily Telegraph* reported that although Arthur's Irish brogue was agreeable enough, 'he is not a convincing illogical Irishman'. Arthur ignored the criticism, relished the part, and Joan later claimed that Father Duddleswell was his favourite TV part of all. He certainly enjoyed the character very much, 'the straight-talking, cynical, Catholic priest,' I was told by Daniel Abineri, who was 19 when he played the part of Duddleswell's young curate, Father Neil, and whose greatest moment of fame had come the previous year when he had given 14-year-old Tatum O'Neal her first screen kiss in the film *International Velvet*.

He really enjoyed the challenge because Duddleswell wasn't pompous, he was fallible. I was terrified of meeting Arthur because he was a very big star. A rather overkeen assistant took him on the first day of filming to a caravan and said 'This is your caravan, Mr Lowe', and Arthur said 'Oh, that's very nice, what an enormous caravan, a Winnebago', and the assistant was so over-excited that he said 'Yes, and we've actually got an even better one than this', and Arthur said 'Oh, really? Really?' – and the next day the Winnebago had gone. He'd obviously gone down and said 'you've got an even better one.'

I was incredibly in awe of him, rather frightened of him, actually, because he was very like Captain Mainwaring, with that no-nonsense brusqueness, and he could be quite pompous, and he could be devastatingly rude and would go quite red in the face. At first people thought he was doing his Mainwaring act and would laugh, which infuriated him. He had a real temper on him – never with me, but I remember we were filming in the Isle of Wight and Joan wound him up because their hotel room was too small, and I remember him standing at the top of the staircase in this big hotel *screaming* abuse at the production manager about his room. But he was terribly nice to me. He was very paternal and protective of my performance, which was in his interest: he knew that he'd got this young bloody actor and if the chemistry between us didn't work and I wasn't right, the series wasn't going to work. I was very young, very green, and he was fabulous in that he would take me aside and say 'Why don't you try that line with a pause there, and play that a little slower?' He taught me the Rule of Three, which is a comedy rule based on three counts: if you leave a beat of three before a good laugh line it's almost guaranteed to get a laugh. He was obsessed with the minutiae of comedy, the technicalities, and loved W. C. Fields and would do little bits of his dialogue and told me how the guy inspired him to become a performer. He said 'I'd love to write an encyclopaedia of physical comedy, every gag you can do with a revolving door, every gag you can do with a hat, with little diagrams', which I thought was a great idea. He was a very adept physical comedian, very dextrous, and he could get a laugh out of anything, really. There's that wonderful dance sequence that he does in *The Ruling Class* – that's his finest hour – and he could be like a little elegant pig.

But he was intolerant of people and his audience. One excruciatingly funny incident was when we were shooting an episode in the studio. He used to go round to the back of the audience and stand underneath their seats and listen and form an opinion as to what sort of people they were. He came back while the warm-up man was doing his routine and sat down with me at the table where we were playing a scene and said 'I've just had a listen to this audience and they're the biggest load of morons I've ever come across. They must have been carted in from a mental hospital.' The hubbub of the crowd was going quieter and quieter, and the warm-up man had stopped, and I looked up to one of the monitors and realised that the camera was on him, and the boom was hanging down, and they'd all heard it. There was this terrible silence with embarrassed giggles, and he looked at me and turned to the camera and said 'I was just teasing you, ha-ha-ha', and got a huge laugh out of it.

But we never got that close and I never cracked the surface with him, though we would sit in his caravan and he would talk about his early career. He said he knew he'd been very lucky with *Dad's Army*. 'I was 47 when I started really to make it,' he said, 'so you've got to hang on in there and keep working.' I think he was aware of the thin ice he was on and that he should make hay while the sun shone.

The second tour that the Lowes undertook together, in the summer of 1978, was in a farce, *Caught Napping*, in which they appeared with Fiona Fullerton and Bill Pertwee, and Arthur played a schoolmaster. It was a very funny part, said Pertwee:

We really enjoyed every moment of that wonderful tour. One of the many wonderful comic moments in the play is when the dotty butler announces that the Aga Khan has come to visit the house. The visitor is in fact a bookmaker dressed as a plumber, so bears no resemblance to the Aga Khan. After the plumber has left, the major general, who is also rather dotty, says quite casually and as a matter of course, 'Funny, I always thought the Aga Khan was a much taller man.'

The play took them to nine towns in 12 weeks, from Leeds and Birmingham to Cardiff and Brighton, and when it reached Eastbourne in August, Pertwee, knowing that both men greatly admired each other, arranged for Arthur to meet the much loved 78-year-old music-hall comedian Sandy Powell, whose catchphrase 'Can you hear me, Mother?' had once been as famous all over the British Empire as Arthur's 'You stupid boy!' From a certain angle Powell looked remarkably like Arthur and as performers they had a great deal in common: both were convinced that clean, wholesome humour was funnier than smut and refused to tell even the most mildly risqué joke, and both had an instinct for farce that was touched by a genuinely comic pathos. They even had 'the same sort of stance,' Pertwee told me,

> both small men, feet wide apart, and Sandy used to put his glasses up in the same way as Arthur did. I introduced them in the glass conservatory of the front of the hotel at about noon and they were still there three hours later. They got blotto together on gin and tonics discussing this and that and making each other laugh. I wish I'd had a video camera to record two masters of their craft in full sail.

Sadly Arthur's narcolepsy was beginning to affect his life seriously. Sometimes he nodded off on stage and Joan would kick him surreptitiously and pray that he would wake up in the right play. When *Caught Napping* reached Bath there was one night when he really was caught napping: he was due on stage at any moment and his dresser rushed down to Pertwee crying 'I can't wake Mr Lowe!' Pertwee

> went upstairs and shook him – 'Arthur, wake up!' – but he wouldn't wake, so we got Joan, who smacked his knee and said 'Arthur, wake up, you naughty boy!' She said 'Open the window' and we got his head right out of the window and she sprayed the soda siphon on the back of his neck. That woke him!

Moments later they manoeuvred him, still dopey but at least already dressed in shorts, T-shirt and plimsoles for his part as a schoolmaster, towards his entrance. This was down a long flight of stairs and to get to the top he first had to climb a ricketty wooden staircase. Somehow they managed to get him, still half asleep, to the top. They held their breaths. 'The curtain went up and Arthur started his descent of the staircase,' wrote Pertwee in his autobiography. 'It took a bit longer than usual for him to descend, but the amount of comedic business he got out of it, most of which must have been instinct, was wonderful to watch, and the audience applauded his entrance even more than usual.'

Arthur was astonishingly careless of his health. Now 63, he ate, drank and smoked far too much and took no exercise at all so that he had begun to become very fat and unfit, a classic case for a stroke or heart attack. 'He wouldn't just have a small omelette at night, he'd have a huge meal and a couple of bottles of wine,' Pertwee told me, 'and as he got tubbier he got lazier in walking, and because he didn't walk he'd get even more slovenly.' Yet somehow he retained a jaunty perkiness and would dress nattily in a loud checked jacket and blue corduroy peaked cap. Nor did he lose his impishness. In Bath he and Pertwee emerged from a Spanish restaurant one night and saw two old ladies waiting for someone. Pertwee told me:

They didn't recognise us, and Arthur suddenly started to play the drunk. He put his hand through my arm, stood on the edge of the pavement, and started looking up the road and putting one foot out and staggering back. It was hysterical. I started doing it with him, and then suddenly he did this little run across the road. One of the old ladies said: 'Those two have had a *skinful* tonight. It's *disgusting*.' Arthur was delighted.

In September the Lowes went off for a month to Austria, where Arthur and Ian Carmichael played two cricket-mad old English buffers in a remake of Alfred Hitchcock's 1938 thriller film *The Lady Vanishes*. The original version had starred Michael Redgrave and Margaret Lockwood as two spy-hunters aboard a train in Nazi Germany as Europe teetered on the brink of the Second World War, and the two silly-ass cricket fans on holiday abroad – and desperate to return to England in time for the last Test match against the Australians at Lord's – had been played by

Naunton Wayne and Basil Radford. The remake starred the Americans Elliott Gould and Cybill Shepherd. Even so, Carmichael and Arthur – who was tweedily splendid in deerstalker hat, bow tie, waistcoat, watch chain and plus-fours – were able to keep their characters as daftly pre-war English as they had been in the original because the scriptwriter George Axelrod left their parts unchanged, admitting he knew nothing about cricket. This had quickly become obvious when Arthur (Vice-President of Hayfield Cricket Club) and Carmichael (a member of the MCC) discovered to their horror that at first the script described the great English batsman Len Hutton as a bowler. Then they learned that the new version of the film was to be set in 1939, not 1938, in which case the last Test would have been not against the Aussies at Lord's but the West Indians at the Oval, and the English team would have been different. The script had to be changed again.

'Arthur was a very amusing, affable man,' Ian Carmichael told me,

and we had quite a good time on *The Lady Vanishes* and it was fun to make except that the director never seemed to know what he wanted. There was one character who was one day a nurse, then the next day an SS man. He couldn't make up his mind what to do with him. The result is a travesty of the Hitchcock film, I'm afraid, but Arthur was a very good actor indeed, an ace farceur with tremendous comedic sense and yet he never really stepped out of character. He played the farcical situations so really and truly that you believed them.

The reviewers were much kinder about *The Lady Vanishes* than Carmichael, though they were not so kind about Arthur's next film, *Sweet William*, in which he played Jenny Agutter's retired army-captain father and managed to wangle a part for Joan.

Arthur rarely ventured into politics but he admired Prime Minister Edward Heath's enthusiasm for the European Common Market as well as his seamanship. He not only allowed his face to appear (along with that of J. B. Priestley and others) on a pro-Europe poster but even turned out in November to open a Conservative fund-raising bazaar in Heath's constituency of Bexley and Sidcup, the sort of celebrity chore that he usually tried to avoid and that he would have sneered at had Clive Dunn done it for Harold Wilson. His presence 'delighted everyone', Heath wrote to Joan later, and helped to raise more than £1,000, a record for the constituency association.

In January 1979 Arthur started four months' work on a new BBC television series, *Potter* by Roy Clarke, in which he played a sweet manufacturer ('Pottermints the Hotter Mints') who has been forced to take early retirement and relives his boredom by interfering in other people's business and causing trouble. Arthur himself remarked that Mainwaring was 'Swindley in uniform' and Potter was 'Mainwaring in civvies'. In some scenes the smug, expansive Potter is barely distinguishable from Mainwaring, as in this scene when a couple of French tourists in England have lost their way:

ENGLISH WOMAN: It appears he's looking for Grasmere Road.
POTTER: *Ah, la rue de Grasmere. Oui*, I remember it well. No bother at all. A piece of cake. *Un morceau de gâteau.*
[*The Frenchman looks baffled. The English woman goes her way.*]
POTTER: *Au revoir, madame.* Take a tip from me, *monsieur*. When in *Angleterre* don't take directions from the English memsahibs. Utter waste of time. Don't make enquiries *par* the British female. Anyone with a sense of direction wouldn't wear a hat like that.

When Joan was asked which character Arthur resembled most of all those he had played she giggled: 'I used to see signs of Captain Mainwaring, but after seeing him in *Potter* that's more like the real Arthur.' But after he died in 1982 she said: 'Looking back, the bossy, pompous Captain Mainwaring of *Dad's Army* captured more of his character than any other part.' In fact Potter is not nearly as pompous and bossy as Mainwaring and his relaxed, chit-chat relationship with the other two main characters – the amiable male-chauvinist vicar and the twitchy antique dealer 'Tolly' Tolliver – and the slow, affable pacc of each episode resembled that of the three elderly, laid-back northern men in Clarke's earlier TV series, *Last of the Summer Wine*. The scripts were much more amusing than those of *Bless Me, Father* and Arthur would have enjoyed the fact that some of the jokes were refreshingly politically incorrect, such as when the vicar remarks airily: 'I liked coloured people until it became compulsory.' In another episode Potter is showing a bewildered group of Japanese tourists around and someone remarks: 'You wonder how they ever found Pearl Harbor.' The lanky, laddish vicar was played by John Barron, fresh from his triumph a couple of years earlier as C.J. in *The Rise and Fall of Reginald Perrin*, who had last appeared with Arthur in rep 30 years previously. Their hapless, henpecked butt, Tolliver, was played by John Warner, who had made a name for himself in the 1950s as the young star of the phenomenally long-running hit musical *Salad Days*. 'We got on frightfully well,' Barron told me,

but he did keep himself to himself. We were doing *Potter* on location and were all thrown together in a hotel for three weeks, but you didn't see much of Arthur. He was drinking or having dinner on his own or with Joan. He didn't join us, not like the rest of us. I don't think it was arrogance. It was shyness, I think, especially with women, with actresses in the cast.

He did, however, keep up with his oldest friends: the Bonds, the Leeches, and some of the cast of *Dad's Army*. 'Pamela Cundell and I would quite often go out with Arthur and Joan for a meal,' said Frank Williams, 'and he would say "I've just done a commercial, I'll pay." He never let one pay. He wasn't mean. He was really very generous.'

By now the narcolepsy had become so bad that Arthur fell asleep even in the studio 'when they were building the set and hammering away under bright lights', John Warner told me. 'And when we were on location in Bournemouth he fell asleep in the middle of signing an autograph.'

To bolster Joan's career Arthur formed their own little repertory company in 1979 so that they could control every aspect of the plays they took on tour. They hired old chums like Honor Shepherd (who had appeared in *Potter*) and Vyvian Hall (who had been in both *Potter* and *Bless Me, Father*) and persuaded their old friend Christopher Bond to direct their first play for them, *Beyond a Joke*, a new comedy by Derek Benfield, even though Bond had not been near a theatre for 30 years. 'Arthur was the actor–manager and he loved it,' Bond told me. 'He liked being in charge and this little company was another pull to keep him and Joan together.' In Derek Benfield's original version of *Beyond a Joke* there had been no obvious part for Joan, but Arthur asked him to change the part of his mother to his sister so that Joan could play it. 'I'd have changed the part into a Japanese wrestler if he had asked,' Benfield told me. 'The great Arthur Lowe was going to do my play! I couldn't believe my good fortune.' Arthur liked the play because it was funny but also clean family entertainment at a time when he said that on stage and screen 'there's either too much violence or foul language or people popping in and out of each other's beds ... People are fed up with that sort of thing.'

The producer of *Beyond a Joke*, John Newman, told me that despite Arthur's reputation for being difficult 'I never had a wrong word with him in three years. He loved acting.' And Arthur acted all the time, even off stage: Stephen remembered that if Arthur served someone with a drink on board the *Amazon* 'he would have a white cloth draped over his arm, once again the steward on the SS *Adriana*'. As for Joan, Newman said,

she'd very much go on stage and brace her legs against the rake and say the lines, but she was fine in *Beyond a Joke*, and playing his sister there were some lovely gags that they got together. What you had to do was to cast her correctly. She was fine as long as you didn't give her Hedda Gabler to play. You gave her a support part that she was going to do no harm in.

Beyond a Joke opened at the Shanklin Theatre in the Isle of Wight in July 1979. Arthur's part – as a businessman living in a country house where people are constantly having lethal accidents – 'seemed to fit him like a glove,' said Benfield. 'The moment he made his first appearance on the opening night – in city suit, bowler hat and carrying a rolled umbrella – the audience applauded and I knew we were onto a winner.' *The Stage* enthused: 'Arthur Lowe excels ... His superb timing and skill in milking every funny situation really brings the character to life. It's a gem from start to finish.' Said Benfield:

He touched every part he played with his own special magic. Once he had learned the part and seen that it worked, then that was how he kept it, but always managed even in a long run to make it appear as if each line had only just occurred to him.

And it was to be a very long run indeed, for after Shanklin the Lowes were to take the play on a successful nationwide tour, then to Australia and New Zealand, and in 1981 they were to revive it for another long tour of English provincial theatres.

Stephen was by now the actual skipper of the *Amazon*, no matter how much Arthur liked to pretend that *he* was, and that summer he sailed the boat to Falmouth to help BBC TV with an episode of *The Onedin Line* and organised a burial-at-sea scene for *Bless Me, Father*. He and his new girlfriend, whom he called Bear, anchored the boat off Cowes so that Arthur and Joan could live on board during that eight-week summer season in Shanklin. Each day they commuted to and from the shore in an inflatable dinghy with Arthur dolled up in a yachting cap and reefer jacket. 'Arthur would usually arrive at the Folly with a wet bottom,' Stephen wrote in his book,

> but with his gusto for disparaging other people's boats undampened …
> 'Look at that poxy little thing,' he would say in a voice that could fill the
> Palladium. 'I don't know how people could put to sea in a tub like that.'
> Or, worse, 'I wonder if that clown knows what he looks like.'

At night after the show Stephen would ferry them in the dinghy back to the boat and on board 'there would be gins and a cold supper with wine, brandies, tantrums, cold beers and standing on the deck in the cool early hours with cigarettes, and in the morning it would all begin again.' There was not much time for proper sailing but in his book Stephen vividly captured the atmosphere of one idyllic Sunday when there was no performance and they sailed down the English Channel with their friend Honor Shepherd, who was Arthur's wife in the play and whose husband was Bob Dorning, Arthur's old friend from *Pardon the Expression*:

> Joan took up her sea-spot on the bench in the deckhouse, her things
> arranged about her, silver bosun's call on a chain around her neck,
> packet of Craven 'A' and gleaming brass Zippo lighter, harmonica,
> newspaper folded open at the crossword. Arthur stood on the bridge or
> took a trick at the wheel, arctic convoy coat kapok-cosy in the hot
> summer sun. Honor elegant beside him, vibrant and romantic, all her
> favourite men short and fat with whiskers.

You can smell the happiness.

In September they took the play on a nationwide tour, starting with the Alexandra Theatre in Birmingham. Stephen, Bear and their friend Alan Cundell battled for four days to sail the *Amazon* across the English Channel through some dreadful weather to Jersey so that Arthur, Joan and Honor could live on board there while they put on the play in St Helier. They revelled in an Indian summer and Arthur and Stephen shared a delight in shopping together for prawns, scallops, crabs and shark steaks. 'Arthur loved to dress crabs,' said Stephen, 'and he would spend an hour or two standing in the galley patiently picking the meat out of every last crevice. These he would proudly present to members of the cast he had invited for lunch. Joan preferred tinned sardines, or baked beans.' After Jersey they flew back to the mainland and the Theatre Royal, Brighton, while Stephen and Bear sailed the *Amazon* across the Channel through the swollen autumn seas and moored it in Brighton marina. Then Joan and Arthur took the play on to Eastbourne, where they fell out with Honor Shepherd. The actors' union, Equity, was holding a ballot asking members to strike over a dispute with theatre managers and the Lowes, who were both rigidly right-wing, were incensed by Honor Shepherd's support for the strike. 'Arthur went potty,' John Newman told me, 'and Joan threatened to throw Honor off the boat.' Daniel Abineri also learned to be careful with his political opinions. He told me:

I was a young left-wing actor and Arthur was pretty far right. He was so happy when Thatcher got in in 1979. He had been to No. 10 Downing Street and had a desk made that was a copy of the Prime Minister's desk [which Chippendale had made for Pitt the Elder in 1760] and he was very proud of it and went on and on about it.

That summer Arthur made a 45-minute silent movie with Eric Sykes, *The Plank*, in which he and Sykes try to move a plank of wood from a carpenter's yard to a building site, and then a second series of *Bless Me, Father*. 'He was terribly nice to me,' said Abineri. 'I had my first child during the second series and he was terribly considerate and said: "Now you get home, don't stay too long in the bar, have a good night's sleep." He was very paternal with me.' As always, he drove himself incredibly hard. He did all 17 voices on a long-playing record on which he read modern adaptations of Aesop's fairy tales, *Aesop in Fableland*, with music by the

London Symphony Orchestra, and he had his little rose garden in Maida Vale concreted over because he said he would never have any time for gardening, which in any case he hated. He was now 64, fat, puffy, unfit – he never took any exercise – and the strain was beginning to show. Joan was looking very ill too. Her mother died just before Christmas and when she went up north alone for the funeral on Boxing Day her sister Margaret was appalled to see how fragile she looked. 'That was one of the things that hurt me,' Margaret Stapleton told me. 'I trained to be a nurse and I wish Joan had confided in me more about her health. She was so thin and so frail. She looked as though she would blow away in the wind.' It was a toss-up whether Joan or Arthur would be the first to suffer some serious illness. At the end of 1979 Abineri heard that Arthur had had a mild stroke and a friend of John Newman told him that he had seen Arthur fall over in the street and get up unsteadily. 'He'd probably had a stoke that he hardly knew he'd had,' said Newman. 'And he still drank a lot.'

After spending Christmas on board the *Amazon* at Teddington, Arthur did take a few weeks off in April. Stephen and Bear sailed the *Amazon* across the Channel through some heavy gales with the idea of taking the boat up the River Seine as far as Paris – April in Paris – and Arthur and Joan crossed the Channel by ferry and met them in Honfleur. They spent three delightful days there and were joined by Bear's brother, Rupert, and the five of them sailed off up the Seine. It was a disastrous holiday. The *Amazon*'s intermediate shaft bearing became extremely hot and needed to be cooled constantly with a bucket of water to prevent it catching fire. Then the boat rammed an iron piling, which snapped the bowsprit in half. French engineers had to be summoned and the boat and her occupants were delayed for three days. They limped further upriver through Rolleboise, Rouen and Vernon, where they ran aground on a mudbank. A French barge tried to tow them off but succeeded only in snapping off the taffrail and ensign staff. Joan 'took immediately to her bunk with a bottle of gin,' reported Stephen. Eventually a Dutch barge helped to free the *Amazon* but the boat had to run more and more slowly to reduce vibration from the dodgy intermediate shaft. 'They accused me,' Stephen wrote sadly in his book.

I accused them. When our big guns were spent we peppered each other at short range with irrelevant little grievances. One sad Sunday, in a beautiful place where the cliffs rise sheer from the river and buzzards wheel on the hot air of the afternoon, I mutinied and would not take the *Amazon* on. 'Look, just get the fucking boat back to England,' my mother said and, with nothing but a holdall and a credit card, Arthur and Joan set off to find their own way home. They must have been terribly, bitterly disappointed.

They returned to England by train. Stephen, Bear and Rupert sat it out in France while the *Amazon* was repaired frighteningly expensively, and eventually they did sail into the heart of Paris and moored opposite L'Isle de la Cité. Arthur and Joan flew out to inspect the repairs and Arthur proclaimed them excellent. 'Joan was buoyed up too,' said Stephen, 'carried along on Arthur's enthusiasm, but I felt she was damaged, we were damaged, our relationship never really to recover from the days that led up to the mutiny.' It was not until the middle of July that Stephen, Bear and Rupert sailed the *Amazon* back up the Thames to her home berth at Teddington.

In 1980 Arthur recorded another *Potter* series and a third series of *Bless Me, Father*, during which 'he was in a terrible way,' Abineri told me.

He would fall asleep in the character of Father Duddleswell and wake up as Captain Mainwaring. "You stupid boy!" he'd say. And he'd fall asleep when you were doing your lines, which was really disconcerting. And he put on a lot of weight and looked a lot older in the last couple of years.

But in August the Lowes were both well enough to attend a royal garden party at Buckingham Palace – where Joan quizzed the Queen about New Zealand – and then to take *Beyond a Joke* on an eight-week tour of New Zealand and Australia with an Australian cast, John Newman as producer and Vyvian Hall as director. The flight took 36 hours but 'we took him out first class and he enjoyed going,' Newman told me.

When we arrived at Sydney we went into the transit lounge and had a drink. Joan had been bevvying quite a bit on the plane and when they called us to go back on the plane we suddenly realised that she couldn't get up. Lots of people came up and said 'Ooh, it's Captain Mainwaring' and Arthur said 'Take one arm, I'll take the other, stiff upper lip', and we took one arm each and her feet weren't actually on the ground and we walked through and he cried 'Long flight, sick woman, long flight, sick woman', and we went straight through onto the plane. It was hysterical.

By the time they finally reached New Zealand Arthur was equally frazzled. The *New Zealand Women's Weekly* writer Amanda Samuel reported that when he and Joan gave a press conference on their arrival at Auckland airport he was red-faced, bloodshot-eyed, crotchety and called a press photographer 'sir'. Knowing Arthur, this was more likely to be due to sarcasm rather than respect. Later he used to remark 'I arrived in New Zealand on the weekend but it was closed'; in those days almost every shop was indeed shut on Saturdays and Sundays. 'Everybody knew him there,' said Newman, 'but we didn't do terribly good business. We just played to sheep, really, as Arthur said.' One cold, damp, cobwebbed theatre had not put on a play for years and Arthur told the local paper: 'It's like opening a disused railway station and expecting the trains to run.' When the company left the 1,800-seat Regent Theatre in Dunedin one of the cast, Alan Fletcher, scribbled in the visitors' book: 'Just think – 1,710 more people and we'd have turned them away.' As for Joan, 'she was pissed every night,' said Newman, and

there was a press guy who really got up Arthur's nose because he'd arranged so many heavy press calls. For one he was required to go round with a camera crew early in the morning to three locations. At the first he was asked to get into a *Bless Me, Father* Catholic priest outfit. Then he went on to where they had a Leonard Swindley outfit with the pork pie hat and the jacket. And the third one was Captain Mainwaring, and by then Arthur wasn't getting on at all well with the director and the cap had no cap badge on it, so he said 'I couldn't possibly do this without the correct regimental cap badge.' The poor assistant stage manager looked astounded and I said to Arthur 'They're never going to find that cap badge', and he said 'Tell them to get some chewing gum and put some silver paper round it and stick it on.'

The PR man was not the only one to get up Arthur's nose: so did 40 Maoris when he had to rub nostrils with them at an ethnic welcoming ceremony.

Back in England Arthur made a speech in Moreton-in-Marsh at a reunion of the Duke of Lancaster's Own Yeomanry which he attended with Bill Bateman. 'He was as warm and friendly as ever and his speech was hilarious,' his old army comrade Nobby Hewitt told me. 'He had us helpless with laughing: nothing blue or suggestive, just real humour, still taking off officers and relating wartime experiences, the same old Arthur.'

The Lowes spent Christmas on board the *Amazon* again and immediately began rehearsals for *Hobson's Choice*, a 65-year-old play, set in 1880, in which Arthur played a mean, tyrannical, northern shoe-shop owner whose strong-minded, 30-year-old spinster daughter, Maggie, played by Julia McKenzie, rebels against him, marries one of his young workers (played by Ronald Pickup), persuades her two sisters to marry against their father's will, and sets up a rival shoe shop that steals most of her father's customers. Joan played Mrs Hepworth, a mysterious woman who helps Maggie and her husband. The play opened in February at the Lyric Theatre, Hammersmith. For once Arthur's performance earned only lukewarm reviews because the critics felt that he was not nearly tyrannical enough, 'not so much a tiger as a grumpy tom', said one.

In the spring of 1981 the Lowes began yet another tour of *Beyond a Joke*, taking it to Darlington, Hull, Lincoln, Peterborough and Cardiff before settling down with it for a long run entertaining summer holiday-makers in Eastbourne while they lived with Stephen aboard the *Amazon* in Brighton marina. 'When they came to Peterborough,' said Christopher Bond,

we were both very shocked by Arthur's appearance. In two years he really had deteriorated. He was enormously pot-bellied, far too overweight, and the bones of his neck had solidified so that he couldn't move his neck. We thought he should really pack it in or not do so much, and of course a few months later he was dead.

'He was a workaholic,' Derek Benfield told me.

He would often travel up to London in the morning to do voice-overs, returning in the afternoon to have a nap before going off to the theatre. I don't suppose anyone could have stopped him, but I remember suggesting that he take a break after Eastbourne, but he was committed to do a pantomime and had then promised to do a tour of *Home at Seven*, and being a man of his word he would not let anyone down.

The numerous voice-overs were for children's *Mister Men* films. That year he also made several children's radio programmes and no fewer than 19 commercials, from Granny Bonds and Concorde lawnmowers to Guinness and Walkers Crisps. In July he and John le Mesurier also recorded a pilot programme for a new radio series about a seaside pier, *It Sticks Out Half a Mile*, in which Captain Mainwaring and Sergeant Wilson meet again after the war but this time Wilson is the bank manager and Mainwaring needs a loan to buy a disused pier. The pilot, written by Harold Snoad and Michael Knowles, was never transmitted because Arthur died before a series could be made; later, 13 episodes were broadcast with Bill Pertwee and Ian Lavender, still in their *Dad's Army* roles as Bill Hodges and Frank Pike, buying the pier instead.

Arthur and Daniel Abineri also went to Holland, where *Bless Me, Father* was a big hit, to make a short comedy film promoting a camera. 'They paid us a fortune,' said Abineri,

and we stayed in a hotel in Amsterdam together for three or four days. I noticed he did like a drop and he asked if I'd been down to the red-light district and said he had been there. He was reminiscing about it and we had a conversation about the hookers.

By now Arthur's narcolepsy was a constant trial. 'On a bad day he could be asleep as much as he was awake,' said Stephen, who was finally divorced from Susan Turner in September. But still Arthur soldiered on. That month at Box Hill School in Surrey he recorded the first of six episodes of his last TV series, *A. J. Wentworth, B.A.*, about a bumbling old 1940s prep-school master whose pupils run rings around him. Sadly it was slow, dull, and not a tenth as funny as the hilarious book by H. F. Ellis on which it was based. Arthur was exhausted, and looked it. When he presented a cheque to the winner of a newspaper competition in December he looked as if he might drop dead at any moment. Joan later claimed that she and others often begged him to take a break but he refused to listen.

Like some awful black joke he was cast in his penultimate film to play the part of an old man dying in hospital. *Britannia Hospital* was Lindsay Anderson's typically manic, but this time amusing, satire on the shambolic state of Britain at the end of the 1970s before Margaret Thatcher came to power in 1979. The country and hospital are paralysed by strikes, corrupt trade union officials, bolshy pickets and bombs exploding in London, yet the hospital is preparing for a visit by the Queen Mother, who is eventually smuggled in past the pickets on a hospital trolley. It is all great fun – one black nurse was wittily named Nurse Persil – and Anderson assembled a superb cast, several of them favourites who had appeared in his films before: Alan Bates as a corpse; Graham Crowden as a wonderfully mad professor; Jill Bennett as his assistant; Malcolm McDowell as a protester who breaks into the hospital; Peter Jeffrey as a surgeon; Leonard Rossiter as a hospital administrator; Joan Plowright as a union representative; Dandy Nichols as a hospital cook; Fulton Mackay as a police chief superintendent. The music, including numerous naff, off-key versions of *Rule Britannia*, was by Alan Price. Once again Arthur's part was tiny: it consisted of just one scene two-thirds of the way through the film and he was on screen for no more than a minute, yet his performance was brilliant. As the advance party from Buckingham Palace is shown around the hospital they open the door of a private room and there in bed, dying, is 'our most distinguished Foreign Secretary since Palmerston' – Arthur – and he is furious with them all. 'You wouldn't listen to me!' he croaks from his bed as they stand in his doorway gaping at him. 'This sceptred isle? This other Eden, demi-paradise? This precious stone set in the silver sea? This blessed plot? This realm? This England?' – and dies of a massive stroke, as Arthur himself was to do so soon. In retrospect his performance looks like a portent.

That summer John Inman had persuaded Arthur to join him and Ian Lavender in December and January in the pantomime *Mother Goose*, which opened at the Victoria Palace in London on 21 December. It was Arthur's first panto – he played the wicked Squire – and at first he was reluctant, but he agreed eventually when Inman promised to let Joan play the Queen of Gooseland. 'There's no such thing in *Mother Goose*,' Inman told me,

but to get Arthur we had to have her as well. She'd put on this posh voice but she was just a middle-of-the-road rep actress and wasn't upmarket really. I think that's something she aspired to. The extraordinary thing was that they didn't share a dressing room: I had number one, Arthur had number two, and she was under the stage with the Goose.

Arthur had to sing and say 'stupid boy!' every now and then, and he had even more trouble than usual remembering his lines. 'At rehearsals he couldn't get into the habit of calling me madam or miss or missus,' Inman, who played Mother Goose, told Bill Pertwee for his 1993 BBC radio programme *The Arthur Lowe Story*,

and when Mother Goose came out of the magic pool and no one recognised her Arthur had to say 'Allow me to introduce myself, dear madam,' and at rehearsals every single day, because I was in a pair of trousers and a jacket, he would say 'Allow me to introduce myself, dear sir,' and I'd say 'No, Arthur, no – it's *madam*, because I'll have a frock on.' On the third night he did it again: there I was with high heels, eyelashes, a big red mouth, a big red wig, and he said 'Allow me to introduce myself, dear sir,' and pulled the place apart. And after all the noise had died out I said 'Well, that's two and a half hours gone for a Burton,' but every year since then I've got whoever is playing the Squire to do exactly the same line so that we get the same laugh.

Arthur now fell asleep onstage all the time and to prevent complete disaster two male dancers stood on either side of him and nudged him if he dozed off. 'His first song,' said Inman, 'was "I think that I will start off with a nice *hors d'oeuvre*, There's really nothing nicer than a nice *hors d'oeuvre*…" and when they nudged him he would stand up within a second and start singing.' The panto was an exhausting mistake and even his admirer Francis King wrote in the *Sunday Telegraph* that 'Arthur Lowe … sadly makes as much impression in all this busy hubbub as a man with laryngitis at an office Christmas party.'

Arthur's last Christmas was not a happy one. He bought Joan a typically imaginative present, an exquisite white jacket with hand-painted silk pockets and a fish across the shoulder, but on Christmas Day his mother died at the age of 96 at Dystlegh Grange, an old folks' home at Disley, four miles from Hayfield, after suffering a stroke and bronchopneumonia. Arthur went north for the funeral at 11 o'clock one morning, missing that afternoon's matinée of *Mother Goose*, but he was back in London in time for the evening show. Nan left him everything she had, a small estate that was eventually valued at £26,575.03 net (about £54,000 now), but Arthur was never to enjoy his inheritance: three and a half months later he was dead too.

Inman lived close to the Lowes in Maida Vale and that winter he, Arthur and Joan renewed the friendship that had begun when all three had appeared together in *Ann Veronica* in 1969. 'I did like Arthur very, very much, and I admired him,' Inman told me.

I went to their flat a few times after the curtain had come down at the Victoria Palace. On a couple of nights I gave them a lift home and he'd say 'Come in and have a little drink.' This would be at about 11 o'clock at night and at four o'clock I used to try and find my way home across the canal. Late at night he would get very serious and they drank a lot of heavy brandy, and he would fall asleep. We'd put the world of show business to rights and he'd talk about Frank Fortescue and old actors and plays. It was always to do with the theatre, never money or politics. I think he thought 'Aren't we lucky? We keep going to work.' They adored each other, but neither of them was at all sexy. I think she might have been a *flirt* – she flirted like Dick Emery flirted – but she probably wouldn't remember being a flirt because of the drink. She used to put her napkin over her food. One of the most expensive things in a restaurant is a Dover sole and she would order a Dover sole and make movements in it and then all of a sudden this napkin would go over the top of it and that would be the end of it.

John Newman told me that he and his wife were invited by the Lowes to

quite a few dinners, which were always rather funny because Joan would attempt to cook even though she didn't eat much. On one occasion she'd done duck and it was so burned that none of us wanted to say anything. Joan was well away on the booze and we all ploughed through this completely scorched food.

From duck to *Mother Goose* again, and Inman was baffled to discover that the Lowes had booked into a hotel near the Victoria Palace theatre even though their flat was no more than a 15-minute taxi ride away, and refused to let him give them a lift home each night. Even a 15-minute taxi ride after an evening onstage had by now become too much for Arthur. The pantomime exhausted him and he vowed never to do another.

When the *Mother Goose* run ended in February Richard Burton flew Arthur to Venice on his private jet for just one day to make a brief appearance in Burton's mammoth new nine-hour film, *Wagner*, about the life of the German composer. The huge cast included Burton as Wagner, Vanessa Redgrave and Gemma Craven as his two wives, and a crowd of other famous names, among them Olivier, Gielgud and Ralph Richardson, who had been persuaded to appear together in the same scene for the first time ever as the Bavarian politicians Pfeufer, Pfistermeister and Pfordten. Arthur played Meser, a part so tiny that he was not even mentioned in the press releases, and he was paid with a case of wine.

Back in England the Lowes began to rehearse what was to be their last play together, *Home at Seven*, another of John Newman's productions, which was to open in March in Croydon and then go on to the Alexandra Theatre in Birmingham and a national tour. *Home at Seven*, in which Arthur played a suburban banker yet again, had been written in 1948 by R. C. Sherriff and was already extremely old-fashioned: not only does the doctor in it offer one of his patients a cigarette, he also remarks to the patient's wife 'Your husband remembers feeling a little queer at Cannon Street station', a line that would surely have caused a titter even in 1982. Despite the unlikely ending the play does have an excellently mysterious start when Arthur's character, the happily married, respectable, bowler-hatted, striped-trousered banker David Preston, returns from work one evening to discover that his wife is distraught because he was been missing for 24 hours. He has no idea where he has been during that time. He is always home at seven every night, but somehow he has lost an entire night and day of his life. And worse: during his absence £515 of sweepstake money has disappeared from the local social club where he is the treasurer and the club's steward has been murdered. Preston is caught out after lying to the police about where he has been and is gradually sucked deeper and deeper into a nightmarish quagmire of suspicion – and this at a time when murderers were still hanged in Britain.

It was a dauntingly long part which had originally been played by Ralph Richardson in 1949. Arthur was on stage throughout all three acts, so that it was an exhausting role for him to take on in his state of health. Joan's own touching part as Preston's loyal and loving wife was also a big one, 'one of the best parts she'd had for a long time', Newman told me, which may be why she did not try to talk Arthur out of taking on such a big part, as she should have done. Newman said:

> The first night was a bit of a frightener because the Director of the Ashcroft Theatre was sitting there and Arthur was asleep on stage. Luckily Joan always knew how to make him wake up on cue and she knew his lines. He often didn't know his own lines but he had this wonderful way of bluffing it out and ad-libbing.

Arthur was obviously ill in March when he presented a BAFTA award at a dinner in London. He muddled his brief speech, stumbled three times over the word 'lyrics', mispronounced a surname and looked embarrassed, but the audience roared with laughter and applause, thinking he was joking. He had only a few more days to live.

In April *Home at Seven* opened at Derek Salberg's Alexandra Theatre in Birmingham, one of Arthur's favourite theatres and cities. On the morning of Wednesday, 14 April he went to the BBC Birmingham radio studios to record a morale-boosting Forces radio broadcast in the character of Captain Mainwaring which the BBC planned to drop on the British Navy ships that were sailing south through the Atlantic at the start of the Falklands War with Argentina. Then he went to do an interview at the Pebble Mill studios, where a bed had been arranged for him to have a nap but where he caused a panic by disappearing for a walk in a nearby park minutes before he was due on the air. Back at the theatre he told Salberg – who had helped to launch his career 35 years previously by hiring him and Joan to join his Hereford rep company – that he was too tired to go to watch cricket with him the following day, but he went onstage with Joan as usual at 2.30 that afternoon to play the Wednesday matinée of *Home at Seven*. During that final performance, as he played Preston and she played his wife, Janet, Arthur looked at her and said: 'Promise me you will go on and be happy', and at the end of the final scene he spoke his last lines on stage: 'You've had a terrible time, Janet … and I'm afraid I didn't help you very much … I'm going to try…' But Janet and Joan were no longer onstage. They had made their exit and he was on his own.

After the matinée the Lowes and Salberg exchanged some banter about Arthur's experiences in *Mother Goose*, and at about 5.30 p.m. the Lowes went downstairs and joined the queue in the theatre's small canteen, where he cracked a few jokes with the other customers. 'He was as happy in his last few minutes as I have ever seen him,' Joan said later. From the canteen he carried a plate of egg and chips back to his dressing room while Joan went to the staff room to watch the latest news about the Falklands. After eating his meal Arthur settled down to read a book before the evening performance at 7.30, after which he and Joan were due to have dinner with Bill and Phyllis Bateman, who were going to be in the audience that night. But just after six o'clock he collapsed, felled by another stroke. Two usherettes heard his groans and Joan was called from her dressing room next door. 'He's done this before,' she said, and was sure he had just fallen off his chair and banged his head, but the management insisted on calling an ambulance and he was taken alone, unconscious, to Birmingham General Hospital. Then Joan did something extremely odd. 'Immediately I had the theatre manager clear his dressing room,' she told Gill Preece of the *Sunday Mirror* three months later. 'Although I refused to believe he was seriously ill, I felt I just couldn't face passing his door and seeing his clothes hanging there' – a strange reaction if she really thought he had simply banged his head and would soon recover.

John Newman asked Joan if she wanted to cancel the evening performance. She said no. 'We agreed that Arthur was such an old pro he would have wanted the show to go on,' Newman told me. Arthur's old friend, understudy and chauffeur Vyvian Hall went on that night in his place. 'He was excellent,' said Newman, 'and Joan was phenomenal. You wouldn't have known anything had occurred.' The Batemans, however, could not bear to sit in the audience and watch Joan on stage while Arthur was lying ill in hospital. 'There *are* situations when the show *doesn't* have to go on,' Daniel Abineri told me, 'and when the whole audience is sitting out there hoping to see Arthur Lowe and he's your husband ... It must have been a nightmare for the poor understudy who had to go on with her while they were packing Arthur into the wagon.' The Batemans left their seats and went to the hospital. 'Arthur was lying semi-conscious on a trolley,' Mrs Bateman told me.

They'd picked him up from the theatre by ambulance, but the show had

235

gone on and there was no one to go with him to the hospital. The hospital didn't know anything about his history at all, Joan was onstage and had just switched off, and when we got there they thought I was Mrs Lowe, and I said 'Oh no, Mrs Lowe's in the theatre', and they said 'Can anyone give us any history?' So Bill said 'You stay with Arthur and I'll go and register him.' Bill admitted him and gave them all the details and I stayed with Arthur. Later we went back to the theatre after the show, collected Joan, took her to the hospital, and then took her home with us.

The doctors told Joan that Arthur had lost the use of one side of his body and would be paralysed if he survived. 'I was devastated,' she told Gill Preece, 'yet I reacted with icy calm. Knowing him so well, I couldn't imagine anything worse than Arthur stuck in a wheelchair. I felt that unless he could recover completely and be himself again, it would be better for both of us if he should die.' Her wish was granted. At about 5 a.m. on Thursday, 15 April 1982 he died in hospital without regaining consciousness. 'I'm grateful it was all over so quickly,' she said. Dry-eyed and without showing any obvious grief, and determined that the show must go on, she went straight into re-rehearsals with Vyvian Hall. She did not even bother to telephone Stephen: he heard about his father's death on the radio. In his book he wrote:

When eventually I phoned my mother I was surprised, hurt, outraged, to find that she was utterly in control, needed me not at all. She wanted and would accept no sympathy but informed me that everything was in hand: she had advised the accountant, solicitor and the bank. Bill Bateman would be taking care of the funeral arrangements and she would be continuing with the tour. There was nothing for me to do at present … Her strength had shut me out, and, selfishly, I retired hurt. Redundant.

As for Stephen's own reaction to Arthur's death, 'I supposed I would now be rich and that I would be able to be more my own man. I wondered about how things would be carved up.' And he added sadly: 'I never knew him, he was always out at work, or on the phone, and then I went to boarding school and away to sea. Only now that he had gone did I realise that he had been extraordinary and that I had missed my chance.'

Joan registered Arthur's death that day, mistakenly telling the registrar to put on the death certificate that he had been born in Cheshire. That night in the theatre she was given the sort of standing ovation of which she had always dreamed, not for her acting but for her courage, and perhaps that affected the balance of her mind and persuaded her that she was a much better actress than she was. Afterwards Newman took her and Hall out to dinner, and for the rest of the week, inflamed by the applause and the newspaper stories and obituaries, she stayed with the Batemans. She even managed to joke that Arthur's possessive, dead mother had at last got him in her clutches again, and she told the Batemans: 'I've got to carry on with this show. I can't let people down. So, look, will *you* arrange the funeral here in Birmingham?'

'But who do you want to come?' asked Bateman.

'Oh, you know who to invite, Bill,' she said, but sadly he didn't. Many of Arthur's closest friends – Richard Leech, the Bonds, Bill Pertwee – were not told where or when the cremation was to be held. Arthur was cremated at Sutton Coldfield on 22 April and his ashes scattered in the ground of the crematorium. 'We had a very quiet cremation,' said Mrs Bateman.

Very few people came. Stephen came up from Southampton with his girlfriend and spent the night with us, and Mike Bullock came, the manager of the Alex, and John Newman managed to come over from Ireland, and Peter Campbell, and one or two odd bods. But Bill Pertwee rang the theatre and said to Mike Bullock 'Where's Joan gone?', and Mike wouldn't give him our phone number because apparently all the press were ringing round every funeral director's in Birmingham, but we used a local funeral director and they had Arthur down under an assumed name until the actual funeral.

Fewer than a dozen people gathered to say goodbye to one of the greatest comic actors of the century, and afterwards they went to a pub for a drink.

Joan did not attend Arthur's funeral. She preferred to stay with the cast of *Home at Seven* in Belfast and to complete the last three weeks of the tour, even though John Newman was able to get back to England for the funeral. 'Apparently Joan and Arthur had had a pact for years that neither would go to the other's funeral,' Mrs Bateman told me. 'This is what she

said. We were a bit surprised, I must admit, but that's how she wanted it.'
A few weeks later Joan explained to Romany Bain of the *TV Times*:

> I could hear his voice telling one of his favourite stories about the old
> Jewish gentleman on is death bed taking a roll call of his family. When
> he found that all his sons and daughters were present, he asked: 'Then
> who is looking after the shop?' On that day my sons represented me, and
> I was looking after the shop.

In fact she was not represented by her sons. 'David didn't come,'
Phyllis Bateman told me.

> We only met David once: the day after Arthur died, he came to the flat
> and took a chair of Joan's back to the cottage and said 'Of course, I
> won't be able to come to the funeral.' It was very odd but that was it. We
> thought it was a bit funny.

Joan's goodbye to Arthur was to have this message written afterwards
on the page of the crematorium memorial book which is opened every
year on 22 April: 'Loved by Millions'.

Many of Joan and Arthur's friends were shocked that she did not go to
his funeral. 'We all felt very bitter,' Pam Cundell told me. 'None of us
understood and I think Arthur would have been upset if he'd known.' John
Inman believed that maybe Joan 'thought everybody was coming in to the
theatre to see her, because she was that sort of lady. She thought she was
a good actress, bless her.' Joan's sister Margaret told me: 'I've buried two
husbands and I wouldn't not have gone. I had to be there, no matter what.'
Said Ian Lavender: 'It was odd. People better qualified than I say that it's
important to say goodbye.' And Richard Leech told me: 'I suppose she
must have been mad. It's a terrible thing to be a widow.' But Stephen
understood. 'Where he was a romantic, she had little sentimentality,' he
said. 'She was not a believer, and to her his body was not the important
thing. The thing that was important to her was the show.' And John
Newman told me: 'I think she felt she was paying her own tribute to him
by keeping the show on the road. He wouldn't have minded that she wasn't
there. They were that old school of actors that said "The curtain stays up." '
Christopher Bond was astonished that she continued with the tour.

'When he died the first thing that you would imagine would be that they would cancel the tour since he was the Name.' But Stephen understood that, too. 'It wasn't just about Arthur,' he explained, 'it was about everybody in the cast, people who relied on the production for their livelihood.' Another who agreed was Edward Heath, who wrote to Joan to congratulate her on her decision to carry on: 'Everyone admires your courage in such a heartbreaking situation,' he wrote, and 'however great the loss, we can all give thanks that in his very full lifetime he gave such immense pleasure to so many millions of people who will never forget him.' David Gatehouse told me: 'She was simply obsessed by being a professional actress. She would have been onstage if her entire family were being buried at that time and if she had broken both legs. She was manic about it. And she didn't believe that a funeral had any significance at all.' Arthur had himself explained Joan's attitude 32 years earlier when he had played the part of Wilson the actor–butler in *Larger Than Life*, his first West End play. When he is asked what makes a star a star, Arthur/Wilson said: 'It's courage, but it's more than that, it's a kind of bigness, a feeling that you're just a little larger than life-size. You believe in yourself, you *must*. That's why the big people in the profession can ride over illness or sorrow or anything.' The show must go on, no matter what.

'We'll never know if things might have been different had he taken a decent break,' Derek Benfield told me, 'but in the event he died in harness, which of course is what he would have wanted.' Stephen agreed: 'I had a great sense of relief and happiness that he'd died still working,' he said, and Arthur himself would not have been at all shocked by the way he died. He had in fact foretold it three years earlier: 'I'm going to embarrass everybody by being found dead in a dressing room somewhere,' he had told Chris Kenworthy of the *Sun* jocularly in January 1979, a remark that he repeated during a radio interview a fortnight before he died.

Two nights after his death the BBC broadcast an episode of *Dad's Army* on television and the following night ITV repeated *Car Along the Pass*. On the cricket pavilion at Hayfield they flew the flag at half-mast. John le Mesurier, Clive Dunn, Ian Lavender and David Croft all delivered sad tributes. He was 'one of the great comedians of our time,' said le Mez. He was 'the funniest man I know,' said Dunn, 'possibly one of the best actors we have had in this country since the war.' He was 'a brilliant and unique comedy talent,' said Croft. And the obituaries in every newspaper were huge and glowing. 'ARTHUR LOWE: THE UNFORGETTABLE LITTLE MAN WHO BEGUILED A WHOLE NATION' was the headline in the *Daily Express* the next day. 'EVERYONE'S FAVOURITE MAD, PRICKLY UNCLE', said the headline in the *Daily Mirror*. Arthur was one of those very few celebrities who are actually loved by the public.

Joan telephoned Clive Dunn and asked him to take over Arthur's part in *Home at Seven*. He was appalled by the suggestion and said no. 'I'd have been on a hiding to nothing,' he told me, and remembered the old theatre story of the two married actors who are staying in digs when the husband dies in the night and in the morning the wife goes to the top of the stairs and calls down to the landlady: 'Mrs Brown? Just one egg for breakfast.' Eventually John Newman persuaded Jack Watling to take on Arthur's part at very short notice.

Joan did attend the memorial service, which was held in London on May 24 at the Church of St Martin-in-the-Fields, appropriately in the heart of the West End theatre district. Among the mourners were Stephen, David and Sylvia Gatehouse, most of the surviving stars of *Dad's Army* (Clive Dunn, Bill Pertwee, Arnold Ridley, Frank Williams, Pam Cundell, Jimmy Perry, David Croft) and his oldest friends (Bill Bateman, Christopher Bond, Bill and Diana Shine, Vyvian Hall, Mary and Dick Francis) as well as Eric Sykes, Julia McKenzie, Ian Hendry, Peter Campbell, John Newman, John Warner, the Benfields and the Snoads. It was a surprisingly Christian thanksgiving service for a man who had been such a blatant non-believer. They sang 'Guide Me, O Thou Great Redeemer' and 'He Who Would Valiant Be' and 'Jerusalem', and Ian Lavender and Sheila Keith read two nautical poems to mark Arthur's love of the sea and the *Amazon*. First Lavender read 'Sea-Fever' by John Masefield:

> *I must go down to the seas again, to the lonely sea and the sky,*
> *And all I ask is a tall ship and a star to steer her by,*
> *And the wheel's kick and the wind's song and the white sail's shaking,*
> *And a grey mist on the sea's face and a grey dawn breaking.*
>
> *I must go down to the seas again, for the call of the running tide*
> *Is a wild call and a clear call that may not be denied;*
> *And all I ask is a windy day with the white clouds flying,*
> *And the flung spray and the blown spume and the sea-gulls crying.*

I must go down to the seas again to the vagrant gypsy life,
To the gull's way and the whale's way where the wind's like a whetted
  knife;
And all I ask is a merry yarn from a laughing fellow-rover,
And quiet sleep and a sweet dream when the long trick's over.

Sheila Keith read Tennyson's 'Crossing the Bar', which exhorts mourners not to weep and ends with these two verses:

Twilight and evening bell,
And after that the dark!
And may there be no sadness of farewell,
When I embark;

For though from out our bourne of Time and Place
The flood may bear me far,
 I hope to see my Pilot face to face
When I have crost the bar.

Harry Andrews, who had appeared so often with Arthur, from *The Ruling Class* to *A. J. Wentworth, B.A.*, read an extract from the book of that last TV series. The eulogy was delivered by John le Mesurier, and Nicholas Daniel and Julius Drake provided a musical interlude on oboe and piano. And when they played 'A Nightingale Sang in Berkeley Square' Joan cried in public for the first time since his death:

That certain night, the night we met
There was magic abroad in the air
There were angels dining at the Ritz
And a nightingale sang in Berkeley Square.
I may be right, I may be wrong
But I'm perfectly willing to swear
That when you turned and smiled at me
A nightingale sang in Berkeley Square.

Epilogue

Arthur left his share of the *Amazon* to Stephen and the rest of his estate to a Midland Bank trust with Joan as the sole beneficiary. In his will he made no mention of David despite his claims over the years that he had always treated David and Stephen the same. He left £205,983 net, which would today be worth about £410,000, surprisingly little for a man who had become a household name all over the world. 'If he'd survived the stroke but had been incapacitated by it, he could well have been quite hard up,' Lawrence Newman told me. As it was Joan did not need to worry about money. She sold Arthur's expensive collection of fine wines and *Dad's Army* was so constantly repeated on television that his posthumous repeat fees were eventually huge. Even in 2000 Ian Lavender was still being paid between £600 and £1,600 for each repeated episode, and 'Arthur got six or seven times more than me,' Lavender told me. 'We've all made more out of the repeats than we did out of the original programmes.' Lawrence Newman confirmed it: 'Arthur earned more after he died than when he was alive.'

Joan finished the tour of *Home at Seven* and out of loyalty to Arthur John Newman offered her a part in an Agatha Christie play, *The Unexpected Guest*, which opened for five weeks at Eastbourne at the end of June. Unfortunately Joan gave herself such airs and graces that she annoyed the leading lady, Pat Phoenix, who was then at the peak of her fame as a star of *Coronation Street*. 'I gave her the dressing room next to Pat so that she felt she was being treated like a star,' Newman told me, 'but Pat was furious because Joan told her to switch her radio off and said to me: 'She might have been Arthur's leading lady but she's not the leading lady in *this* cast.' Harold Snoad also gave Joan a part in a new TV series, *Don't Wait Up*, but after that she was offered no more parts. Stephen moored the *Amazon* in St Katharine's Dock in the East End of London and for a while provided on-board corporate lunches for which Joan took bookings at the flat in Maida Vale. Later he offered the *Amazon* for charter and for sailing functions, especially during Cowes Week regattas in the Isle of Wight.

In July 1982 the first of the six episodes of *A. J. Wentworth, B.A.* was broadcast and *The Times* critic Dennis Hackett got it right, sadly, when he reviewed it under the headline 'A WASTE OF LOWE'S TALENTS.'

A year after Arthur's death John le Mesurier saw him in a dream and was terrified when Arthur said cheerfully: 'Come on, Johnny, we're all waiting for you.' Le Mesurier was by now very ill and, white and trembling, he sought refuge in his wife's bedroom. 'He had woken up in a sweat of fear and gone downstairs,' Joan le Mesurier wrote in her autobiography *Lady Don't Fall Backwards*. 'It was only about six o'clock on a fine summer morning. He opened the french windows and a blackbird hopped into the room. I went cold when he told me.' A few weeks later John le Mez was dead. Four months later so was Arnold Ridley. The old *Dad's Army* platoon was well and truly demobbed.

Joan Lowe saw few of their old friends after Arthur's death. 'I used to see her quite a lot going to Victoria Wine just past the end of the close and then coming back,' John Inman told me, and although Bill Pertwee and Richard Leech tried to keep in touch with her she was often unwelcoming. Clive Dunn and the Bonds never saw her again. 'She felt there was no reason for Arthur to have died so young,' said David Gatehouse, 'and she felt a powerful grievance against specific doctors for failing to realise that he had something that was going to kill him. She felt that he had been let down. She also felt desperately lonely. Perhaps she couldn't face people.'

She drank more and ate even less than ever. 'She once said to me "I smoke too much and I drink too much and I don't care!"' Phyllis Bateman told me. 'After Arthur went she said "Give me five years",' and it was five years later, in 1987, when Joan was 65, that she left London and moved up to Hayfield to live alone and all but friendless in Arthur's parents' gloomy little cottage at 3 Chapel Road. Perhaps she thought it might somehow make her feel closer to him, but it was a dreadful place to waste the last two years of her life. The Batemans would come from Manchester and take her out for a meal, though she ate very little. 'She thought a prawn cocktail was a meal,' Ann Middleton told me. Bill Pertwee, who was working in Manchester a lot, also came to see Joan as often as he could, but otherwise she lived like a drunken hermit and saw almost no one except Nan Lowe's cleaning lady, Alice MacDonald, who shopped and cleaned now for Joan, and the village taxi-driver Trevor Middleton, who liked a drink himself and would sometimes drive her out into the countryside for a change of scenery and a pub-crawl. 'Stephen used to come to see her, but David didn't come often,' Mrs MacDonald told me. Stephen also remembered to send Joan flowers on Mother's Day, but he believed that she was 'testing her friendships to destruction' to see who cared enough to come to visit her, and he wrote in his book: 'If David or myself went to see her, we couldn't stay long or else the conversation would move away from the acceptable and towards confrontation. Without Arthur she was, simply, desperately unhappy.' And he added: 'In many ways their love had been the Destroying Angel, and it destroyed her now.'

'It was awfully sad to see her go down like that,' said Phyllis Bateman. 'We were very worried about her stuck up there on her own in this tiny, dark cottage. It was awful, but she said "I'll be all right: I've got Alice, I've got Trevor."' In the two years of life that were left she did not see even her sister, Margaret, who told me:

My first husband went to see her in Hayfield and he was upset about her being there. He didn't think she should be there by herself and said it wasn't a fit place to live in. Maybe she was always depressed and Jane's death brought it out, or maybe she was depressed that her career wasn't as successful as Arthur's.

Joan was told that she had stomach cancer but refused to have any treatment or to go into hospital. 'I want to die here, on my own,' she told Stephen angrily. 'She was in a terrible state and a lot of pain,' Pertwee told me. 'She had also fallen out with Stephen over the *Amazon* because he wanted to sell it, though he came back to her just before she died and she phoned me and said "We've made it up."' To help to ease the pain Joan took up with a Scottish actor in his thirties, Robbie Macnab, whom she and Arthur had befriended in London, and she asked Pertwee to introduce him to directors. 'I wouldn't have thought he was her lover,' said Pertwee, 'but who knows?' The villagers, however, joked that Macnab was her toy boy. 'She said he was her nephew!' Helen Higginbottom told me, and Trevor Middleton said: 'Robbie enjoyed a drink as well, and he stayed with her in the cottage, and there was only one bed, but I really don't know if he was a boyfriend.' Mrs MacDonald claimed that Joan was 'financing' Macnab, and Middleton added:

She certainly wasn't skint and she never asked any prices, she'd just write a cheque out. She always paid for the drink and on one occasion when Robbie had a small part in a theatre in Worthing, Joan paid for a taxi to take him from here to Worthing. It cost about £120: it would be more than double that now.

But even with Robbie she had vociferous arguments.

She was rarely seen in the village, but everyone there knew that she drank far too much and that she was notoriously unsteady on her feet and had hurt her leg when she tripped over a stone. Of all the witnesses I interviewed only Bill Pertwee refused to believe that she was almost permanently drunk. 'We went out to lunch one day and she had half a glass of wine,' he said, 'and there was no reason to believe that she'd been drinking before I met her.' Everyone else, however, told me that by now Joan had surrendered herself to the bottle. 'She literally drank herself to death,' Richard Gatehouse told me. 'She fell down the stairs at one point and spent the rest of her life walking with a frame. David said it was very bad. It was a terrible life, a sad ending. I've often thought about why Joan was so unhappy, but I don't know why.'

Trevor Middleton and Alice MacDonald confirmed that Joan had become a hopeless alcoholic. Middleton told me:

She drank gin neat and she smoked very heavily. When I went to the village store for her one Saturday lunchtime I bought her a bottle of gin, a bottle of brandy, a bottle of whisky, and 200 cigarettes, and on the Monday she sent me back to get another bottle of gin. And she dressed like a tramp.

Mrs MacDonald said:

It was pathetic. I don't want to see anybody else like that. She was a very nice person and I got on well with her, even when she was drinking – she were never nasty, she was very generous and she wasn't poor – but she was no use without Arthur. She really loved him very much. She was very unhappy without him and after he'd gone she couldn't care less. She was lost completely and was never sober. She never watched TV or read books, she'd just drink all day and she'd drink raw from the bottle. It was awful to see her. She had vertigo and she was all over the place. She let everything go. Her hair was awful, she didn't eat anything, she didn't worry about her clothes, and she wouldn't go to bed: she used to lie all night in front of the gas fire.

Occasionally Mrs MacDonald would try to persuade her to brush her hair, change her clothes, or sit in a chair, but Joan's usual response was to tell her to 'piss off'. When Stephen visited her he often found her curled up on the floor 'like a wounded animal, drunk and bleeding inside. She lived on the floor.' The night before she died, said Mrs MacDonald, Joan 'was lying in front of the fire and I pleaded with her to go to bed that night. "It'd do you good to rest yourself properly," I said, and she did go to bed that night – and she died.' Said Stephen: 'Maybe she knew her time had come.'

Joan died in her cottage on 1 July 1989. The stomach cancer had invaded much of the rest of her body. She was 66, the same age as Arthur had been when he died. 'Five days earlier she told me that she'd had a lovely life but she was ready to die,' said Middleton.

She'd had enough. She'd given me a key to the cottage and I saw the curtains drawn at about 10 o'clock on this Saturday morning. I unlocked the front door and she'd managed to get herself to bed and she'd peacefully gone to sleep in bed.

David was in the Far East and decided not to come all the way back for the funeral at Stockport crematorium, but his wife, Sylvia, was there, and Stephen, and Joan's sister Margaret, the Middletons, and Robbie Macnab. Joan left everything – £331,778 net (about £430,000 today) – equally to David and Stephen, but Stephen bought David's share in the *Amazon* and continued to charter it with dwindling success. They also inherited trunksful of Arthur and Joan's memorabilia. At the end of 1989, after a row with his headmaster and after 20 years at the school, David lost his job as the director of music at Stowe and the big house that went with it, and in 1990 he sold at auction three tea chests full of Arthur and Joan's diaries, letters, theatre programmes, press cuttings and photographs because he said he would no longer have room for them all in a smaller house. 'Arthur would have been heartbroken,' he said at the time and Phyllis Bateman agreed. 'It was rotten of David to sell off their letters, she told me. 'I think Arthur'd be very hurt.'

In 1992 Stephen became engaged to a second Susan, a 37-year-old ex-nurse from New Zealand, and the following year she gave birth to his second child, a girl called Nina. They settled in Scotland in a cold, damp, run-down, untidy, rented cottage near Inverness, at Clachnaharry on the Caledonian Canal, where they opened the *Amazon* as a floating museum and where one local woman swore that she saw Arthur's tubby little ghost on board. Becoming a father and marrying again mellowed Stephen. For many years he had blamed his father for Joan's boozing and unhappiness, feeling that Arthur had been weak and should have stood up to her more, but in 1996 he told Deborah Ross of the *Daily Mail*:

I've learned that my father was actually a saint. He worked incredibly hard, bringing pleasure to millions, while enduring all his family problems without any violence or disrespect, and at huge cost to himself. And no one could have made my mother happy. She wasn't the happy, contented type. But Arthur did more for her than any other man could have, would have, or possibly should have.

That *Daily Mail* interview, which appeared when Stephen's memoir of Arthur was published, shocked his parents' friends. It was published under the headline 'WHY DID MY FATHER ALLOW HIMSELF TO BE HUMILIATED BY MY DRUNKEN, SEXUALLY DEMANDING MOTHER?' and announced in large type that 'Arthur never did have other lovers. It's just that my mother had a big appetite for men.' It appalled everyone who knew them. 'Clive rang me from Portugal,' Bill Pertwee told me, 'and Pam Cundell was crying on the phone.' Pam said: 'I was incensed. All right, in the last years she did drink, but what she did for Arthur more than compensated.' Margaret Stapleton told me: 'Stephen's book hurt me very much. He said some very nasty things about my sister. I shall never understand or forgive Stephen for the things he said about his mother. They were very unnecessary and hurtful.' David Gatehouse said he was 'surprised by the bitter tone of Stephen's book because I really don't detect any bitterness when I talk to him. I can only imagine that he was depressed or thought it was a good way to sell a book, or perhaps his publishers thought it was a good way to sell a book.' Ian Lavender told me: 'I was shocked by the book. Stephen always seemed to be reacting against Arthur's fame and success.' Clive Dunn agreed: 'Stephen never forgave Arthur for certain things. Maybe as a child he felt abandoned.' So did Ann Middleton: 'Stephen seemed to resent having a famous father, which is rather sad.' Daniel Abineri reckoned that it was common for the child of somebody famous to feel resentment: 'It's a very common story among star actors' kids. You're born in the shadow of somebody who's considered special and it's very hard to match up to that.' And Harold Snoad said: 'The last thing Arthur would have wanted would have been to have had that sort of thing said about Joan.'

Stephen's book is well written, touching and vividly evocative but sometimes startlingly inaccurate. He says that his mother was born in 1923 when in fact it was 1922, and that she died in 1987 when it was 1989. His grandmother, Nan, was 96 when she died, not 99, and she died four months before Arthur, not two years afterwards. Even Arthur's first appearance on the West End stage is said to have been on 7 February 1951 when it was actually 27 April 1950. A letter from John Laurie is said to have been written by John le Mesurier. And so it goes on, with names, dates, places and minor details often slightly wrong and passages that are fictionalised for no obvious reason.

Stephen told Deborah Ross that although he had never known security as a child he had found it now and was happier than he had ever been. He chose to live in his run-down cottage, he said, not because he was poor but as an act of rebellion because his father had always revelled in luxuries and possessions. He still owned the *Amazon* but it was costing a fortune to maintain and he had been trying to sell it for several years, gradually dropping the asking price from £285,000 to £185,000 in 1994. He finally sold it to Ted and Melody Morgan-Busher in 1997 for 'just £50,000', Steven Lowe told me. Since Arthur had spent the modern equivalent of £420,000 on it, the *Amazon* was not in the end the profitable investment he had thought it would be. Today the boat is moored in Malta. Free of the boat at last, Stephen became a computer buff and electronic publisher, and emigrated to New Zealand with Sue and Nina to become a multimedia teacher at Aoraki Polytechnic in Timaru.

As for *Dad's Army*, a British survey in 1993 reported that it was the most popular TV comedy ever, and when it was repeated at prime time on Saturday nights in 1996 it attracted nearly 10 million viewers while *Baywatch*, its sexy rival on the ITV channel, had only 7 million. In 2001 both the BBC and satellite TV were still broadcasting prime-time *Dad's Army* repeats and David and Stephen were still sharing Arthur's huge posthumous royalties. 'If the BBC repeats an episode of *Dad's Army* Arthur's estate would get about £1,350,' Bill Pertwee told me. Arthur would have been proud of that. He had always loved money.

So how good an actor was he?

Of all the scores of actors, producers and directors who worked with him – not to mention the critics who wrote about him – only his very first director, Martin Benson, was less than ecstatic about his talent. 'I wouldn't say that he was a great actor,' Benson told me.

All the characters he played were the same character. They weren't even a variation. He wasn't really a character actor: he was a quirky little personality who was just versatile enough to fit into many characterisations that were all the same. This is not denigrating him. It's great good fortune if you're like that.

Nor was the owner of the Hereford repertory company, Derek Salberg, exactly euphoric about his talent. Asked whether he had realised back in 1947 that Arthur would become a star, Salberg confessed that he had not. 'I realised what a most useful type he was, with such a definite personality,' he said, but 'in fact, I think he was a better TV than stage actor.'

There were others who agreed that most of Arthur's film, theatre and TV roles were very similar. 'I'm afraid that this is what makes a star,' said John Warner. 'Robert Morley was the same and so was Gielgud. People like to see what they know.' Jimmy Perry believed that Arthur 'represented every pompous man that ever existed', and Derek Granger told me:

What Arthur succeeded in doing in his marvellous lifetime's work was creating one single character, this wonderful, quintessential little middle-class Englishman, and he did it with extraordinary finesse. He created a type which transcended your liking of those characters. He gave it an extraordinary comedy and sympathy but marvellous accuracy.

John Inman agreed:

He did play the same part, and it was only a hair's-breadth difference between every character he played, but he was quite brilliant. He was a great actor. John le Mesurier did the same: when John was asked to what he attributed his own great success he said 'Always play the same part and if possible wear the same suit.'

Almost every actor who worked with Arthur considered him to be outstanding, from his humble colleagues in provincial rep and the West End to the rest of the casts of *Coronation Street* and *Dad's Army*, and Laurence Olivier, John Gielgud and Ralph Richardson, who were generally considered to be the three greatest English actors of the late twentieth century, admired his acting very much indeed. So perhaps the last word should be left to the man who was in 2002 widely acknowledged to be Britain's greatest living actor, Paul Scofield, who appeared onstage with Arthur in *A Dead Secret* in 1957. 'He was a seriously brilliant actor,' Scofield told me, and

Dad's Army proved to be the complete realisation of his gifts, because not only was he funny but he also gave us, as Captain Mainwaring, a very lovable and vulnerable human being. It was a deeply serious performance. When I watched him on television I felt strangely proud that I had worked with him, and had had a close-quarter knowledge of his rare talent.

No actor could hope for a better review or a more qualified critic. Little Arthur Lowe, the railwayman's son from a Derbyshire village, had revealed himself as a comic genius and had fully deserved the thunderous 1,387-gun salute that had greeted his birth.

Index